MALACHITE
A Journey in Africa

Paul Marketos

MINERVA PRESS
LONDON
ATLANTA MONTREUX SYDNEY

MALACHITE: *A Journey in Africa*
Copyright © Paul Marketos 1998

All Rights Reserved

No part of this book may be reproduced in any form
by photocopying or by any electronic or mechanical means,
including information storage or retrieval systems,
without permission in writing from both the copyright
owner and the publisher of this book.

ISBN 0 75410 058 8

First Published 1998 by
MINERVA PRESS
195 Knightsbridge
London SW7 1RE

Printed in Great Britain for Minerva Press

MALACHITE
A Journey in Africa

About the Author

Paul Marketos was born in Johannesburg. He attended the University of Cape Town, where he studied for a BSc in Computer Science and an MA in English Literature. After spending several years working and travelling abroad he returned to settle in Johannesburg. He remains incurably optimistic about the new South Africa. *Malachite* is his first book.

To J.A.L.P.

Chapter One Maun

The road from Francistown to Maun is long and straight, and certainly not the most interesting in all of Africa. It is flanked on both sides by dry, level sands whose monotony is broken only by coarse scrub and the occasional hardy tree. But to us it was beautiful. That road marked the start of things for us, the platform from which we were stepping off into the unknown. As our tyres rolled along its striped back, closing regularly over its even white markings, they hissed a single, unchanging word up to us: "Freedom," they sang. Our journey across Africa to London had begun.

The road had led us into a temporary limbo. With all past cares put further behind us with every mile of its length we travelled, and the future beckoning brightly, we were free to enjoy the present, to revel undistracted in the now. The days had lost their names. We were so excited, lifted with a moonwalking weightlessness. I turned the music up. Simply Red was playing, and the stars they sang of became the stars that lured us forward. Northern stars, hidden beyond the equator. Stars and constellations that would light the Saharan sky above us: the Big Dipper, Polaris, Drago, Cepheus, Ursa Minor. We were on our way north, to turn innocence into experience and names into memories.

Two months before I had resigned from my job, sold everything I owned and cashed in my pension, in exchange for a quarter share in a large Bedford truck. And this intoxicating freedom.

★

We had bought the truck off friends of James who had driven it down from London the previous year. I was sitting in the kitchen of James's digs in the student suburb of Observatory in Cape Town, chatting to his housemates, when he burst in to call me.

"Paulus! They're here! They're here! The truck's arrived!"

As we rushed outside my initial impression was overwhelmingly one of size. The truck seemed to fill the narrow street in which it was parked, dwarfing the cars next to it. Everything about it seemed big, from the sound of its diesel engine, throbbing low like a tractor, to the massive bar of steel that was the front bumper. Its exotic shape suddenly brought a little closer to reality all James's passionate but distant ravings about this trans-Africa trip that we must do. We opened the rear of the truck, a huge yellow box, and I inhaled the traces of far-off smells. Diesel mixed with desert sand and wood smoke. Mud and damp, food and canvas. I was gripped by a longing to go where it had been, to feel that mud and sand under my feet, to breathe in strange smoke and air.

The truck was ungainly. A heavy platform had been added above the roof of the cab, anchored to the chassis. Huge bars were mounted on the front to support this structure. Poles and the exhaust stuck up from the back of the platform, like horns. It reminded me of those microscopic creatures that haunt our skin, magnified a millionfold. Its head, the cab, was squat, sunk low over the wheels, as though squashed down by the weight above it. Huge bars encaged it, like a protective armour shell.

Excitedly, I explored the cab. On each side sliding doors opened into the interior. Above the stairs, two in each door-well, were four chairs. The front two were the original chairs, simple, made with low, firm backs. The two in the rear were of Italian leather, from a crashed BMW M5 sports car. They were mounted on poles welded to the floor and swivelled or reclined for comfort.

The dashboard had a few basic adornments. A button for the hooter and large round switch for the indicator were positioned next to the broken speedometer and milometer. In the centre of the dashboard was a gauge indicating the pressure in the on-board compressor we would use to pump the tyres. The starter button was inside the cubby hole. The engine sat between the front two seats, beneath a carpeted cover. Behind it were three levers, for the gears, four-wheel drive and the engine-driven winch.

Two 200 litre fuel tanks were situated between the cab and box. The main tank leading to the engine sat below them and had a capacity of 118 litres. A spare wheel was mounted above the tanks, behind the cab. Each tyre was more than half my height. On the side of the aluminium box, the carapace of this awkward-looking beast, someone had painted a small silhouette of Don Quixote on his mare, a gentle reminder of folly.

Soon after, we accompanied three of the four who had driven down from London – Robbie, Doug and Dave – on the final leg of their journey, the sixty or so kilometres to Cape Point. The truck thundered down Constantia Neck like a juggernaut, seeming to take the full width of the road. I watched impressed as Robbie drove it so coolly, like a seasoned horseman riding a fiery but tamed steed. The day when I too would know the truck so intimately seemed a long way off. The trip itself did as well. We wouldn't be ready to leave for almost a year, and I wondered if I'd be able to retrace the steps of these callused, sun-darkened men, who spoke so lightly of the roadblocks and unpaid, gun-toting soldiers they'd come across, of sandstorms in the desert and how they'd spent thirty days on a floating village of a barge, inching their way upstream into the Congo Basin. And who became strangely reticent when talk turned to their arrest and temporary incarceration in Cameroon.

*

And there I was, almost exactly a year later, headed for Maun, the small town at the foot of the Okavango Swamps, the trip a reality at last. Right up until we left there had been something chimerical about it, as though some chance misfortune could snatch it away from us. After the initial excitement of seeing the truck wore off, routine life managed to relegate thoughts of the trip to a seemingly ever-distant future. Work and study pressures left James and me little room for more than the occasional get-together to discuss dates and plot routes. Even as we talked about places we had to visit and encouraged others to join us, I somehow couldn't dislodge the entire trip from the realm of fancy in my mind. It held a fictional quality for me, something to be read about. Uncertainty reminded me that I could always just decide not to go.

Like a pulsar, the trip brightened and faded. People joined up with us, gung-ho and enthused, and then pulled out, for financial, business or personal reasons. We would excitedly take the truck on outings, down to Hout Bay for sundowners with ten people on the roof, or for a Sunday drive around the Cape peninsula, and then not even set eyes on it for three weeks. But time rolled steadily on towards our departure date of May 1993, James returned from England with the *carnet de passage*, the temporary importation documentation, and I committed myself by resigning my job.

Suddenly, two of the crew who had been definites pulled out. With only three months to go before we were due to leave there were only the two of us left. Thoughts of abandoning the whole thing entered my mind. Echoing there too were the admonitions of friends and the fears of family. Political and economic collapse has made Africa far harder to cross now than thirty years ago. Anxiety about what bandits or illness we'd meet, and whether the thirty-two year old truck would make it across 30,000 kilometres of unforgiving roads, tugged at my conservative inclinations.

But with James as eager as ever, I couldn't desert him. We would go, even if it meant just the two of us together. Other reasons too for going had begun to cement themselves inside my mind, outweighing my misgivings.

I had a vision of myself as a seventy year old man looking back on my life, and knew that if I chose to forego such an opportunity I would look back only with regret. The deep reticence of spirit I had learnt in my childhood had been steadily eroded by the invigorating currents of university life, and while a cautiousness remained in me, I tried to live by the axiom that, whenever in doubt, I should go with experience. I had begun to see that invariably we regret not what we do in life but what we don't do. By choosing the path of passivity we are left with an unanswerable wondering. Shying away from experience leaves a hollowness inside, the knowledge that once past such moments are unreclaimable.

Growing up as a young white boy in apartheid South Africa, mine was in some ways an artificial childhood. The government's suppression temporarily held down the lid on the historical disquiet and tension that our country's troubled past had been unable to resolve. As a six year old I would walk the three kilometres home from school without any fear and this security and protectedness was the pattern right through my schooling. By the end of university I had seen very little of life's darker side, and of my own, both because of the artificially sheltered environment of my upbringing, and because I had been since a child submissive, conciliatory, and had always sought to avoid conflict and confrontation. A trip like this, I knew, would help me to grow up.

I was also being drawn by the mystery of Africa itself. The apartheid propaganda machine had effectively blanked out black Africa. It was not that I thought of the rest of Africa as a breeding ground for terrorists. I just hadn't given it much consideration at all. It was somewhere I'd never be able to go. I had visited Zimbabwe almost once a year since childhood, and loved going there, but the Zambezi acted as a border that was both physical and mental. Then, with the beginnings of political reform in 1990, as white South Africa began to peep between the wheels of its laager, Africa became visible once more. I visited Kenya for three weeks in 1991 and loved it. I began to want to see more of the vast continent that had lain hidden above us. Like other South Africans, I was learning to be proud to be African, to have a home continent and not just a home country. I wanted to learn about Africa, and to learn from it, as people like Laurens van der Post had done in the days before the Nationalists slammed the door on the world.

Underlying these other reasons was my friendship with James Pitman. We had become closest of friends in our first year of university after being given next door rooms in our residence, Smuts Hall, despite – or more likely because of – our vastly different temperaments. Where I was passive, James was hyperactive; where I was cautious, he was reckless; and as such we were foils to each other. I helped him to control his excesses, and he invested me with a greater vitality and lust for life, shaking me out of my conservatism. James's healthy disrespect for authority helped me to overcome the unquestioning obedience I had learnt at school.

We balanced each other out. While I showed him the insanity of leaping drunk into the fir tree outside his fourth floor window, he showed me the fun of driving brazenly into Fernwood, the parliamentarian's club in Newlands, to make use of their tennis court or swimming pool. I was perhaps more confident in myself, in who I was, but James was certainly far more confident of himself, of what he could do. When committing some small misdemeanours such as stealing pears or going jogging in someone's private estate, I noticed that while I quailed inside in fear of reprisals, this kind of daring made James more alive. He revelled in these acts of lawlessness, where I found them stressful.

The fact that we were going together was a comfort to us both. Without the security of this friendship I doubt either of us would have gone on with the trip. This made the courage of our three other travelling companions more admirable by contrast. Until a couple of months – or weeks in one case – earlier, they had been complete strangers to us. There was no doubt that over the next seven months we'd get to know them well, perhaps too well.

In order to get through the Central African jungle before the rainy season we would have to leave in mid-May at the latest. So it was a great relief when, at the end of January, my friend Cameron told me he knew someone who was eager to join us. Robbie Hoard had surprised all his friends by deciding to give up his job, leave behind Bridget, his girlfriend of seven years, and join two strangers on a journey into peril. I met him twice in Cape Town and immediately warmed to his enthusiasm and sharp if rather dry wit. Robbie would join the truck in Johannesburg as he'd need to work right up until our departure date in order to finance the journey. Our initial costs had been quite low, as we'd bought the truck fully-equipped for only R8,000 – about $2,400 – and we thought we'd each need another

R12,000 or so, if we travelled on a shoestring – and if everything went smoothly over the seven months that lay ahead.

We had insisted that anyone joining us buy into the truck itself, so that we would all have not only a vested interest in it reaching London, but an invested one too.

When Robbie joined us in Johannesburg the day before we were due to leave, he wasn't in the best of shape. He had flu, a hangover, and his stocky frame was beginning to assume a profile more suitable to a corpulent and office-bound banker than a rugby player. None of this diminished his enthusiasm, however, or prevented him from vigorously defending the trailer-load of personal effects he expected us to load into the back.

"Come on, Robbie, you can't seriously be taking all this stuff," said James pointing to his rucksack and his long brown army kitbag, which were surrounded by a small mound of other bags containing a camera, binoculars, chairs, a tent, books and a short-wave radio.

"They're vital essentials. You'll be praising my name for having brought them before we even get to Malawi," he replied, stowing his bags away on the lowest of the three bunks and in one of the many lockers that filled the left-hand side of the well-designed interior.

Robbie's banking experience had automatically elevated him to the status of truck accountant. Amongst all the paraphernalia was an accounts book. There was also, testimony to his attitude toward what lay ahead, a large, empty diary emblazoned on the front with the letters T.O.A.L! Trip of a Lifetime!

Juliet Oliver had similarly heard about us through the network of friends we'd asked to look out for prospective travellers. She was also very enthusiastic and had happily sold her Mini Minor to pay her way. An English doctor out in Africa to gain experience, she was eager to see more of

Africa and had been able, in her capacity as a doctor, to obtain for us a large box full of medical supplies. Juliet was planning to go only as far as Kenya as she needed to return to a job in England in August. I thought it was probably a good thing that she would not be attempting the hardships of the jungle and desert, as I had begun to harbour a few doubts about her resilience after the first shopping expedition in Johannesburg. There Juliet insisted on lowering into the trolley several large bars of chocolate and bottles of olive oil.

Those were the four of us travelling to Kenya. There we were to be joined by a classmate of mine, Sandy Young, who would take up the fourth berth until London. Although we thought we might well come across other travellers who might join us *en route*, it was not an ideal complement. We had hoped, mainly so as to cut down on costs, to have a five person crew the whole way.

We also had tentative plans to meet up with others we knew of who were doing a similar trip, in particular two friends of James and mine from university: Derek Hume, who would be leaving South Africa a month after us on a motorbike, and Andrew Birrell, who was driving up in his Land-Rover with three others.

When James and I were fixing up the truck at his family's farm in Balgowan, Natal, and having to spend what seemed to our student mentalities to be large sums of money, financial concerns were at the forefront of our minds. This inspired us to invite the regional newspaper, The Natal Witness, to interview us, in the hope of renting out the sides of the truck as large mobile billboards. The full-colour, front page article that appeared did not entice a single corporate director to throw sponsorship our way, but it had the fortunate side effect of attracting the attention of Bronwyn Tuck, an impulsive New Zealand physiotherapist who had come out to fulfil a lifelong dream of living in

Africa and who had been working for nearly a year at Edendale Hospital in Pietermaritzburg.

As chance would have it, the Saturday morning she read the article found her at the house of three young doctors with whom James and I had been at university in Cape Town. "Go for it, Bronwyn!" they exhorted her, and this was all the prompting she needed. Undaunted by the fact that we were due to leave in just over a week.

James had met Bronwyn once already by the time I first met her. "She's rather unconventional," he warned me, "but I think she'll be excellent to have along." When she met us at the bottom of her block of flats, I saw what James meant. It was obvious that she felt a little awkward in our presence and was filled with nervous energy. Dressed in bright ethnic clothes, with a shock of curly light brown hair tied loosely on top of her head, she distracted herself through providing tea and animated conversation, swearing freely and unaffectedly as she spoke. Clearly the enormity of what she had taken upon herself was weighing on her, but a bubbling excitement affirmed to herself, and us as well, that she was doing the right thing.

We mentioned that she would need to contribute R2,000 towards the truck. "Half a mo'," she said, and disappeared into her bedroom where she retrieved a wad of R50 notes from under her mattress. With that she was in. I left feeling pleased but a bit bewildered. She was certainly like none of the women I knew. Whereas South African girls are brought up to be sweet, quiet and submissive, Bronwyn seemed loud, forward and wild.

From early childhood Bronwyn had had a fascination with all things African, and had come to South Africa as soon as she had saved enough money for the ticket. She had a fearlessness bordering on insanity. Or perhaps *naïveté* had more to do with it. Shortly after arriving in Johannesburg, she had leapt into a taxi for Soweto only hours after having been divested of a large amount of money in downtown Jo'burg. Undeterred by her initial experiences, she continued to see Southern Africa up close, hitch-hiking throughout South Africa and Zimbabwe, befriending people wherever she went. Although she did not conform to any type I'd met before, I was heartened by her total lack of pretension. Pretentiousness, to me, is the least attractive human trait after malice. Bronwyn, I could tell already, was completely down to earth. And from what our medical friends told us, she would be loads of fun to have around.

*

For James and I the trip started in March 1993, when we drove the truck from Cape Town to Balgowan, a small farming town in Kwazulu-Natal where we would spend a month conducting the necessary repairs to the truck. It seemed a fitting way to start, just the two of us, as it had been our trip for almost a year now. And even though we hadn't done all that much in terms of planning, other than organising the carnet in England and writing to people we hoped to stay with, routes and conditions being something we felt confident we'd find out about on the way, the drive consolidated the spirit of support between us.

The first day of the trip turned out to be the longest daylong drive the truck would make. We woke before dawn. James turned the ignition key and I pressed the large black starter button. The engine, housed under its cover between our seats, struggled briefly against the chill morning air before throbbing into life. The occluding lack of sleep I felt was soon drawn aside by the wind that whistled into the cab, blowing before it the excitement of experience yet uncovered. Our weak headlights, one yellow, one white, illuminated the walls of houses and shanties as we drove from the suburbs and past the squatter camps, heading for

Nieu Bethesda, an almost deserted town in the heart of the Karoo, the semi-desert that stretches across the interior of the Cape.

Climbing slowly over the Hottentots-Holland mountains to Worcester, we came across a coloured family whose car had engine trouble. James immediately stopped to offer our help. We were unable to assist them other than to offer the unhappy diagnosis that their engine had seized, but the interaction was warm and friendly and filled us with optimism for the futures of both our trip and our country. Before we left they pressed upon us a box of grapes from the Paarl farm where they worked.

The rapidly-encroaching darkness was already draining the warmth from the dry hills around us when we arrived, after fifteen hours and 800 kilometres of continuous driving, at the farm of friends of James's, the Kingwells. James's mother, Vicki, was there, with his two brothers. Our hopes for the country, which was at that stage involved in a delicate process of negotiations on the road to full democracy, had the wind knocked out of them by the blow of what we saw on the television news.

> *'Good evening. This is the eight o'clock news. Chris Hani, leader of the South African Communist Party and head of Umkhonto we Sizwe, was murdered today outside his home. Police have arrested a fifty year old white man in connection with the crime. Witnesses say the gunman approached Mr Hani...'*

We listened to the end of the broadcast in stunned silence. My heart sank into my stomach. "Christ, there's no hope for this bloody country," I said, shaking my head. "After Mandela he's about the last person we could afford to lose."

"I hope it doesn't prove the catalyst for a series of revenge murders," said Vicki.

"Ja, it could be the start of a complete bloodbath," agreed James.

"Hell, it's depressing," I said. "It makes me quite keen to escape from the politics of this place for a while."

It did raise for us a more immediate concern as well. We were due to travel through the Eastern Cape and the Transkei over the next two days, and our hosts warned us that the mood of the people we'd be passing might be vengeful. Undeterred, we set off at mid-morning the next day, on what we now thought might well be the most dangerous section of the entire journey. All fears proved unfounded, however, and after spending a night on the stud farm of the family of Craig Birch, an old housemate of ours, in the sleepy farming district of Dordrecht, we arrived at the Pitman's farm, Bridford, in Balgowan late on the 13th April, 1993.

There followed a month of cleaning, shopping, repairs and modifications. The truck had been well looked after on the way down and was in good condition. The main problem, we'd been warned, was that the viewing platform above the cab, which was bolted onto the chassis, had proved too heavy for the front springs, causing several to snap. It had also bent the front right tractor joint that connects the axle to the wheel, giving the truck a lopsided, slightly lame look. Loath to take down the platform, which gave the truck so much of its character, as had been recommended, we decided to have the front leaves re-tempered and an extra one inserted for strength. We would also scour the scrapyards of Pietermaritzburg for spare springs and a new tractor joint.

Our truck was built 1961, making it years older than the oldest person on board. It was a Bedford RL that had started out as a fire tender on a military base near London and had moved on to become a grit spreader before being bought by the crew who drove her down. Known as Green

Goddesses, similar trucks had been exported to all corners of the former British Empire, so it was with a degree of confidence that we set off in search of spares.

With great excitement, we soon ventured across a scrapped Bedford that, although not quite our vehicle's twin, was certainly a close cousin. We thought our dreams had been answered, but our visions of cannibalising it for all the spares we could possibly need were soon dashed by the surly and abusive scrapyard owner who asked an outrageous price of us. After further attempts at bargaining we left, though James did manage to filch the insignia from the centre of the steering wheel that our Bedford was missing. Other Maritzburg scrap dealers proved of a similar ilk, and eventually our search for spares took us to a vast scrapyard north of Pretoria where we found acres of veld littered with the hulks of Bedford trucks, most of them old army vehicles. The proprietor here was more friendly, and allowed us to salvage the parts we needed for very little.

We found the experience a bit disquieting, however, when we discovered that he was in fact the brother of the man who had assassinated Chris Hani only three weeks before.

*

Haunted by the spectres of student loans and eight months without income, we endeavoured to spend as little as possible on camping gear, relying on using the battered pots and dirty, torn tents we had found in the back of the truck. The only luxuries we bought were a three-legged cast-iron potjie and three cheap foam mattresses to supplement the two already on board. Whereas trips we had read about had discussed such useful means of conserving space and weight as breaking the handles off hairbrushes, the expansive rear of the truck allowed us the luxury of taking almost anything we wanted. In addition to the tools and spares, the large gas bottle and stove, ten water jerrycans, tents, chairs, pots and plates that had come with the truck, we piled in a library of fifty or so books, Bronwyn's guitar, a cricket bat, a skottelbraai, and the extra mattresses. Two mountain bikes were tied down on the roof-rack.

In comparison to the eighteen months of dedicated attention the truck had received prior to its southward journey, our preparations seemed meagre and hasty. Robbie Enthoven, one of those who'd driven south, was out on holiday from London.

"I thought I might as well say goodbye to the truck now," he said casually to James. "Odds are I won't be seeing it again."

"Stuff you, Robbie! If a bunch of misfits like you lot could drive it across Africa, there can't be much to it. And we've sorted out all the mechanical problems now. She's running sweetly."

"You haven't seen the roads yet," he said, shaking his head. "The truck might be okay now, but it took quite a hammering on the way down. I don't know if it'll handle another hard journey. The suspension's the main thing. If I were you I'd have cut that viewing platform down. But that's just mechanically. A group of people is a lot harder to hold together over seven months than nuts and bolts."

The list of modifications and minor repairs grew steadily as the truck became more our own and we stopped wondering how those who had driven her down had managed. But the chores that needed doing, from mounting lights in the rear of the truck to making the back door burglar-proof, and strengthening the winch brackets, threatened to delay our departure by at least a week.

We drove north to Johannesburg where we met Robbie and discussed whether we should stay there until satisfied with the state of the truck. By now the desire in all of us to end the preparation and begin the experience was so strong that we decided unanimously to leave on schedule, and worry about the long list of Things to Do some time in the future.

The departure from Johannesburg was a flurried day of shopping, packing, organising photographs for visas, and getting inoculations. I packed my personal belongings in half an hour, throwing clothes, stationery, toiletries and extra books into a large rucksack which I bundled into the back. Anything I'd forgotten I could buy on the way, or do without.

We were frustratingly delayed at the last minute after discovering that the alternator bracket had snapped: not, we hoped, a portent of things to come. Eventually we left two hours late and, in our eagerness to get away, the trip nearly met with tragedy not five kilometres out of Johannesburg. A yellow Volkswagen Golf slowed suddenly in front of us and I watched in horror as James, grim-faced, pumped the foot brake and pulled up violently on the handbrake, bringing us to a shuddering stop just inches from the small car below.

The truck's momentum gave it a gyroscopic forward impetus and we had a second narrow escape the following day, just outside Gaborone. Juliet had taken the wheel for the first time and, coming upon a bend to the left, had discovered that the truck's steering was far heavier than her Mini's. We were heading straight for an old Land-Rover when her frightened yelp caused James and Robbie to reach forward from the back seats and wrench the wheel to the left, thereby extending by a number of years the life expectancy of the terrified Land-Rover driver.

I have friends who have killed people. A drunk hobo stumbling into a car's path, a head-on collision on tired night roads. There is a deep guilt, even with innocent deaths. What is irreversible leaves scars whose pain time dulls but cannot erase. The lumbering momentum of our truck would kill a child with ease, crumple a car like a tin can under a fist. In the back of my mind was the fear that we might confront such finality somewhere on the crowded, spontaneous roads ahead; that a dark cloud would descend over the trip, and remain to shut out light long after its end.

James had already begun to have a nightmare that would recur for weeks. The truck plunged uncontrolled down a road in darkness. He was behind the wheel, helpless. The noise of impact and his screams would jolt him awake. Already the responsibility for the trip, especially the burden of having to look after our ancient truck, was beginning to weigh down on him. That first night he wet his bed for the first time since infancy.

We stayed for the night, the first we had all been together, with the family of university friends, the Lawrensons, in Mafikeng, in the then homeland of Bophuthatswana. So well were we entertained there that I feared we'd been spoilt for the trip. We left after a fine breakfast, bearing gifts of beer, sherry and whiskey and the cab filled with the aroma of an immense picnic hamper given to us by our hosts. The next night saw us quickly adapt to the camping lifestyle, however, amongst a clump of trees just off the road sixty kilometres south of Francistown.

On the third day of the trip we were up early, anxious to cover the 550 kilometres to Maun by eight o'clock, as we'd arranged to meet Ross Douglas, an old school friend of James's then, in a pub called the Duck Inn. We wanted to spend five days or so exploring the Okavango Swamps before heading east to Zimbabwe.

We stopped for lunch, the remains of the picnic hamper given to us by the Lawrensons, under the shade of a baobab tree in the Makgadikgadi Pan. The peacefulness of the place, and its open empty space, made Johannesburg seem more than two days behind us. Stopping like that, attracted by some feature of the roadside more interesting than its surrounds, adopting the place as our own for a while, we felt the excitement of children in a new home. Like an enormous garden the land stretched out around us, its sand and stone ours temporarily as we interrupted our nomadic course to the north.

One of the repairs we hadn't been able to effect was to fix a wobble the truck developed as soon as it exceeded fifty kilometres per hour. To counteract this, James developed the technique of weaving the truck to one side and then, as soon as the wobble threatened to appear, veering across to the other.

Now, with evening drawing in and Maun moving closer, the stresses of leaving dissipated, replaced by exhilaration. The erratic weaving of the truck bore us ever onwards into Africa. "I loooove Botswana!" cried Bronwyn. The truck's drunken behaviour was rapidly being augmented by our own. It wasn't just freedom we were drunk on that afternoon. We'd been making serious inroads into the vast quantities of alcohol generously given us by the Lawrensons and were all singing jubilantly, much to the bemusement of the six hitch-hikers we had picked up and who were packed onto the roof-rack and in the door-wells.

The euphoria lasted into the night, which was one of wild revelry and dancing in dimly remembered nightclubs and shebeens all over Maun. We awoke the next morning, hungover but still excited, in a camping spot Ross had led us to in the early hours of the morning. It was a barren field covered with paper thorns and duiweltjies, the four-pointed thorns that bedevil Southern Africa. "God, this place is heinous," said Bronwyn. "But I love it!"

Chapter Two

The morning was spent mooning around in Maun. With difficulty we turned our alcohol-soaked brains to the logistics of gathering enough provisions for two days' camping. At some stage during the night it had been decided that we would spend time relaxing at a secret lagoon that Ross would take us to on the far side of the Buffalo Fence that acts as the boundary of the Okavango Nature Reserve.

Ross took James aside. Having seen our old vehicle and the wildly contrasting natures of the people on board, he was harbouring grave doubts about the trip. "What the hell have you got yourself into, James?" he asked. "Do you really think this lot will make it across Africa? And the truck? The bloody thing's ancient, man, and none of you is a mechanic. What are you going to do when it breaks down?"

Ross's scepticism, like Robbie Enthoven's, aroused James's quick competitiveness. "Don't project your own shortcomings onto us," he replied. "We'll make it across. Just watch us." These open doubts only strengthened James's outward resolve. But deep inside him uncertainty smirked.

An hour's lethargic shopping later we were following Ross down a thin sandy road, heading north towards the Okavango Swamps. The swamps form the world's largest inland delta, a vast network of shallow streams and lakes surrounded by low islands. The waters of the swamps first come together in the mountains of Angola, a thousand kilometres to the north west, to form the Cubango River, whose downward yearning never finds the satisfaction of the sea, dissipating instead into the unslakeable thirst of this dry place. Even when the waters flood, they flow only until the Makgadikgadi Pans where they shimmer briefly before being sucked away into the heat of the air and sand.

The road was flanked by mopani and acacia trees, and those travelling on the roof had to nimbly move about to avoid being scratched by their long thorny claws. In places the sand thickened, dragging at our wheels and causing the engine to strain, but by keeping our speed up and wheels straight we were able to avoid getting stuck and could leave the four-wheel drive prop shaft in the back of the truck, where it had been left to save on fuel.

We rounded a corner to find the road disappeared briefly beneath a small river. "Hell, James, do you reckon we're going to need four-wheel drive?" I asked. "The river bed could be quite soft."

"It looks quite deep!" exclaimed Bronwyn excitedly.

"We'll cruise through," James affirmed confidently. "Go for it!"

I engaged second gear and accelerated down the slope. Like a mother elephant plunging into the water our yellow truck splashed its way across, inexorably, easily. We were all impressed, and beginning to feel quite proud of this vehicle that was our transport and our home in Africa.

After the frenetic pace of the last three days, which had been spent mostly in the cab driving, it was a relief to stop in one place for a while. We set up our first proper camp, pitching all the tents, digging out the collapsible chairs from the truck's darker recesses and sliding out the large wooden table from between the rear box and the chassis where it was kept. We made a fire and ate a meal of braaied meat, salad and baked potatoes beneath a star-bedecked sky. We went to sleep that night to the grunts of hippo and the occasional whoop of hyena, primeval African sounds.

The next day was spent exploring the area. At the Buffalo Fence we came across an elderly blind man who seemed to be the authority in the area, Mr Dintho, and his son Sepho. We all shook his hand and laughed uproariously when he looked towards Robbie through his sightless eyes and said, "Ah, so you're the fat one!"

*

Revitalised after two days without driving, we headed back to Maun and set off from there to The Swamp Thing camp. Whereas many exclusive private camps, accessible only by air, are to be found in remote parts of the 15,000 square kilometres of the swamps, The Swamp Thing, located at the southern end, is the only camp catering to budget travellers. And it is accessible by land. Land and one large river, that is. Just before the camp, as dusk was setting in, we found our way barred by a river thirty metres wide and one and a half deep.

"We'll definitely need four-wheel drive here," said James.

"Maybe we should just park here and carry our things across," I suggested.

"Nah, we'll cruise through. Trust me."

We put the prop shaft in for the first time and held our breaths as we drove the truck in up to her headlights. Again she forded it with ease, and we smiled a bit smugly at other campers ferrying their gear across to cars parked on the side we'd just crossed from.

The main complication of the crossing was that water had splashed into the fuse box, causing our headlights to short, a problem that was to recur soon after with near-disastrous consequences. We also found that we couldn't disengage four-wheel drive. James eventually realised the fault lay with the second-hand tyres we'd bought cheaply in order to conserve the off-road tyres (two new and four old) that had come down with the truck. As these front tyres were larger than the rear ones, when four-wheel drive was engaged the wheels were covering different distances with each revolution, resulting in tension being stored in the prop shafts, diff and half-shafts. To prove his theory, James jacked up the front of the truck and we watched the wheels spin wildly as the tension was released.

After a potjie meal we went to bed, planning the next morning to head into the swamps in *mekoro* for a three day safari.

I lie back in the mokoro, reaching out to touch the reeds that drift gently past. The sun is warm on my body. Dragonflies dart and stop above the water; weavers disappear through the bottom doors of their nests and emerge singing; jacanas pad earnestly across lilies at the water's fringes, heads down. It is soothing to be here. Our guide, Hekulehelo, poles us forward, the long, smooth branch sliding through his hands, with the steady rhythm these swamps have felt for centuries. The gentle splash of the pole entering the water is followed by the murmur of the dugout moving forward and the muted plops of droplets falling off as he swings the pole forward again. These are the moments I love in Africa, moments that are timeless, that could be found at any point in its history.

We had been warned that only the central, more expensive camps offered good game viewing. Fortunately this turned out not to be the case. Almost immediately we saw two adult elephants and a calf ford the stream only thirty metres ahead of us. Crossing slowly, their trunks raised like periscopes, they clambered out ponderously on the far side, their flanks below the water line gleaming darkly in the sun.

All around us the swamp's bird life sang and flew. Fish eagles, white-cowled and solitary, cried their majestic call, while lilac breasted rollers shot through the air, dazzling as they banked, and red bishops sat curiously, bobbing slowly on thin reed stems. Upon reaching our camp for the night, our guides took us on a game walk during which we saw two jackals in furious pursuit of some smaller creature, a family of warthogs, and herds of impala, tsessebe and wildebeest. A low drumming sound alerted us to the presence, over a small kopje, of a vast herd of buffalo, two thousand at least, heading across the veld under a thin cloud of dust. We crept up as close to them as possible, speaking in excited whispers, awed by their massive bulk, the girded potency behind their curved horns.

It was so much what we had come to see, and we returned to the camp in high spirits. There we met five Israeli tourists and shared a log fire with them as we cooked dinner.

It was fast becoming apparent that there were certain fairly significant ideological differences amongst the members of our crew. These had been bubbling beneath our conversation for the first week, and came out now in a heated argument that centred on whether South Africans ought to be patriotic, before spiralling off into related areas.

Though never aggressive, attitudes were forceful, fuelled by a bottle of unbelievably bad whiskey called Highveld from a case my mother had donated for the bribing of corrupt officials.

"I don't feel any patriotism at all towards South Africa," said James.

"I can't believe you can say that, James! Surely you feel something, some kind of pride. What about when the Springboks run onto the rugby field?" asked Robbie.

"I feel rocks. On all these rebel tours I supported the other team. You just have to look at those boneheads in the crowd to see the attitude that's stuffed South Africa up."

"But don't you have a love for your country?"

"What's there to love? Our cultural heritage? Our history of civil rights? Okay, I love the place, the geography of it, its mountains and beaches and all that. But I love it here too and I'm not a Botswanan."

"I don't understand how you can say that. How can you be indifferent to the place and the people you were brought up with? You must feel something towards it, a feeling of belonging."

"Look, Robbie, just because you've been brainwashed by the army doesn't mean I can't see the whole set-up for the corrupt and racist, shameful mess that it is."

"Who said anything about racism?"

Bronwyn joined in, saying that every white South African she'd met was racist, and this riled me into expressing the frustration I'd been feeling at her unforgiving attitude.

"But you have to see where these people are coming from. If you're force-fed racist propaganda from the cradle onwards, and if the only blacks you ever meet are uneducated servants, if your cities are white by night, it's a rare person who can see through it all and emerge without some kind of race prejudice."

"There's just no excuse for racism."

"I don't want to excuse it at all. I just wish you'd try to understand what it's been like in South Africa. How pervasive the government's propaganda has been. How difficult it is to unlearn the programming of eighteen years, even for someone like me who went to a liberal university, let alone some kid out on the platteland. I know. I feel it in myself at times. I hate it, but can't deny it's there."

"All the blacks I've met have been wonderful. Why don't the whites just go out and start getting to know them? I think it's just because you've had it so cosy and couldn't be bothered to change the way things are. That's why you're getting so uptight now."

"You're not understanding me at all. I don't condone racism in the slightest. I just wish you'd stop being so bloody judgmental. People are shaped by their environment from the first days of childhood. It's arrogant to think that if you or your friends had been brought up in South Africa you'd still have emerged non-racist. Children are born innocent and learn what they are taught. It's more complicated, more tragic, than happy whites on one hand, oppressed blacks on the other. If you look more deeply at these racist whites you'll see how wide the tragedy of apartheid really is. They aren't happy in themselves at all, brought up as they have been on hatred and fear. All discrimination stems from insecurity. You can't be happy if you're so insecure you need to create as diabolical a system as apartheid."

The arguments continued to rise in volume, drowning out the night sounds, and to veer away from the abstract towards more personal criticisms. Juliet refused to get involved, and the five Israelis watched bemusedly this minor eruption of the passion that underlies South African politics. They were even more bemused when, after the rest of us had retired to the tents, Robbie turned to them as an earpiece for his by now very drunken frustrations. Lying in our tents, we could hear his tireless diatribe rising into the night.

The next morning, as we returned to the main camp, saw no acrimony at all between us. It had been good to give vent to our feelings, to get things off our chests. But the night had shown that we were five very different people.

Back at The Swamp Thing we met five other South Africans heading overland across Africa. Two of them, Richard Gush and Greg Short, were old school-friends of James. The other three were Rich's girlfriend Lucy Chambers, his sister Kate, and their friend Alison Mitchell. Their vehicle was a white, snub-nosed, forward-control Land-Rover christened The Beast and, as we discovered, by amazing coincidence they had also set off for London from the small Natal town of Balgowan not a week after us. Their itinerary was almost identical to ours, and we were to bump into them several more times in similarly exotic spots.

As ever, after we had been in one place for a while, it was good to be back on the road again. We returned to Maun the next morning and headed towards Nata, the road junction 300 kilometres to the east, where we'd passed through six days before. The wheel shake was proving a great exasperation as it limited us to travelling at fifty kilometres per hour. At our lunch stop, taken amongst round granite rocks just off the road, James and I tightened all the U-bolts and reset the wheel alignment. Both attempts at stopping the shake proved fruitless.

Lunch was sandwiches filled with tomato, onion and bully beef. Juliet had managed to delay as long as possible the moment when we bit into our bully beef stocks, saying it looked far too much like dog food to possibly be healthy. We bullied her into trying a sandwich. Her verdict, unhappily for her, and much to our amusement, happened to coincide with James's tackle (for he'd forsaken all underwear on the trip) slipping into view. "It tastes okay, so long as I don't look at it," she said.

★

"One of the problems with orthodox medicine," I was saying, "is that it too often treats the symptoms and not the cause. Take psychiatry for example. Say I'm depressive. They take me aside, do all sorts of neurological tests and announce that the reason I'm depressed is because I've got too much of some chemical in my head. So they then give me some other chemical, to counteract the first one. It's obvious to me that the chemical imbalance is there in the first place because of some or other emotional imbalance – so why not concentrate on that, and try to resolve the actual causes of the problem instead of treating it as some kind of physical ailment?"

"It's not so easy," countered Juliet. "Sometimes treatment with chemicals is the only way to prevent people doing themselves or others harm. If the drugs restore them to some kind of equilibrium, then great."

"But the problem is that the medical profession draws too distinct a division between the mind and body. They don't approach healing holistically. This whole mind and body thing, what is it anyway? Just a useful division coined by some Greek philosopher. There's no such tangible thing as 'the mind' and another 'the body', they're inextricably interlinked. The state of one can't help but affect the other. I reckon almost all illness is psychosomatic."

"What?" James leapt in, sensing an easy argument. "So you mean to tell me that if you get malaria it's not because a mosquito bit you but because you're emotionally disturbed? Or that if your mind's okay the mosquito will leave you and go off to bite someone who's down in the dumps instead?"

"I don't know if I'd go that far. All I know is that when I'm emotionally well I never get sick, but when I'm stressed out I do. Who knows – maybe it takes more than just a mosquito bite to get malaria. This world's stranger than we think. Perhaps the immune system has to be weakened. I was reading a book by Louise Hay in which she puts it down to being out of balance with nature and with life. There could be something in that."

There was scorn in James's reply. "And horoscopes too. I can't believe you can believe in such irrational rubbish. What about the millions who are suffering from AIDS, or the children who are born HIV positive, or with any disease for that matter? They don't even have thoughts. You can't tell me their illnesses are psychosomatic.

"Everything comes down to chemical reactions. We are essentially organic machines. Viruses are able to exploit weaknesses in our immune system because their molecular structure enables them to. If I were to inject you now with HIV, there's no doubt you'd end up HIV positive. No matter what thoughts or emotions were in your mind."

Rationally I found it hard to counter James's arguments. They made logical sense. Yet there was in me also a sense that what happens is explicable and not random, that beneath the everyday misfortunes and coincidences of our lives a deeper pattern is unfolding. That there are lessons to learn and that we are offered the experiences through which these lessons can be learnt. But how to reconcile these divergent beliefs, the one rational, the other emotional? Rationally it is easy to sympathise with the view that such emotional beliefs, or feelings, might be born of fear, mere security blankets to be clutched onto in the face of the ineluctable and uncaring march of evolution, while emotionally those feelings, or intuitions perhaps, do exist – and who's to say our current scientific paradigm has all the answers anyway?

"Look, let me put it this way. I'm not saying that all illness is necessarily psychosomatic. All I'm saying is that I live my life as though it were. So if ever I fall ill I take it as a sign that there is imbalance in my life, and use the time for self-reflection, to work out how I need to change the way in which I'm living my life to make it more balanced. I can't be prescriptive and say that it's the truth and the way to live, only that as a philosophy it's worked well for me so far."

*

The next morning, as we were packing up camp, the Israelis, who happened to pass by in their car, stopped to warn us (erroneously, as it turned out) that the border post at Kazangula, where we were hoping to cross into Zimbabwe, closed at noon. Knowing we'd never make it, even without the crippling wheel shake, we consulted the Michelin map and decided to change tack and try to get into Zimbabwe at the dot on the map with the quaint name of Pandamatenga. Diversions like this were easy to make. At the outset we'd decided to leave our route as open as possible. There were certain places we had to get to – Vic Falls, Zanzibar, Nairobi, London – but how we got there would depend on whim, chance meetings and *coups d'état*.

Pandamatenga turned out to be a sleepy, two-cars-a-day border post. The only problem we had, other than convincing the officials ours was not a commercial vehicle, was politely ending the conversation their boredom would have let them continue all day. Our experience at border posts so far had been altogether more pleasant than we'd hoped, filled as our minds were by the echoes of the horror stories of bribery, corruption and imprisonment other travellers had told us. The fact that none of us had the necessary heavy-duty driver's licence didn't seem to matter at all. It was as though possession itself granted us licence to drive the truck, and we never had to convince anyone that the truck was actually a camper-van as our carnet, to cut down on temporary insurance costs, suggested.

It had also been straightforward obtaining visas. We'd left South Africa with not a single visa stamped into our passports, planning to get them at the borders until we reached Tanzania. Whereas James and Robbie had South African passports, I had been able to obtain a Greek passport as well as my South African one, being Greek by blood. Although most countries had acknowledged the breakdown of apartheid by lifting tourism sanctions, we had heard that some countries, such as Sudan and Algeria, were still refusing South Africans entry. If worst came to worst those of us not on South African passports could always drive through while the others flew on ahead.

Scared that swapping passports might lead to complications at immigration posts, I had decided to travel only on my Greek passport, a passport of convenience more than an indicator of identity.

Chapter Three — Harare

The detour via Pandamatenga had the fortunate advantage of diverting us through Hwange National Park whose dried grass and autumn cover provided for excellent game viewing. We spent two hours driving slowly along its sandy tracks, exchanging looks with impala and giraffe, before reaching the main road on the far side of the park where we turned north.

We arrived at Victoria Falls in mid-afternoon. After enquiring about prices at the local campsites, we trundled down Zambezi Drive to the National Parks Lodges. I had discovered the year before that if you arrive in the evening when the wardens are about to go off duty, they will allow you to hire the lodges of people who have failed to keep their bookings.

While we were waiting, we heard terrified, high-pitched squeals coming from the bushes nearby. Hurrying over, Robbie and I found a baby bushbuck. Its blue entrails hung out messily below its frantically beating heart. Red flecks of blood were splattered over the pretty white dots on its fawn coat. It had been eviscerated by a large male baboon who stared at us from a distance, intent on retrieving its prey.

"Ag, shame! The poor little thing," said Robbie. Then, picking up a stone a hurling it at the baboon, "Go on, *voetsek*!"

"We should put it out of its misery," I said.

"I suppose we could use the axe," Robbie suggested. "I'll go and get it from the truck."

"Jesus, I dunno," I replied, looking uncertainly at the thin brown neck beneath shocked, staring eyes. "What if we miss or don't kill it cleanly. We'd cause it even more suffering. Best to let nature take its course."

"I think you're right. I wouldn't be able to do it anyway. Poor thing. At least it doesn't look like it'll live much longer."

We returned to the front gate, telling ourselves that such cruelty is an inherent part of nature, but weighed down all the same. A few minutes later there was more agonised squealing, and then silence, as the baboon returned to kill the bushbuck. The park warden said the baboon probably wouldn't even eat the buck, and killed merely for the sake of it, like some cats do with mice.

He also said we could have one of the unclaimed lodges. We were jubilant as at Z$70 – about $10 – for the night it was cheaper than the campsite. It was infinitely more pleasant too. Sleeping six, the lodge had a fully-furnished kitchen and dining room, and a front lawn that sloped down to the Zambezi. We sat on the veranda drinking sundowners and watching a family of warthog trotting busily past, tails up like aerials. The setting sun painted the clouds purple and pink, and we got enjoyably drunk on gin and tonic and the heavy evening air.

We had seen the Israelis in town and invited them over for a party. They arrived and discovered all five of us in the bath together. An argument with Bronwyn over who would have our first bath in ten days led to me leaping in fully clothed to thwart her. She plunged in after, and from there things got steadily out of hand. As defences dropped and inhibitions eased we felt closer, more of a team, in this together.

Our excitement proved infectious, and the Israelis joined in the merrymaking. It soon became obvious that what they had told us about hardly drinking at all in their culture was true. A few glasses of wine and they became deliriously, obliviously drunk, in the way that happens only the first few times you get drunk on alcohol. We had brought the truck's speakers in from the cab and a soon as Queen started singing "I want to ride my bicycle," Yariv, the youngest and drunkest of them, leapt onto one of our mountain bikes and careered randomly around the house before crashing into a door and passing out, much to our amusement.

We had decided to stay at the Falls for two nights, and spent the next day swimming above and viewing the Falls and then going on a game drive. The waters of the Zambezi were high, causing a vast spray to be sent upwards and fall as a gentle rain. From one of the viewing points Robbie pointed out a rainbow arcing the spray. "Look," he said, "it's a little bushbuck rainbow."

On the game drive we came across two elephants just past the giant baobab known as the Big Tree. Eager to get close-up snaps, Robbie and Bronwyn crept up to the elephants but fled terrified when the large male made a mock charge toward them, ears flapping angrily at their temerity.

We had been told that the view from the Zambian side is better than that from the Zimbabwean, so the next day, while Juliet went for a flip above the Falls in a microlight, the four of us took turns cycling our two mountain bikes across the bridge. The view is better from Zambia. The paths are plain and unfenced and an outcrop, called the Knife Edge, seems to take you right into the falls themselves.

Standing at the side of the Falls under their unsteady shower, I thought of how wondrous it must have been to come across such dramatic and majestic natural beauty for the first time, as Livingstone had in 1855. And how odd that the original, and far more evocative name, *Mosi-oa-Tunya*, 'smoke that thunders', should be superseded still by the sterile name of some faraway and long-dead Queen. In this simple fact I saw how far-reaching and strong the octopus arms of that Empire were. And though its arms might now have withered, the beating of its heart still plays the bass of the score of our African lives. It was no coincidence that London was the destination we had chosen.

★

It was getting late, and still Juliet hadn't returned from her microlight flight. At last she came into sight, walking across the bridge from the Zambian side.

"Jesus, Jules, where the hell have you been?" asked James.

"We wanted to leave ages ago," I added.

"We crash-landed in Zambia! Something went wrong with the engine."

"Shit! Are you okay?"

"Fine, fine. Just a bit shaken. We had to walk for miles through a game park to get back to the car."

"You're pulling our leg, aren't you."

"No, seriously. He even gave me my money back if I promised not to tell anyone."

"Well I'm glad you've come out alive," said Robbie, "there's not much space in the back of the truck for a coffin."

Once again, a bad habit that had been formed on our first night, we drove on after dark, something we'd wanted to avoid altogether on African roads. The moon was up when we stopped on the side of the road near Deka. The conventional route from Vic Falls to Harare, in northern Zimbabwe, is to detour via Bulawayo, the main city of Matabeleland, the south-western province; but we'd decided to take the direct route, a dirt road running parallel to Kariba Dam, which lies below the falls, to Karoi, despite having been told it was badly corrugated and potholed. Robbie was eager to get to Raffingora where he was to stay with Bridget his girlfriend's family, and woke us up early with his not too gentle coaxing.

"Come on, come on, up, up, up! Here's some tea. It's nearly lunchtime already. Come on, Jules. What on earth are you up to? Right, where's that cattle prod?"

The truck started easily. I engaged second gear and it moved forward, shuddering slightly under its own weight, accelerating slowly before enough speed had been gathered for me to push in the heavy clutch and change into third. Elevated like that, looking down on the road, with my hands on either side of the steering wheel, as though holding reins, it felt more like I was riding the truck than driving it, guiding its dangerous weight along the path of the road.

"Never drive with your thumbs on the inside of the steering wheel," James had warned us. "If we hit a rut and the wheels are wrenched sideways the steering wheel will spin round wildly and rip them off!"

We stopped for breakfast in the hills above the small town of Binga, looking down over the blue tail of Kariba's flattened coelacanth shape. The arms of drowned mopani trees reached upward from the water in supplication, their rock-hard wood offering silent testimony that the water of this man-made lake wasn't always here like this.

The road was far better than we had been led to believe but we passed only four other vehicles the whole day: two buses, one of which crabbed alarmingly, as though in a permanent skid, a 4x4 safari Land-Rover and an old army truck, V-shaped for protection against landmines.

Again we drove on into the night, and into near disaster as well. I was at the wheel, driving downhill when suddenly the light fuse blew as it had done in Botswana, plunging our world into darkness. Driving by the after-image in my mind, I pressed down on the brake, angling the truck out of the centre of the road lest another vehicle crash into it. After agonising seconds the brakes managed to halt the lumbering momentum of the truck. Getting out, we saw that we had come to rest only a couple of inches from a culvert over a six foot drop.

We rewired the fuse, which was only a thin strip of wire stretched across a plastic board, like those found in old farmhouses, and continued gingerly to the first site suitable for camping.

*

"There's something magical about this place," I was saying, "something you just don't find overseas. Being Africans, we'd struggle to live outside of Africa permanently."

"But you're not Africans," interjected Bronwyn.

"What? Of course I'm an African, just like you're a New Zealander. What else could I be?" I asked, indignantly.

"You're a European," she replied.

"No, I'm not!"

"I've never even been to Europe," said Robbie angrily. "All my grandparents were born in Africa. We've had bugger all to do with Europe for generations."

"To me Africans means Blacks," said Bronwyn.

"So what would you call Mike Tyson. Do you consider him an American?" asked James, joining in.

"He's an American Negro."

"And Negro just means black, so why can't we be white Africans?"

"'Cause you're not African. Everything about you is European."

"You're mad, Bronwyn. You might as well be saying that only Maoris should be called New Zealanders."

The argument continued with increasing frustration and no resolution. In the past Afrikaners called English-speaking South Africans 'souties', short for 'soutpiels' or 'salty dicks', because they had one leg in England, the other in Africa, and their 'piel' dangling in the Atlantic. But this pejorative had fallen into disuse by our generation. Yes, our culture was very Anglocentric and this had been exacerbated by apartheid, which had prevented any movement towards a more homogeneous culture; but to us there was only one place we could call home and that was Africa. We resented Bronwyn's easy dismissal of us from the continent we called home.

And yet, deep down I could not help but feel a slight discomfort at what she said. We had been brought up in the West, culturally and cognitively. While I knew and spoke critically about the fact that the First World disparages Africa, is unwillingly to relax its rigid, self-righteous stance and listen to what it might have to say, I knew too that the rhythms of Africa in us had been drowned out by the assertive voice of the Reasoning West.

*

Bridget's family farmed in Raffingora, a town near Banket, the farming district where Doris Lessing was brought up. After dropping Robbie off at the turn-off to Raffingora from where he would hitch-hike to their farm, we continued south through Harare to the farm of my uncle and aunt, Pete and Jackie Bekker, in Marondera, a busy, expanding town sixty kilometres to the east of the capital.

While Juliet and Bronwyn went hiking in the Chimanimani Mountains, a beautiful range which lies along the eastern border with Mozambique, James and I, with the help of my cousin Brendon, completed the repairs and modifications we had started in Balgowan. Apart from getting spares such as U-bolts made up and fixing the wheel wobble, the most important concern was to strengthen the brackets supporting the engine-driven winch. These had been buckled hauling the truck out of soft sand in the Namib Desert on the way down, and we knew that it would be a vital component if our route were to take us into the jungle as we hoped.

Even though we had been together for only two weeks, it was with something of a relief that we separated. You can relax completely only with people you know intimately, when your allusions are recognised, your humour understood, your memories shared. The period apart gave us time in which to assimilate what we had done, and planned to do, to gather breath for the next step of the journey.

The shared responsibility of looking after the truck's mechanics made the frustrations and setbacks of the repairs easier to bear, and brought us closer together. Although I didn't have as great an aptitude for mechanics as James, part of me delighted in working with the huge tools that had come with the truck, ratchets a foot long and shiny chromium sockets that sat heavy and comfortable in my hand, the largest the size of a small pot. Working on the truck required physical effort, a refreshing change from deskbound studying or office work, as we jumped on the wheel spanner to loosen the wheel-nuts or pulled like rowers to tighten the U-bolts fastening the suspension.

Changing tyres was a demanding task, not without its dangers.

"Each year in Central Africa more people are decapitated by three-rimmed wheels exploding apart as they change them than die in truck crashes," James was fond of warning. His lore of trucking might not have been exactly true, but we were careful to keep clear as we let down the air from the wheel before releasing the interlocking rims and then levering away the stubborn rubber of the tyres, which was glued to the hub by the heat of driving. Using soapy water as a lubricant, we would force two heavy crowbars into the crack between hub and tyre, bearing down on them with all our weight.

During the nine days that we stayed at Mitengo Farm, I read Thomas Pakenham's absorbing history of the colonisation of Africa: *The Scramble for Africa*. My mind was filled with images of what we might see ahead, of the Ituri rainforest, so dense that Stanley had "zigzagged through it for 160 days without seeing a green field the size of a cottage floor"; of mighty green rivers slicing their way through jungle and plunging over cataracts and waterfalls; of endless tracts of barren sand and dunes shimmering beneath a remorseless sun.

There were other images too, still threatening to travellers in an Africa a hundred years older: of crippling fevers, dysentery and malaria; of murder and theft; of bloody accidents and personal hatreds. The price paid for freedom is insecurity. They walk into an uncertain future hand in hand. The trip so far had been through places that were safe and we knew well. Now the unknown and the trepidation it evokes waited for us, and the excitement I felt as I looked to the experiences that lay ahead was tinged with a thin grey streak of dread.

★

The repairs we'd made to the truck boosted our confidence as we resumed the journey north. Small additions had made travelling more comfortable too. A welder at Brendon's fencing factory had fashioned a short ladder for us out of cast iron which made getting into and out of the back of the truck easier. Proud of his work, he had scorched his name, Kitembo, into the metal. We had also fetched from Harare airport a parcel of music tapes which had been left behind in the chaos of leaving Johannesburg.

James was forever tinkering with the truck, tuning the engine or finding ways of streamlining our camping and driving. We had been warned that on the way down the fine dust on the roads had choked a few cassette players to death, so he mounted ours on the roof of the cab, as far away from the pervasive dust as possible. With the number of hours we would be on the road, music was crucial to our sanity, and between us we had a great variety of tapes which we cycled through repeatedly, their sounds reverberating from the two massive hundred watt speakers that were mounted on brackets next to the driver and front passenger.

Foodstuffs are cheap in Zimbabwe and were even cheaper for us as James had managed to strike an excellent black market exchange rate with a pensioner anxious to get money out of the country. We did a massive shop at the Farmers' Co-op in Karoi, filling the back of the truck with biscuits, tea, coffee, bags of flour, maize meal, sugar, milk powder, and hundreds of cans of tinned meat, sausages, Sumu tomato and onion mix, sweet corn, condensed milk and jam.

We then spent two days at Pamwechete Farm in Raffingora, a beautiful estate of 12,000 acres of rippling green wheat fields owned by Robbie's 'in-laws', Jo and J.C. Nicolle, who were wonderfully generous hosts, and treated us like family. Keen to capitalise on the cheap price of agricultural diesel (J.C. offered us eight litres per US dollar), we loaded a forty-four gallon drum into the rear of the truck. This was to result in the back, and all our possessions, becoming indelibly impregnated with the sharp odour of diesel, but it increased our fuel capacity to 850 litres which we reckoned, at a conservative four kilometres per litre, would take us as far as Tanzania.

When the Nicolles waved goodbye to us, it was with grave doubts about our truck's ability to pass muster on the African roads ahead. Reversing onto their gently sloping lush green lawn, we were unable to drive off. Our wheels slipped haplessly beneath us. Even engaging four-wheel drive didn't provide sufficient traction. What was to have been a glorious send-off, five young adventurers journeying into the unknown, became an embarrassing exercise in how to operate the winch as we looped its cable around a jacaranda tree and slowly pulled ourselves off the lawn.

We headed north towards the Zambezi River, driving through the endless expanse of unspoilt bushveld that covers northern Zimbabwe. The view from the roof-rack was magnificent. Dense clusters of trees stood amid the dry grass that covered the long, undulating hills, dark green on yellow, like the flanks of a leopard. Only the road, thinning to the horizon, disturbed the ancient feel of the land, its unmastered beauty.

Filled again with the excitement of heading north, further into adventure, we clambered down into the cab and back out the door and up again like sailors in the rigging of a ship, revelling in being young and out of doors, with the sun on our skin.

Friends of the Nicolles, the MacMillans, had offered us the use of their riverside house in Chirundu. We were met there by the caretaker, who helped us to settle in. His name was Robson. Naturally, this immediately became Robbie's new nickname. The afternoon we spent on the verandah overlooking the swift brown waters of the Zambezi was a strange one. While we were camped near Binga, James had gone off for a walk and come back carrying a large shopping bag stuffed full of dope, which he'd swapped for two old T-shirts.

"And he would have given it to me for one! What economics! We both reckon we've scored the best deal of our lives!" he exclaimed. James was keen to store it away and smuggle it into Zambia and a heated argument followed.

"I refuse to go anywhere near a border post with a truck full of dagga," I protested.

"What are the chances of them finding anything? There are a million places we can hide it."

"I don't care. It would be bloody stupid to risk the whole trip for one old T-shirt. It or me, you choose."

So we decided to get rid of the dope, but only after consuming as much of it as we could this side of the border. Having a deep aversion to smoking, I'd never tried dope before, but from what I'd seen at university, its effects seemed safe and it was about as addictive as alcohol, so I'd been curious to try it, given the right environment. There couldn't have been a much safer environment for such experimentation, set as we were in the middle of nowhere, without any responsibilities or commitments, and we began kneading dough for what emerged from the potjie an hour later as a steaming but distinctly green-tinged loaf of bread.

The problem with eating dagga is that you have no way of monitoring or controlling its effect because it is significantly delayed, unlike with smoking it. Unfortunately for us appetite overcame reason and we gorged on the delicious bread, smearing it with butter and apricot jam and then baking more. For almost two hours it seemed to have no effect. Evening drew in, softening the river from brown into silver. An occasional splash marked the movement of a large bird or crocodile below. The thin, puffy clouds above us reflected pink the fading light of the sun. The day's heat remained behind, warm and comforting.

All of a sudden, ordinary events became hysterically funny. I started giggling uncontrollably. Like an endless spiral of dominoes, our laughter sparked off more in each other. A falling leaf produced a bout of hysterics. An inane comment brought about an eruption of chortling. Through the thin gap still open to my consciousness I could see my own idiotic behaviour but could do nothing to stem the flood of unfocused laughter. It seemed to me that whereas alcohol makes people in some ways more real, stripping from them their masks and inhibitions, removing the controls they've clamped over their emotions, dope made me into someone else...

"I don't feel myself at all," I said, weakly. "I don't feel normal."

"Ah, but normality is relative," replied James.

"Absolutely," said Bronwyn.

Chapter Four — Lusaka

And I never knew
What my house looked like
Until I
Took a walk outside

Jools Holland's voice flooded the cab. His would become one of the trip's theme tapes, and we danced and sang to it on our way down the road to Lusaka.

Leaving the countries we knew, it seemed that at last we were getting into Africa. Whatever that might mean. Is there an essence that is Africa? Can it be said that Cape Town is less African than, say, Mombasa? Perhaps it is just that since Roman times Africa has been symbolic of what is new and different, and for us the African experience grew stronger the further we travelled into the unfamiliar.

Apart from our brief foray across the border at Vic Falls, none of us had been to Zambia before. What I had heard about it was mostly negative, stories of muggings and robberies, but I had heard also of the beginnings of economic recovery under the new president Chiluba and I was keen to see for myself the extent to which the country was undoing the decades of corruption and mismanagement it had suffered under its first incarnation as Northern Rhodesia, the poorer cousin in the federation with Southern Rhodesia, and subsequently during the twenty-seven years as independent Zambia under the rule of Kaunda's single party.

We had planned definitely to spend time in Malawi. To get there we could go either through Tete Province in Mozambique, to the east, or west through Zambia. Our route was decided for us by Robbie. Studying the Michelin map, he had spotted South Luangwa National Park a short distance off the main road from Lusaka to Malawi.

"That's it, we have to go through Zambia. There is no wildlife in Mozambique anyway – it's all been shot out during the war."

Robbie had already expressed the desire to visit every game reserve we passed within a hundred kilometres of. Without specific preferences of our own, the rest of us were happy to go along with his passion.

The bank Robbie had worked for had recently produced an economic report on South Africa's neighbours, and he read out extracts to us which confirmed what we had heard about Zambia's poverty.

"Inflation is at 200%, interest rates 138%, GNP per capita $290. The population is only 8,000 000, the same as Malawi's, although in size Zambia's four times as big as Malawi."

Evidence of the country's poverty came first in the main road from the border to Lusaka. Although being repaired with the help of US aid, it was severely potholed, with frequent dusty, corrugated detours veering off into the bushveld. As we drew nearer to Lusaka, we saw a sadder and more incongruous reflection of its economic troubles. All along the side of the road people were sitting behind small cairns of white stones which they appeared to be selling. Quite where the demand for this gravel came from was a mystery to us, and we surmised that perhaps it was used in the manufacture of the roads. But even if this was the case, there were so many people selling the same thing, and each had so little in front of them, that we couldn't see how they could possibly profit from the exercise. All the way into Lusaka we didn't see anyone selling anything else. Only these small mounds of little white stones.

Lusaka reminded me of a smaller and poorer version of Harare. Like Zimbabwe's capital it was green and well-wooded but it had a run-down air and was strewn with litter. We found out about a new campsite called Eureka on a farm to the south and retraced our path through the endless detours that wound caduceus-like around the southern road.

The camp was neatly laid out, with braai areas and thatched roof shelters set in spacious kikuyu lawns. We met a group of white Afrikaans-speaking South Africans around the communal fire. Disenchanted with the political change in South Africa, fearing and hating the ANC, they were looking for land they could farm in Zambia. In the spirit of their ancestors they were trekking north, going to a place where, as they said, "the shit has already happened." We found their negativity tedious and retired early, moving our sleeping bags into the open shelters where we slept to avoid the chore of putting up tents.

★

The next morning was spent in town shopping, moving from stall to stall in the open market, buying tomatoes here and oranges there, the smell of sun-warmed vegetables mingling with that of the dust scuffed up by our feet. Robbie bought an oil painting off a local artist which he thought wonderful but which the rest of us reckoned was pretty lame. One of the ideas that we had raised excitedly was to divide one side of the truck into panels and have a local artist from each country we went through fill a panel in whatever way they wished, transforming the truck into a mobile collage of African art. But already we realised that finding sufficient time and skilled artists would be impractical and regretfully shelved the idea.

An idea we had put into practice was to paint a huge map of Africa in black on the side of the truck. Our progress had begun to be recorded across it in red. At every major junction Robbie would climb onto one of the camping chairs, paint pot and brush in hand, and carefully extend the erratic, winding line that, we hoped, would ultimately reach the blue label just below the roof of the truck that said "Mediterranean Sea."

The red line snaked its way 200 kilometres eastward that day. Leaving Lusaka, we popped in out of curiosity to look at the University of Zambia which we happened to pass by. The grounds were extensive and beautifully kept but we were struck by the contrast between the old, prefabricated residences we saw and the Burmese teak and brick residences we had lived in as students. Soon after, we came across the first of the notorious Zambian roadblocks. We approached it with dread but it, and the two that followed as well, proved to be amicable affairs. Nearing one, James lit up a Madison cigarette, pretended to smoke it and offered a few to the policeman who accepted them cheerily and waved us on through.

The countryside we passed through was spectacular, endless high hills of green bush and trees stretching out to the horizon. We camped in a clearing just off the road. In the evening Robbie and I went for a slow jog. Returning into a blood-red sun, and seeing the smoke of the campfire rising slowly into the still yellow air, we were awed by the beauty of the place. Other than the road, there was no sign of human interference. And although there was some comfort in this thin road cutting through the bush, I felt a different comfort in the proximity of Nature. Camping like that, going to sleep on the earth and under stars, to the sound of cricket symphonies, I felt something deep within me resonate faintly in response, echoing the calling of Nature's voice. Away from business, culture, entertainment, sport, education, buildings, I was offered a simpler, less distracted view of myself. There stirred in me whispers that I belonged to something more than just my human society.

The morning was warm and quiet. James returned from a run, bare-chested and vibrant, sweat glistening on his muscular body.

"God, it's great to be here!" he shouted, his arms aloft and palms upturned. "You should have seen the sunrise. It was magnificent! Like the first day of the world."

Bronwyn watched as he started doing press-ups, cords tightening on his back and arms as his muscles tensed under his skin which stretched over his body paper-thin, like the skin across the bridge of your nose. With a satisfied grunt, an awareness of his lean strength, James stood up, clapping his hands to remove the dust. "Come on, Bronnoes," he called energetically, "let's get stuck into those eggs."

After a leisurely breakfast we packed and left. A few miles down the road we passed the place where, two days later, the crew of The Beast would be stoned and forced to leave after a hasty and frightened packing.

*

The road east was empty of vehicles. Only the occasional tin-roofed shop dispelled the rural feel of the land we drove through. Small boys herded cattle, flicking at them with sticks as tall as themselves. Cooking smoke curled thinly above the thatch roofs of village huts. The eyes of adults turned briefly away from the fields to watch our passing.

Within the cab our eyes would move from the surrounding countryside back to the books we held tightly as we bobbed and swayed over them. Bursts of discussion would be sparked by some observed thing or newly-read fact or idea. As the conversation rolled onto political or philosophical shores the tone of it became more argumentative, its ground held onto more firmly. But for the most part the conversation was bantering, Robbie joking about his days of shirking in the army, Bronwyn recounting animatedly her many humorous escapades at university.

More personal conversations were those held on the roof of the truck, where three chairs were mounted. The seclusion encouraged a sharing that was less approachable in the seemingly critical confines of the group below. As the wind flicked our hair behind us and half-shut our eyes, we shouted our histories above it, saying who we were, slowly building up the trust in each other that this knowledge brings.

We would continually clamber out from the cab and up onto the roof, swinging one-handed around the door-well and up onto the fuel tank behind the cab, a grey sea of tar blurring beneath us as we climbed. Even here though, or in the intimacy of the campfires, guards were raised against too open a revelation of ourselves. Such a trip would naturally attract people who are self-reliant, but it seemed as though, beyond this, the uncertainty of the future before us made us less willing to reveal, and thereby potentially weaken, ourselves. The unknowns of the long months to come lay not only in our interactions with the world around us, but in the dynamics within our group as well. Trust could not easily be granted, lest it be broken.

We reached Petauke, a sprawling village south of Luangwa National Park, at lunchtime. Too lazy to siphon diesel, we filled up at its only garage. While we were eating bread rolls we'd bought we decided to leave the main road and take a short cut to the park, heading up the thin white line we could see on the Michelin map.

At one o'clock the next morning, exhausted and hopelessly lost, with Robbie at the wheel, grimly intent on reaching the camp, we were bitterly regretting the decision.

To begin with the road was easy to follow, but we soon came to a fork not reflected on the map and out of nothing more than a hunch, took the right-hand path. We began to feel unsure of our route and stopped to ask some people we passed if we were on the right road. We discovered that they were Mozambican refugees who were living in a camp nearby. As they were new to the area themselves they couldn't assist us. We drove on.

"I'm sure we're heading due north," I said, much later.

"The only direction you could be sure we're heading is due forward," replied Robbie, who had begun to notice the lack of a homing-pigeon instinct in me.

"Hey," said Bronwyn, "doesn't that signpost look familiar?" And it did. We had just completed a two hour, sixty kilometre loop around the refugee camp. We felt frustrated at the wasted time and decided to press on, thinking we could still make the camp by eight or nine o'clock. With a reddening sun growing fat on the western horizon, our day was just beginning.

Half an hour later we stopped to get directions from a soldier and discovered we were again heading in the wrong direction. We should have turned left up a barely noticeable track we'd passed a few kilometres before. We were halfway through a ten-point turn when the truck suddenly spluttered and stalled.

"We must have run out of fuel," I offered.

"No, that's impossible," said James. "We bought diesel in Petauke. There must be an airlock or something."

Probing the depths of the tank with a torch confirmed that we hadn't run out of diesel, and we spent almost an hour blowing into the fuel tank and bleeding the injector leads, in an attempt to release the blockage and extricate the truck from the centre of the road where it sat widthways, like a sphinx, barring the road ahead.

Emotion is relative, and our frustration at the delay, and anxiety for the truck's health, caused the return of its deep throbbing voice to fill us with joy where before we had taken it for granted. As we drove on, jubilant at having been up to the challenge confronting us, we had no idea that the ghostly spluttering had not been exorcised at all. Driven away temporarily, it would soon return to haunt us.

The night was black and moonless. The pool of light cast by our headlights revealed a road that was steadily worsening. We drove slowly, skirting potholes, hemmed in by the window-high grass that bent into the road ahead of us. Grass seeds and stems, torn off by our passing, fell into the cab, their sharp smell mingling with the fresh night air and the fine dust kicked up by our tyres.

Suddenly ahead of us the road seemed to end abruptly. I braked, staring at the line in the road ahead where our light ended and the blackness began. We climbed out and went forward to inspect the chasm in front of us. It was a dry river bed, about ten foot deep and twenty wide, carved by long-absent waters into a groove the shape of a large skateboard ramp. It seemed we'd definitely get stuck in it. Not wanting to be the one to drive the truck over the steep edge and into the soft sand and darkness below, I handed over the driving to James. I held my breath as we accelerated forward and then nose-dived into the pit, the truck lurching forward violently and then rearing up almost immediately, bucking and straining as we mounted the other side.

The road wound haphazardly through the grass and trees. The grass in the centre of the road was almost as high as that on the sides, witness to how little the road was used.

It fell forward like wheat beneath a harvester as we drove resolutely through. We were tired by now, but Robbie was insistent on reaching Mfuwe Camp, the destination in the reserve we'd picked out on the map.

"Just think about it," he encouraged us. "We can all have a warm shower and some tea and we'll be able to relax the whole of tomorrow. It can't be far. Only another half hour or so."

At eleven o'clock, after another hour of dongas and potholes, we found a military camp where a sleepy guard directed us to a turning we'd missed two kilometres back. We asked him about camping in the area. "No camp," he said, "too much hyena."

The week before we had seen the Mortal Enemies documentary on the savage nocturnal battles fought between lions and hyena. Visions of these scavengers, with their bloody and powerful jaws and ruthless pack instinct, were fresh in our minds. We decided to carry on.

The road ended abruptly. A new road was being built on top of the old one, obliterating it. Sand had been shaped into a flattened mound, like a long mine dump, in preparation for the new surface. Tall poles wedged into the sand marked the course of the road. We looked around for a detour, but there was none. We tried driving on but got stuck in the thick sand and had to dig and winch ourselves out. Deciding we couldn't continue, we began to turn around but slid backwards down the steep bank at the edge of the road. The winch came out again. It was now past midnight, we'd left more than sixteen hours earlier, hadn't eaten for eleven, and were fast becoming disheartened. The thought of retracing the way we had come, of doubling back along those forty kilometres that had taken five hours to cover, sapped our will. We tried again to go forward but got stuck for a third time.

Woken by the noise, two local men came up to offer assistance. They spoke smatterings of English, and we learned from them there was no detour and that we were on the right road. They seemed to think there should be no problem with using the road and showed us the path to take, pulling the marker poles out of the ground and tossing them aside as they walked forward. We approached the roadworks again, at greater speed this time, and made it across, the steering wheel spinning wildly beneath James's hands as the truck slewed its way forward, its wheels wrenched sideways by the grasp of the thick sand.

We found ourselves in an open wood. In order to widen the road, trees had been felled at its side. They had been burnt down, not chopped, by fires set at their bases. The stumps of the trees glowed brightly in the night, like dozens of unblinking, red, malevolent eyes. Their trunks lay dead beside them, smouldering, and we had the feeling of having been transported to some other time or place, as though we were in Delville Wood, or some newly-blasted war zone in Bosnia. It was surreal, the scene around us, and held a stark beauty. But it was eerie too, ominous. We wondered where the people responsible for the construction and destruction all around us were. We'd seen only three people and no vehicles or habitation for hours.

It became impossible to see where the road led. It split and branched continually into a maze of tracks and paths that might have been created by animals or vehicles, we couldn't tell. Robbie had taken over driving, and he steered this way then that, intent on finding the camp. Eventually, nearing two o'clock, with tired, gritty eyes, wearied by the continual driving, and not even sure if we were heading in the right direction any more, we persuaded him to stop. We felt vulnerable in the silence and darkness of the night. The coughs of lion and whoops of hyena led to us putting up only one tent, with three sleeping in or on the truck.

Having drawn the short straw, I lay down inside the tent, but fell asleep immediately, exhausted.

The next morning we drove the remaining thirty kilometres to South Luangwa National Park, along fishnet roads that parted and rejoined, all leading, ultimately, to the knotty confluence of the camp. On the way, twenty giraffe walked across the road in front of us, and then broke into the fluid, slow-motion run that makes them so graceful despite their size. They and the impala and waterbuck we saw were outside the camp, roaming as freely as any animal ever did.

At Mfuwe we met a couple who were heading towards Lusaka. We easily dissuaded them from taking the short cut to Petauke. They in turn advised us that the best place to camp was Flatdog Camp, run by an ex-overland driver called Jake da Motte. The camp was gloriously positioned, on the high southern bank of the Luangwa River. It had the additional advantage of being next to Mfuwe Crocodile Farm. The mud below us was filled with the motionless lengths of crocodiles who had escaped their captivity.

That afternoon we watched amazed at what seemed to be a fight to the death. The centre of the river was the arena for the duel. Two huge crocodiles, at least three metres in length, would float slowly towards each other. Suddenly the river would explode into spray and limbs as the two massive tails twisted and writhed upwards and around each other, thrashing violently, kicking up depth-charged plumes of water. We watched the battle subside and re-ignite for two hours, engrossed. Later we found out that this was crocodiles' way of making love.

*

At dusk we went on a night game drive, with Jake proving a very knowledgeable and entertaining guide. "The elephant population," he was saying, "is 6,000, 100,000 less than ten years ago. Poachers have had a free run of the place until recently. They'd come in and mow down whole herds with machine-guns. One of the strange side effects of this is that 20% of females are tuskless, as opposed to only 4% ten years ago. It's natural selection perverted by human greed. The tuskless females are abnormally aggressive too. They have to be to chase other females away from trees they have knocked down and ripped apart with their tusks."

Different animals inhabit the world of night, and we saw civet, genet, porcupines, owls and hyenas, but no large cats, which Jake assured us was very unusual. Hippos were out too, grazing in their dozens. They look so different out of the water, their pink feet and bellies exposed. With their wide mouths and small, blinking eyes, they seemed somehow embarrassed at being seen naked, running quickly away on their short legs. Nightjars flitted silently through the fast-cooling air as we turned back towards the camp. The sky ahead of us blazed white as a shooting star seared, seconds long, its way into the atmosphere.

★

We spent two more days at Flat Dog Camp, reading, writing and relaxing, and then headed towards Malawi. We stopped for lunch in Chipata, the last Zambian town before the border. We found a restaurant called The Hot Spot where we ordered chicken and spoke to the local patrons. The people were friendly and treated us no differently to anyone else. It made me long for the day when the people in my own country further south could interact within equality, when an enforced humility would be replaced by pride.

Robbie went off to search for a money changer, as we'd heard the rates for kwacha were better in Zambia than

Malawi. He entered the first Indian shop he passed, and there met Iqbal, a pleasant if rather shady man, who offered us 7.5 kwacha per US dollar.

"What about the customs officials?" we asked. "What'll happen if they find the money?"

"Oh no," Iqbal reassured him, "the police are our friends. When they want money they also come to us."

Chapter Five

When Hastings Kamuzu Banda held sway in Malawi, tourists were regularly harassed at the country's borders. Long-haired young men were shorn of their locks, woman refused entry for wearing shorts, and anyone carrying the backpacker's Bible, *Africa on a Shoestring*, had to look on helplessly as the offending Malawi chapter, critical of Banda's autocratic rule, was torn out in front of them. When we got there, the President for Life's star was waning but was still, we had heard, the guiding light for most border officials. So we hid our three copies of *Africa on a Shoestring*, dressed Juliet and Bronwyn up in kikois – sarong-like wraps – and hoped our hair didn't look offensively long.

Our troubles came from a completely unexpected source, however. I'd entered Zimbabwe and Zambia on my Greek passport and, mistakenly thinking I didn't need a visa for Malawi, presented it again to the Malawian official.

"Greeks need visas."

"What?"

"Yes, you cannot enter Malawi."

"Can't I get one here?"

"No. You'll have to go back to Lusaka. You can get a visa there."

"Oh, God. Are you sure?"

By this stage the others had gone through easily enough on their South African and British or New Zealand passports, so I tried a different tack. "Look, uh, I'm actually not that Greek. I'm really a South African, and come to think of it, I'd prefer to enter Malawi on this passport," I said tentatively, showing him my blue South African one.

"What?" he asked, scrutinising the two passports intently, his eyes glinting at the thought of apprehending an international fraudster. He looked deeply sceptical. "I will not accept this passport. You'll have to enter on the passport you used first. You can get a visa in Lusaka."

"Are you sure I can't *buy* a visa here?" I asked, speaking what I supposed to be corrupt officialese.

"No. Only in Lusaka."

"I don't know what to do," I said to Juliet who had just finished her immigration formalities. "This guy's straight and a complete bureaucrat. Rules is rules and he's not going to budge."

"Let me have a go," she replied. "We'll see what I can do." Two minutes later I'd had my South African passport stamped and was through, not a penny poorer and grateful for the strange kind of power women have in a patriarchal system.

★

We were not in the best of physical shape, heading towards Lilongwe. Bronwyn and I had slight diarrhoea, Robbie was in discomfort, having managed to split his bottom on the morning after our dehydrating night of dagga and booze on the banks of the Zambezi, and James was feeling sick from the Lariam he'd taken.

Malaria had filled many of our conversations. Robbie and I had started taking paludrine and chloroquine, but I soon changed, after realising I could not reliably remember to take pills every day. So, like James and Juliet, I moved on to the mefloquine-based Lariam, pleased that it was only one pill a week, but a bit wary of the lengthy list of side effects the little notice inside the box warned about, and the caution of a doctor who'd advised against taking it for more than three months – "because it begins to affect your central nervous system. You start going mad."

James and I hated taking the drugs. It seemed to detract from the freedom and healthy living we sought on the trip. Bronwyn decided to take no prophylaxis, preferring to treat malaria if she caught it. And there was the unvoiced thought in the back of our minds that malaria was something other people got.

The signposts in Malawi were of an identical design to South Africa's, obviously having been imported from there. The only difference was that they had all been perforated, presumably to make them less attractive to thieves. Driving into Lilongwe, the nation's newly-built capital, we passed dozens of cyclists returning slowly to the city with firewood piled three metres high in wooden baskets mounted on their pillions. In the poorer areas on the outskirts a thin haze of smoke drifted listlessly over tightly packed tin roofs. By contrast, the city itself, and the inner suburbs, were modern and spacious. We found the house of Lou and Rusty Markham, friends of my family, who had offered to put us up for the night, and were warmly welcomed.

We drove early the next day to the Old Town where we had a large bolt engineered to replace one that James had noticed had rattled loose from the gearbox bracket, leaving the gearbox hanging awkwardly. With a potential disaster averted, we drove south to Blantyre, the commercial and industrial centre of the country, passing endless groves of tropical and citrus fruit. We camped at the sports club, played golf – nine holes for the princely sum of two kwacha, $0.27 – and went shopping at the market.

It was a noisy, bustling place, alive with the sounds of livestock and people selling their wares. It seemed that you could find anything you needed on one of the wooden tables that stretched endlessly under the confusion. Fruit and vegetables were being sold alongside motor vehicle spares and primus stoves; live ducks and chickens squawked in wooden cages piled behind tables laden with building supplies. Apart from basic groceries we bought a wooden bowl, a voodoo mask and a spiced chicken's head which James and I ate out of bravado.

Robbie bought a political T-shirt. The country's first democratic elections were drawing near and the ageing Banda sought to reassure his voters through distribution of shirts emblazoned with photographs of him at least twenty years younger. On the back was a rooster, his party's symbol. This is what was written on the shirt: "Peace, Progress with Kamuzu. Vote for the Cock."

*

While planning the trip, James and I had imagined it would be seven months of leisure. If we passed an interesting mountain, we would stop and climb it. We'd live in the present, no longer servants to time. Somehow this dream slipped through our fingers. Before we started, the seven months ahead of us had seemed eternal. Now already, five weeks into the trip, it was apparent reality was not mirroring expectation.

Although we had taken our watches off on the first day, we soon discovered that it was difficult to stop being goal-directed. Already the tension between travelling and arriving, which would increase later in the journey, was being felt. Those interesting mountains were driven past because we had a long way to go, and needed the satisfaction of getting part-way there. As though to make up for those missed mountains, we planned to spend four days hiking in the Mulanje mountains in the south, and it was towards the Mulanjes that we headed from Blantyre.

The drive to Likhabula Forest Station where the hikes started was beautiful. We passed through brightly coloured towns set amidst expansive, even fields of tea. Thunderclouds hung low in the sky, edged dark grey, spitting occasional heavy drops at the ground. The rays of the late afternoon sun streamed below the clouds and reflected off them. Softened into yellow, they enriched the vivid tones of the forests and tea fields, deepening their greens and drawing into orange the fertile earth of the roadside and farm tracks.

Before supper, we had a drink at the local bar in Mulanje town, and learnt to play the board game *bawo*. *Bawo* is played on a board containing four rows, two for each player, with eight hollows in each row. Each player starts with two beads in every hollow. To move you pick up all the beads in any hollow and move in any direction, dropping one bead in each hollow as you go.

If the last bead ends in an empty hollow your turn is over. If the last bead ends in a hollow containing at least one other bead, you can pick up all the beads in that hollow and continue in the same direction unless the last bead landed in one of the end two hollows. In this instance you pick up the beads in that hollow and start again in the end hollow in front of it. If your final bead ends in a hollow with at least one other bead, and your opponent has beads in their opposite hollow, all their beads in the hollow are collected and distributed, in the direction of the previous play, from the end hollow. The loser is the person whose front row is cleared.

The game seemed to fit Africa. Its outcome appeared to be random as control was swept from one player to the other suddenly and unpredictably, and it could take anything from five minutes to four days to complete a single game. Strategy was subservient to chance, it seemed, as we manoeuvred beads away from us by whim, only to watch them desert and come flooding back behind our lines. Compared to chess or draughts it seemed unstructured, capricious.

Watching the experts play, though, their deft fingers flitting over the board, scooping up and depositing the beads like bees transporting pollen, I began to realise that underlying the seemingly random events there was a complex pattern I wasn't quite able to grasp.

★

Driving up to the camp, we were mobbed by teenage boys wanting to be our guides and selling curios. The night air was washed in the rich smell of the carved cedar we were offered, the soft wood shaped into boxes and figurines. Harder woods had been fashioned into hippopotamus-shaped pipes and small tables whose three collapsible and interlocking legs were ingeniously carved from a single, unbroken piece of wood. We bought several items, and chose two guides, Neston and Austin, arranging to meet them at dawn the next morning.

The first day's climb, to Chambe Hut, was a steep ascent in wet, misty weather, passing first through scrub and indigenous forest and later through extensive cultivated forests of pine and cedar. Twice we came across small thatch-roofed huts selling tea to passers-by, either hikers like ourselves or men working at the cable station that brought huge swinging pine trunks down from the upper reaches of the forest. The tea was fourth grade, very strong, and made by pouring hot water through a mound of leaves held in a strainer. It cost only thirty-five tambala per cup, about $0.05. Neston and Austin each sank three heaped teaspoons of brown sugar into their mugs.

I'm sitting straddling a huge uprooted tree trunk, in one of Nature's most beautiful gardens. Before me, Mulanje's old peaks hunch in the sky, their shoulders dressed in shawls of mist, their flanks covered by blankets of pine and cedar. Around me lie the bodies of fallen pines, brought crashing to the ground by the weight of age or in some past, awful storm, some dragged down perhaps by the clasping arms of their drowning brothers. My feet sink into Mulanje's shaggy blanket, a tapestry of rusty pine needles inches deep, emerald saplings breaking through their cover, and gnarled wooden limbs, spotted with blue-grey moss and lined in the burgundy and red of their ripped bark and splintered stems. Between the trees, tiny in the distance, I see the squat shapes of cottages, roosting like mothering hens over the people inside. I am at peace. It feels right to be here, to be doing what I am doing.

We met other travellers in the hut, Zimbabweans and South Africans, including a woman named Emma but called Bucket, and spent the evening playing cards with them. A roaring log fire warmed the room as we sat and chatted, identifying our shared acquaintances and experiences. Several of the group were smoking Malawi Gold, a high-grade dagga, laughing easily under its influence.

As it filtered into her blood, Bronwyn felt no such relaxation. Sitting amongst us, she began to imagine everyone was conspiring against her. Conversational fragments twisted together into dismissive slurs, people's laughter took on the tones of derision. Alarmed by this sense of veiled menace that confronted her, she fled into the second bedroom where she lay down. There she became filled with a terrible anxiety about being alone and was forced back into the main room. Again no comfort was to be found within the group. Her sense of isolation deepened, draining away her confidence, like a black hole sucking in the light around it.

None of us noticed her plight. Bronwyn spent the whole evening shuttling back and forth, spinning between one room and the other, like the copper coil of an electric motor, repelled by the opposing force of each magnet it is alternately driven towards. "Never again," she swore the next day, pale from her sleepless night.

*

James and I had decided to climb to the top of Sapitwa, one of the range's highest peaks, while the others walked a flatter route to the second hut. We took Neston along as a guide. Halfway up, the mist descended and the wind began to strengthen. Three quarters of the way up we were being buffeted about by a gale as we scrambled up loose rocky slopes flooded by small rivulets born out of the pouring rain. Ten minutes from the top we hid from the elements in a narrow wedge-shaped cave. Neston had turned a strange purple colour and was shivering violently under the now-drenched layers of clothing we'd lent him. James's fat-free body too was beginning to blend in with the blue of his jersey, and I was losing sensation in my feet from tramping around in James's sandals, which I had swapped with my wet boots which had begun to chafe.

After a meagre lunch of bread and cold baked beans, and an abortive attempt at lighting a fire, we decided to be sensible and headed down the mountain. As anyone who climbed trees as a child knows, going up is always easier than coming down, and we slipped and skidded down the muddy paths, knocked off balance by blasts of the gusting wind and soaked by the rain.

Seeing the others as we crawled, drenched and dirty into the hut after our eight-hour ordeal was like coming back to family. They put us in front of the fire, wrapped us in blankets and fed us while we told them slightly embellished tales of our near-death experiences.

After a night of deep sleep in the log-fire warmth of the hut, we awoke refreshed. The air, scoured by the night of rain, gleamed. Birds trilled from the high boughs of the pines as the drenched earth steamed beneath the heat of the new sun. Filled with vitality at being in the mountain's embrace, amongst its rivers and trees and waterfalls, we all ran down the mountain to the base camp and our home the truck, hurtling past startled woodcutters and hikers as we careered down the path.

★

"You've never been to Zomba in your life?" James was asking Neston at the bottom. "It's only 160 kilometres away. Why don't you come with us?" Neston, who by this stage had good reason to be wary of any escapades led by James, looked hesitant.

"Come on," said James, brooking no opposition, "we'll get you a lift back somehow."

And so we were six in the cab as we headed towards Zomba. The usual five and a slightly bewildered Neston. Zomba is the original capital of Malawi, a scenic old town nestled at the base of the 2,000 metre high Zomba Plateau, on top of which we planned to camp. It had begun to rain heavily, making driving up to the top – along a steep, winding road not much wider than our truck – extremely hazardous. Robbie was at the wheel, and the drive up was punctuated by shouts and squeals as we strayed dangerously close to the rocky cliff wall on the one side and the precipitous drop on the other. After half an hour of switchbacks and stress we arrived at the top. Robbie sat staring fixedly ahead, knuckles still white on the wheel. "I haven't blinked for sixteen kilometres," he muttered.

We were beginning to appreciate the forethought of the people who had designed the truck for overland use. One of the additions was a huge awning attached to the side. Unfurled, it gave us enough cover to keep the tents dry while erecting them. The rain continued to cascade down, like an upended lake, and we retreated into the shelter of the truck.

There were three bunk beds in the back. The middle one was held from swinging down by two old seat belts and could be raised, making the lowest bunk into a long bench. The six of us huddled together in the confines of the box, the smell of wet clothes and the rain mingling with the nsima and soya and cabbage sauce Neston and Robbie were cooking for dinner. We felt a primal excitement and relief at being warm and secure against the exigency of the weather outside. The rain poured relentlessly, and after a quick dash to the tents we went to sleep to the sound of rain drumming on plastic and dreams of deluge.

The next day dawned misty but dry. James got up early for a jog.

"You'll never guess what I've just seen!" he said excitedly as he returned. "Coming up the hill, a beautiful woman emerged from the mist ahead of me, riding a snow-white horse. And a hundred yards behind her trotted a sable antelope!"

"Sure, James. That Lariam really is affecting you, isn't it," I said sceptically.

"I think I saw the same donkey last night on the way up," ventured Robbie.

"I'm telling you, that's what I saw! May God strike me dead this second if I'm not telling the truth!" James exclaimed, his hand pointing to the sky. "The sable came up to the horse and put its chin on its flanks. It was completely tame. I can't believe you won't believe me!"

As Neston had expressed an interest in getting back home before he found himself in London, he and James cycled down to Zomba town to arrange his trip back. James returned an hour later leading a trio of young boys, Francis, Clement and Martin, who had offered to show us around the plateau. Francis was just tall enough to reach the pedals if he straddled the crossbar, but the other two had to be pushed along, balancing awkwardly on the saddle, when it was their turn for a ride. Mostly it seemed to be Francis' turn, though. Young Clement and Martin accepted that it was their lot to push the leader of their small gang almost all the way up the hill from Zomba town.

To James's pleasure one of the first sights the boys showed us was the tame sable antelope owned by a family who bred dressage show horses.

The top of the plateau is densely forested and the views are magnificent. Looking south, over Karoo-flat plains, we could see the Mulanje Mountains a hundred miles away, uneven grey clouds at the horizon's edge. We spent the rest of the afternoon walking along the neat paths leading from viewpoint to viewpoint with names – 'Queen's', 'Empire's', 'King's' – redolent of a past age.

We looked down from our aerial perch on low chains of hills rising up from the back of the plains below like vertebrae, and rough clumps of woodland meeting the smooth geometric lines of agricultural land. Ant-sized houses clustered together haphazardly next to reservoirs like small puddles. With such views extending out to all parts of the country, it seemed the perfect sight for a country's capital. I would have left it there.

The three boys took us also to waterfalls cascading over time-smoothed rocks, and silent, still lakes that mirrored the browns and reds of the seasonal trees and the greens of the perennials that grew on their shores.

It was hard to leave so beautiful a place. And Robbie and I nearly didn't. Hurtling down to Zomba town on bicycles the next morning, down the tarred 'up' road, we were forced off the road by a fast-moving Isuzu truck that suddenly burst out from around a corner ahead of us. We skidded to a halt inches from a sixty metre fall and had to stop to calm our nerves before continuing down at a far less reckless speed.

*

The next five days were spent at the beaches of Lake Malawi, at Nkopola and Cape McLear. The lake, the most southern of the series of lakes marking Africa's Great Rift Valley, occupies one fifth of the country's area and provides fresh water, fish and a livelihood for much of the population. Lined by golden beaches, the lake invites relaxation. Our days were filled with snorkelling in its clear waters, reading, listening to Bronwyn play her guitar, and playing beach cricket in foot-deep water at the lake's edge. The rules we devised for the cricket were simple. You could be out caught or bowled (we used two water-filled jerrycans as stumps) and the main aim in batting was to hit the ball as far as you could into the lake for the bowler to go and fetch, which created some entertaining rivalries.

At the Golden Sands campsite at Cape McLear James met a man called Fickson Mvura. They remembered each other from James's stay four years before, and soon organised an outing to one of the islands in the boat of a friend of Fickson's. We went snorkelling and ate grilled *kampanga*, or catfish, and lapsed into an unstressed torpor on the hot rocks at the water's edge until it was time to return.

"I'm going to swim back," James announced. "Who's going to join me?"

"Not me," said Robbie. "I'll be a lot happier in the boat."

I looked at the shore, just under a mile away across the water. "I'm not going to either. It's too far."

James set off, swimming steadily. We kept the boat close enough to help if necessary. A third of the way across I decided to join him. There's a dread that comes up when swimming far from shore. The water suddenly seems less supportive and a rising hysteria thrums against your nerves, urging panic and the explosive release of energy, the irrational desire to get to that distant shore as quickly as possible. I chattered to James to quell the fear in me and concentrated on swimming methodically. The boat left us to ourselves, but we stayed calm, swimming together to the shallows, where we emerged exhausted.

The days slid past, sun-filled and carefree. We met other people: a German cycling south, a South African cycling north, and an Exodus group of twenty young English, New Zealand and Australian travellers; got invited to a toga party; went for long walks up the coastline; and slowed to the gentle pace of life that pervades Malawi. At night the camp chef, Foster, cooked for us *chambo* fish curries or roasted chickens we'd bought at the market. Bronwyn began experimenting with baking in the potjie and was soon producing light pumpkin scones for pudding. At around R15 – $4.50 – for a meal for five of us, even with our tight budget we could afford these treats nightly.

Like insects trapped in honey, we struggled to extricate ourselves from the lake's grasp. It was only early July, and we had more than five months yet to reach London: aeons, it seemed. Yet in six weeks we hadn't got very far north, and already I was beginning to feel the first flutterings of anxiety over the speed of our progress. Trafalgar Square seemed a long way off.

★

We returned to Lilongwe via Dedza, driving up the Golomoti road that winds steeply over the escarpment of the Great Rift Valley, much of it in a lumbering first gear. A loud crack signalled the snapping of the truck's right shock absorber bracket. Fortunately we could carry on, but it meant having to find somewhere to get it repaired the following day.

Although we had been away for only six weeks, we were eager for news from home.

"So how many letters do you reckon you'll have waiting, Robbie?" Bronwyn asked.

"At least three from Bridge, and probably a few others. Half a dozen or so I expect."

"I'll get more than that," bet James. "Five kwacha says I get at least eight. How about you, Bronski?"

"Well, I wrote off to nearly all my friends just before I left SA, and the Markhams in Lilongwe was the first address I gave, so there must be a good couple of letters waiting, especially from my dearest and maddest friend, Helen McRee. God, I wish she was here to have a bloody good yarn with."

We all bolstered our hopes by betting on the number of letters there would be waiting for us, links to the world beyond the vacuum we were temporarily in. When we arrived at the Markhams there was post for everyone except Bronwyn. Having looked to these letters from old friends for the affirmation and acceptance she did not receive from us, she was devastated by their absence and became uncharacteristically withdrawn.

Our distance from home also made us keen to watch the rugby test match between South Africa and France being played that afternoon. We managed to get ourselves invited to a house with a satellite dish. There we met the worst of South Africans, one of whom was the military attaché in Malawi. Faced by their racism, arrogance and aggression, we were almost pleased South Africa lost, just to pain supporters like them. Robbie was cornered for half an hour by a drunk, self-pitying woman who had left South Africa and who told him endlessly of her problems losing weight while I had to listen to her husband, her most severe critic, spit vitriol at all around him, and all of his past too. We left as soon as we could.

There is in Malawi a similar, but more intense, air of decadence to that in Zimbabwe. Drink dominates the culture of the small, rich white communities that huddle together in pockets around the country. There seemed to be an unhappiness hidden beneath the comfort of their lives. I felt it in the imbalanced roles of the sexes, in the conservative bar-room conversations, in the discrimination that betrayed an inner insecurity, in the reliance on mateship. The rowdiness hid an emptiness. Beer was being swilled into the vat of their boredom.

★

We stayed that night and the next with a couple, Glenda and Spot MacKay, on a farm forty kilometres out of Lilongwe. We'd met them by chance earlier in the day, and they had generously offered to have five strangers stay. Glenda, a New Zealander, had travelled extensively herself when younger and understood the yearnings travellers begin to develop for home comforts. We slept in soft beds, ate roast lamb for lunch, and had our clothes washed for us.

Spot took us to the very colonial sports club whose manager became quite agitated because Juliet wasn't wearing a skirt and James was barefoot. Spot had returned early from a fishing trip the day before after contracting malaria, but seemed to think nothing of it. He had taken three Fansidar and a few beers, gone to bed and woken up the next day feeling well enough to play golf with Robbie and drink enough beer to make me have to drive his car home.

Spot had asked his local mechanic, Mr Kahn, to help us with our repairs. He welded both shock absorber brackets without charging us, and we left Lilongwe for the second time. We headed north towards Salima, unaware that in eight days' time James and Bronwyn would be back.

★

We spent a night in Salima, at The Wheelhouse campsite, and got up early the following day to drive to Nkhata Bay. To get there we passed through Nkhotakhota, famous as Malawi's biggest dope-producing area, and later through vast plantations of rubber trees, their thick, dark green foliage forming a dense canopy overhead. Each tree had its bark sliced in a number of downward-curving incisions spanning the trunk's circumference. At the bottom of each cut was tied a small wooden cup used to collect the foul-smelling resin that would be converted into rubber. The plantations, dark and shadowy with their mutilated trees, cast an eerie, forbidding atmosphere, in contrast to the light friendliness and security we had found in all the other parts of the country we'd been to.

Although we had already experienced the delights of the lake, we had been told that Nkhata Bay, a small fishing town towards the north, is unmissable if in Malawi, so thought we'd stop there for a day or two. As it turned out, we were there for five. Less commercialised than Cape McLear, it was like a Pacific paradise, all white sand, clear water and palm trees, with cheap fruit and beer being sold on the beach. The people of Nkhata Bay didn't seem to cater for tourists, they just abided them, treating them no differently to the local inhabitants. There wasn't the scent of avarice in the air. The place was seemingly uncorrupted by Western ways, its people happy to live on the fringe of the Western World. Muremba, the old watchman at the campsite, said it had been even better in the past. "Ten years ago," he told us, "anyone could just take fruit from the trees. Now it has to be bought. Everything needs money nowadays."

We spent our time swimming at day and at night, playing more beach cricket, and going for bicycle rides over the jutting headland separating the beach from the town. Bronwyn plaited a long, multicoloured braid into Robbie's hair. We ate pizzas and banana pancakes at Fumbani Restaurant in town one night, and bananas and naartjies all through each day. The time passed lazily, easily, wrapped in the tranquil spell of Malawi's eternally summer days.

I learnt a lot more about Zaire. An American named Ross, who was travelling south with his wife Anne-Marie, had worked for five years as an overland driver and had driven between London and Nairobi half a dozen times. He gave us good practical advice and also told us chilling tales of robberies and breakdowns, an accidental death – a traveller crushed beneath the heavy trailer they were towing – and the decision to take the corpse out with them.

"It's only got worse since I was there," he warned, "what with all the political upheaval. The military haven't been paid and they're trying to get money by whatever means they can. You should budget, for Central and West Africa, on paying about $200 each in bribes, if you go that way. But if I were you I would seriously consider the other option of heading north through Sudan, Ethiopia and Egypt."

A young Australian there had spent two weeks hitch-hiking in Zaire two months before.

"I'd go some other way if I were you, mate," he told me. "You won't believe the roads there. They're bloody terrible. You get these huge holes filled with mud. We got stuck in one for two days. The truck had to be dug out with spades, inch by inch. We were told it gets worse further in too, 'cause it's wetter. And by Christ, the insects! You get eaten alive!"

I found all this talk disheartening. Dark clouds began to build up on the horizon and move across the blue skies we'd been living under. I was becoming anxious to get a move on, to confront that which I feared. The anticipation, I'd learnt, is almost always worse than the event itself. But the stories about Zaire scared me and I began to think we should rather take the northern route. Robbie proved an ally in this but James was intent on heading West. He wanted to see the jungle, and to retrace the steps of his friends who had driven the truck down.

"They're exaggerating," he assured us. "It won't be that bad. Anyway the other way would mean going through Sudan which is also in complete chaos. Zaire and Sudan span the continent, remember. We've got to go through one or the other to get through."

"I don't mind which way we go," offered Bronwyn.

"I suppose we just can't decide yet. We need to find out more," I said. "We only have to decide in Nairobi. Let's wait till then."

We drove out of Nkhata Bay still discussing the demerits of the different routes: the cost of driving through Europe, the likelihood of Nigeria erupting into civil war, the possibility of having to ship from Dakar. We even began considering shipping from Mombasa to Saudi Arabia and driving on from there. London remained our fixed goal. Whether we went around Africa's bulge or along its horn, we planned to reach Dover and drive from there to Westminster in the truck.

The veil of uncertainty that obscured the future made me impatient to move forward, to get past the point where we had to decide one way or the other which way we would go.

Chapter Six Malawi

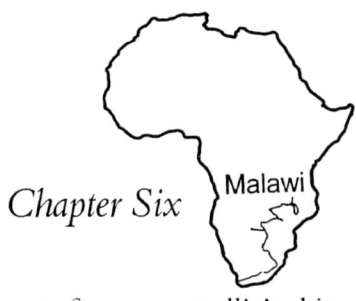

"Come on, it's hardly out of our way at all! And it says here that the game viewing is fantastic. There aren't any lions or elephants so you can walk all over the park." Robbie had spotted Nyika National Park on the map and was busy reading up on it and convincing the rest of us to pay it a visit. We all eventually gave in to his forceful persuasion, even though it meant a detour over roads which, the map indicated, generally saw very little traffic.

We stopped at Mzuzu, the largest town in northern Malawi, to exchange money and buy groceries. Also busy buying supplies were the crew of the Afrika Odyssey expedition led by Kingsley Holgate, a group of twenty or so South Africans who were engaged in negotiating most of the major waterways of Africa in rubber ducks. From across the road Kingsley saw our truck and strode towards us. He was a huge man, six foot four at least, with an enormous beard, and everything about him from his booming voice to his heavy stride exuded energy and confidence.

"What a fantastic vehicle!" he cried after introducing himself, my hand swallowed in his. "Where are you taking her?"

"London," I replied.

"Wonderful! Getting into the true spirit of Africa! We're doing a similar thing, but on water."

We chatted about our experiences so far. As Kingsley spoke my concerns about future difficulties dissipated. His love of adventure shone in his eyes as he told us of where they had been and where they were headed.

"After Kenya, we'll be going north through Sudan, heading up the Nile."

"Do you think there'll be any problems for South Africans getting visas for Ethiopia or Sudan?" I asked.

"None at all! I've no doubt we'll be granted visas."

"We're also considering going west through Zaire, but we've heard a lot of negative reports about it. What do you reckon?"

"No, you'll be fine. And it's worth seeing the jungle, I can assure you. Okay, it might be a bit adventurous. But isn't that the point?"

The problems he'd encountered on his own expedition, especially the fourteen cases of malaria they'd had so far, didn't seem to faze him at all. He bade us goodbye with a firm handshake and an encouraging stare, and strode away leaving me feeling inspired, eager to encounter what the future held in store.

We entered Nyika National Park in the late afternoon. We had climbed to over 2,000 metres and the air now had a cold edge as it poured through the windows. A few kilometres into the park the engine misfired, spluttered and died, as it had done before in Zambia. Not too concerned, we slowed to a halt, parking the truck at a slight angle on the side of the road. There was no sign of human habitation. In all directions we were surrounded by long yellow grass and gnarled acacia trees. We lifted the engine cover, and began the process of bleeding the fuel system that had remedied the situation previously. The engine remained unresponsive and with dusk closing in we decided to camp at the roadside and try again in the morning. We went to bed that night next to the silent hulk of the truck with a sense of foreboding. Hundreds of miles from anywhere, we could hardly have chosen a worse spot to have a serious mechanical breakdown.

Our fears were exacerbated the next day after a fruitless hour attempting to get the truck started. With one battery flattened and the other on the way out we were forced to cease our attempts at starting the truck. Ross, the overland driver we'd met at Nkhata Bay, happened to pass by and stopped to offer assistance. Drawing on his long experience with Bedford trucks he confirmed James's diagnosis that, because we could see diesel moving all the way along the fuel line, the most likely source of the problem lay in what was the most expensive part after the engine itself, the fuel injector pump. As we were unable to continue trying to start the engine by bleeding it, the logical next step was to have the pump tested, in either Mzuzu or Lilongwe.

"There's no point in us all going back," said Robbie. "It makes sense for us to split up. Of course James will have to head back with the pump. I'll go with him if no one else wants to, but I'd really like to head on to Chelinda Camp to see the game."

"I'd also like to go to the camp," Juliet asserted. "I've only got a couple of weeks of the trip left and I'd rather spend them game-viewing than hitch-hiking."

I saw that the next assumed division would be for me to accompany James. "I'll stay here and look after the truck," I offered, hoping no one else sought the solitude I was after.

"By yourself? Are you sure, Paul?" asked Bronwyn. "We could be gone quite a while, especially if we have to go all the way to Lilongwe."

"Yes, I'm fine. I reckon I'll enjoy it. And we can't just leave the truck here. Someone will have to stay."

"So that's that, then," James summed up. "Juliet and Robbie will head off to Chelinda, Bronwyn and I'll take the pump to be checked out and Paul will stay here. Everyone seems happy enough with that. Come on, Paulus, let's get to it then! Help me get this bloody pump out."

The rest of the day was spent removing the fuel injector pump, carefully tying plastic bags over the ends of the leads we'd unfastened so as to keep dust out, and then watching the road for cars we could catch lifts with. We waited in vain. Since Ross had left at ten that morning not a single vehicle had passed either way. Eventually, late in the afternoon, two vehicles heading north bore Robbie and Juliet off to Chelinda Camp.

Soon after our arrival a large group of people, mainly children, had gathered to observe us, laughing and exclaiming whenever one of us did something unusual. We watched the road for cars. The children watched us for entertainment. The day drew to a close. We went to bed early, shortly after the children. As they were leaving, one of them called to us, "Goodbye. See you tomorrow."

The next morning saw the scene repeat itself. The children watched, we waited. James handed out some old clothes and sweets which were enthusiastically accepted. Just before noon a dull growl heralded the approach of a southward-bound car and James leapt into the road to ensure it did not pass. The driver turned out to be a friendly fellow, a lab technician from the university James and I had attended in Cape Town. He was completely lost, having intended to exit the park at the opposite gate. Nevertheless he offered James and Bronwyn a lift to where their paths diverged and I was left alone. If you exclude the dozen fascinated children watching my every move, that is.

*

I had been secretly pleased when no one else expressed an interest in staying with the truck. My motives were by no means altruistic. After almost two months of constant companionship I was beginning to crave time to myself. There is in humans an eternal conflict between the opposite and simultaneous needs for bonding with others and for independence. Our natures are both, and at the same time, solitary and gregarious. This is what can make marriage so hard. And harder still is living with strangers, sharing with them the more primitive functions of our lives, the sleeping and the eating, the drowsy minutes upon waking. We had all been getting on surprisingly well so far, but there were always minor irritations, the need to be tolerant, and I seized this opportunity to just be, to live for myself, affected by no one else's needs but my own.

Most of the children went off elsewhere at lunchtime, except for three little ones who remained sitting shyly a short distance from me. I chatted to them, and found out that their names were Miriam, Gwyn and Button. When they saw me collecting firewood they gathered bundles of sticks together which they offered to me silently. I gave them some sweets.

The day passed in silence. I read and wrote letters and cooked simple meals over the fire. The evenings were cold, the heat leaking from the air as soon as the sun dropped below the horizon. I went to sleep early, just after dark. Not wanting to further drain our dangerously depleted batteries, I had resolved not to use our electric lights at all. I would live simply, by the sun.

The second day was much like the first. There were more people watching me, and small children kept adding wood to my by now considerable stockpile, for the sweets I would give them. Mostly I read and wrote and enjoyed being by myself. I did find it irksome at times to be watched constantly. After all, it wasn't as though I was being particularly entertaining, sitting there reading my book. I didn't mind the children, but thought the adults surely had better things to do. I told myself I was judging from a

Western perspective, but this didn't make me any less irritated.

Towards evening a middle-aged man came to greet me. His name was Pearson Mhango, and he was accompanied by his son Moffat. He said, rather formally, that I was welcome to stay as long as I liked and asked if there was anything I needed. We got to chatting and he told me that he and his family had come over from Zambia some years before in the hope of finding better employment, and that he was now a teacher at the local school. I was thrown into a quandary when he told me that he had been ill in recent nights, sweating and shivering, and suffering from terrible headaches. "I was near to die," he said. It sounded like malaria, but I couldn't be sure and so didn't know whether to give him some of the anti-malarial pills we had or not. In the end I gave him a packet of paracetemol and waited until the next day to see if the symptoms had changed.

Moffat returned the next day, saying his father was feeling somewhat better, and bearing two eggs as thanks. I felt humbled by his gift as I suspected I might have been of better help, had I given them some of our limited supply of anti-malarial drugs instead of just headache pills. Moffat then showed further kindness, asking if I wanted to buy any honey from the park gate, as he was heading that way. He returned with two jars of honey and carefully filled-in park receipts for the six kwacha each had cost.

Another day and a half went by without word of the others. The few cars that passed each day would cause me to get up expectantly and then resume my solitude as they drove by. I entertained myself by writing rambling, incoherent letters to friends, pretending my Crusoe-like loneliness had sapped my sanity. Although I was getting into my solitary way of life, and still enjoyed the quietness it offered, I was beginning to long too for people I knew to talk to, to laugh with, for music and for the freedom to move again.

In the evening of the fourth day after the breakdown, a small car containing a French family stopped to tell me James and Bronwyn were on their way. They arrived late the next morning. Excited at our reunion we hugged and let loose the torrent of questions that had built up over the days we had been apart.

"So is it fixed?" I asked immediately.

"It didn't have to be. There was nothing wrong with it," replied James.

"We've just done a 900 kilometre round trip in four days, for bugger all!" said Bronwyn, laughing. "It'd be tragic if it weren't so funny."

"Shit, Paulus, you won't believe what we've been through," said James. "The guy you saw pick us up took us only to Rumphi. We then caught a second lift to Mzuzu and found out there that we'd have to go to Lilongwe to get the injector pump tested. Luckily, we caught another lift almost immediately which took us all the way to Rusty Markham's front door."

"Poor sod, we had to wake him. He must be sick of us by now," said Bronwyn.

"Anyway, the next morning he took us to a friend of his who tested the injector pump for free. There's not a thing wrong with it. It's one hundred per cent."

"So where does that leave us now?"

"I've got some ideas I've been mulling over on the way back. And God we had enough time to think, getting back. When we left the workshop three days ago, we thought we might be lucky and get back that day, but it's been a complete nightmare ever since. How many lifts did we need to get here, Bronwyn? About ten?"

"At least. There were five to Mzuzu, including one in a truck which exploded..."

"What?"

"It was un-fucking-believable!" continued James. "The handbrake got stuck without the driver knowing it. Eventually the brake drum got so hot that the tyre just burst into flames. I could feel the heat on my face as I looked out the window. It was completely ablaze. I thought the whole truck would go up for sure. We managed to put it out eventually with the extra radiator water, but the brake drum continued glowing in the dark for about twenty minutes. We were bloody lucky the whole thing didn't blow up, taking our passports with it."

"We decided that was enough hitching for one day and spent the night in a church rest house," said Bronwyn. "We got up next day at the crack of dawn and took three lifts to get to just forty kilometres away."

"God, it was frustrating being so close. Three cars passed without offering us a lift. Eventually we just stood in the road and forced a French family to stop. There were four kids in the back and the poor driver kept saying, 'Only one, only one.' We said we just wanted him to pass a message on to you."

"I got it last night. Thanks."

"So we camped in someone's garden for the night, and caught the bus out here this morning. How has your time been?"

"Not nearly as exciting, I must say, but I've enjoyed it. So what on earth are we going to do about the truck?"

"We're going to set up a gravity feed," said James assertively. "I've been thinking about it as we travelled. We'll bypass the fuel line altogether and feed fuel straight into the injector pump from a jerrycan."

"You know how to do this?"

"Not really, but I'm sure we can work it out."

★

We lifted the lid of the lowest bunk bed and searched through the huge stock of spare parts that had come down with the truck for bits and pieces that might be useful. Armed with lengths of transparent tubing, hose clamps, a funnel, various screwdrivers and spanners and a litre Coke bottle, we set about redirecting the flow of diesel from the pump and overflow pipe into an empty jerrycan, and feeding diesel from an elevated pipe into the fuel pump.

Under James's direction we unscrewed bolts and tightened clamps, decanted diesel and squeezed tubes onto nozzles. Eventually it was all set up. The inside of the cab looked like a deranged chemistry lab, with coiled and coupled pipes looping everywhere and various vessels, empty or filled with diesel, poised in readiness. I turned the battery switch on, pushed in the kill switch and got Bronwyn to hold down the starter button and accelerator while I poured diesel from the Coke bottle into the funnel which was jammed into the top of the tube leading to the injector pump. James started tightening the injector lead connections. Three cylinders started firing. Then four. Then five. With a final twist of the spanner the engine sang out on all six cylinders.

The smell of diesel was everywhere. I'd spilt litres in my eagerness to ensure no air entered the fuel line, as I poured diesel into the funnel to replace the fuel being consumed by the engine. We didn't care and whooped with joy. Almost superstitiously, lest the daemon inside drop dead, we decided to leave it running for three quarters of an hour, to make sure. This would also recharge the batteries. I submerged the end of the pipe I was holding into a full jerrycan. The jerrycan itself was balanced high up near the roof of the cab, between the two rear seats. The vacuum created by the engine ensured a constant flow of fuel, and we sat back to relax and listen to the low throbbing diesel music we'd missed these past five days. Later, confident that we could at least get moving again, even if it meant two jerrycans of diesel sloshing around inside the cab, we cut the engine.

"Let's just put it back to how it should be," said James. "We can then start narrowing down the source of the problem."

So we dismantled the gravity feed, restored the original design, and pressed the starter motor. The engine turned over effortlessly as though there had never been a problem. We were too excited to even consider the irony of it all, and decided to celebrate by buying a chicken from the local people to roast in the potjie. The chicken we were sold was a black cockerel with a bright red comb, and very much alive.

"Right, looks like we're going to have to kill it ourselves," I said hesitantly. "I'll, uh, get the axe, shall I?"

The cockerel seemed to start at the mention of the word axe and struggled wildly in James's hands in a frantic bid for freedom.

"Hell, James, how are we going to keep it still enough to kill it cleanly?"

"Don't worry," counselled James, "you can hypnotise chickens easily. You just put their beaks on the ground and then draw a line several times in the sand away from them. Like this. They'll lie there perfectly still, just staring at the line. We've done it on the farm hundreds of times. Just watch!"

The cockerel seemed even more terrified of the line James was drawing in front of it repeatedly than when I had mentioned the axe, and struggled more violently than ever. "Strange, it's not working for some reason," said James. "I'll have to hold it. Just watch my fingers."

Beheading the chicken was not the most pleasant task as I was unable to make a single, clean blow of it for fear of removing several of James's digits. But soon enough we had a carcass which we got Bronwyn to pluck, saying we had done our share of the dirty work. We were cleaning off the layers of diesel, oil, dust and blood when the familiar shape of The Beast came up the road. It was exciting to see Greg, Lucy, Rich, Alison and Kate again and we chatted for a while, swapping stories of exploits in Zambia and Malawi. Saying goodbye, we asked them to relay our good news to Robbie and Juliet and tell them to expect us early the next morning, and then sat down to a celebratory dinner of potatoes, rice, vegetables and chicken.

The next morning we left early and drove to Chelinda Camp. We had with us Moffat who had asked for a lift to Chitipa. We met Robbie and Juliet at the camp, as well as the crew of The Beast, and the French family James and Bronwyn had stopped, the de l'Épreviers, who invited us to stay with them when we got to Paris. After listening to Robbie's wildly exaggerated and passionate tales of marauding hyenas and how the park officials had kept him waiting for seven hours for the lift out to the truck that they'd promised him, we set off for Tanzania. We weren't too sure what we had accomplished in those five days, but we'd overcome adversity, the truck was mobile, and it was good to be together and on the road again.

Chapter Seven

We drove off Nyika plateau along the road that marks the open western border between Zambia and Malawi. It was alternately severely corrugated and covered in thick drifts of sand, making for slow progress as we crawled down and then up the steep folds of the low mountain range. After dropping Moffat off at Chitipa, a small town where we bought diesel, we drove on until evening, stopping to camp a hundred kilometres short of the Tanzanian border. The bumpy road had opened cupboards and dispersed their contents all over the back of the truck. The floor was a chaotic soup of books, tents, tools, and the contents of a smashed mixed spice bottle. We cleaned up and settled down to our first night together for almost a week.

The next day we tried to buy vast quantities of sugar in Karanga, the last town before Tanzania. Overland drivers we had met at the lake had said you could easily make four times the money spent by selling the sugar in Tanzania. There was evidence of this everywhere. Trucks laden with sugar were driving brazenly towards the border. A bureaucratic quirk had left the customs house twenty-five kilometres from the border post. Evidently all that the truck drivers said when questioned about their cargo was that they were merely delivering goods to the tiny village called Songwe at the border itself. Our intentions of becoming smugglers were thwarted, however. We couldn't find sugar anywhere. It had all been smuggled already.

So it was with clean consciences that we approached the border. The Malawians were friendly, but in the Tanzanian officials we met the bullying and corruption we'd heard so much about. We were *naïve* then in the art of extortion negotiations, and I paid $10 for a visa despite having been assured by the Tanzanian High Commission in Harare that I did not need one. Customs went surprisingly smoothly, and we thought we were in the clear when we were told we had to have our vaccination certificates checked in the shack labelled Health Office.

The man behind the desk, fat and sweating heavily, motioned for us to hand over our certificates, saying nothing. He scrutinised them slowly and then dropped them carelessly onto the table.

"There is a problem," he drawled with a slow shake of his head. "Your cholera and yellow fever shots were on the same day. This is not allowed."

"Why not?" asked James.

"It is not allowed, that is the law. They must be at least ten days apart."

"Look," said Juliet, "I'm a medical doctor and there is nothing wrong with taking both vaccines on the same day."

The official looked at her coldly through yellow eyes. "This is Tanzania. Here it is not allowed. You must have another vaccination here."

There was no way we were going to have needles inserted into us amid the dust of the border post, and he obviously knew that. "Oh, come on!" exclaimed James, exasperated. "It's obvious that you can have both vaccines on the same day, otherwise our doctors would never have given them to us. They're completely separate. They don't interfere with each other at all."

The man stared away disinterested. Robbie, his face reddening in anger, made to speak but held his tongue, for fear of his temper bursting through. A long silence followed. The minutes dragged by. We could see no way out. We were powerless, completely in the control of this malevolent man who sat disdainfully across from us, a practised, patient spider watching us struggle helplessly in the old web he wove anew each day. Eventually James broke the uncomfortable silence. "So what do we do now?" he asked.

The man shifted in his chair, to face us. He knew he'd won. "Well, if you each pay $10 I will be prepared to overlook the matter."

James managed to beat him down to $10 in total, but it was the principle more than the money itself which left us feeling disgust at the blatant corruption we'd fallen foul of. We had been mugged, albeit with a pen and not a knife.

Outside again, Robbie immediately set about faking a second cholera stamp in our vaccination certificates, using the stamp kit bought on the truck's first journey specifically for such purposes. James signed as doctor: Doc Holliday, M.D.

★

We hadn't travelled far into Tanzania when James, who was driving, said that the truck wasn't running properly. "It's underpowered. I think the brakes might be binding." The engine did sound like it was straining, as we chugged slowly uphill and we weren't travelling as freely as usual downhill. I had an irrational desire to disbelieve James, as though ignoring the problem long enough would make it disappear, like a child crying itself to sleep. Reason intervened, and we decided to end the day's driving where we were and have a look at the truck.

Lying beneath the truck, James could find nothing wrong with the brakes. But, as so often seemed to happen whenever we had cause to examine the truck's parts, he noticed something else amiss. A bolt holding the shock absorber to the chassis had been stripped. James and I made a temporary fix, using as a washer a large nut we had to cut in half on the vice mounted on the front bumper, and abandoned our search for the original problem, completely puzzled by it all.

It was late in the afternoon of what had been a very frustrating day. The experiences at the border, the concerns about the truck, and the fact that we were more than 150 kilometres short of where we had hoped to be, left us all feeling weighed down. We decided to lift ourselves out of our gloom by starting a new fitness regime. A long jog and various frenetic exercises later, we felt much better, and able to appreciate the spectacular beauty of our campsite. We had parked at an elevated siding which looked down over the flat basin of the Rift Valley. Tropical vegetation – palms, banana trees and cycads – formed a dense green cover over the hills that rose up towards us from the valley. We sweated easily in the humid air which held the faint smell of wood smoke curling upwards from the evening fires of the villages nearby.

We had lost our portable shower somewhere in Malawi, so had to shower under refreshingly cold water poured from jerrycans tilted over by someone standing on top of the truck. Robbie's Malawi tan made his white bottom stand out brightly in the dusk like a waterbuck's, much to the hilarity of the villagers who were watching. James bathed the sores on his legs. His sandals had chafed him severely on his run down Mount Mulanje, and the cuts hadn't healed. In fact they had deteriorated, suppurating and spreading across his ankles and feet. I also had cuts that wouldn't heal, and we began to suspect they might be an undisclosed side effect of the Lariam we were taking.

★

The road to Mbeya was the worst we had yet experienced, more like the moon than a highway. We winced repeatedly as the truck jolted and bucked its way through the potholes, springs squeaking in protest against the jarring force of its own weight. The road was of badly broken tar, which made the drops more sudden, angling steeply downwards at the tar's edge. It took three hours to travel a hundred kilometres. We arrived at Mbeya tired from the continual buffeting, and the stress of imagining what it was doing to the truck's suspension.

At Mbeya Robbie changed money – at the Bureau de Change because, surprisingly, there was no black market in Tanzania – and we bought diesel. While I was in the back of the truck, fetching the funnel we used to filter the diesel we siphoned, one of the crowd who had gathered around stole the large padlock we used as our rear lock. I wondered why. It was useless to them. I still had the keys for it in my hand. Perhaps it was the thrill of theft itself, or just to have possession of a strange artefact? I asked the man helping us refuel. He shrugged and said, curiously, "They're just Africans."

*

The truck still lacked power. James thought it might be that the timing was either too retarded or advanced and started scrutinising the smoke being emitted for clues. "Looks a bit white," he said, confidently. "We'll retard it tonight when we stop." I was impressed yet again by the extent of the mechanical lore James seemed to have picked up from occasional tinkerings with tractors in his youth. More important than his mechanical expertise, though, was his ability to inspire in the rest of us faith in the theories and explanations he devised. Chiefly, I think, because he was able to convince himself of them so readily.

The uncertainty about the truck's condition made me paranoid. The shake we'd never been able to get rid of completely suddenly seemed worse. I began to hear bad omens in every gear change or alteration in the engine's pitch. We never discussed what we would do if the truck broke down irrevocably. We spoke of delays and repairs, but there was always the assumption that the truck would be with us throughout. In many ways it was the trip, the focal point, our *sine qua non*. It had been the catalyst for the whole adventure in the first place, and any thoughts of having to abandon it were quickly pushed from our minds.

*

The relations between us at this stage had settled into a friendly, but not intimate, accord. Apart from James and myself, who had an old friendship, individuals kept their innermost thoughts to themselves. We did confide in one another, but only to an extent. Beyond that were barriers against the recurrence of hurts. The balance between affection and an intrusive closeness was maintained partly through teasing, although this did at times blunder over the line between jest and vindictiveness.

Bronwyn in particular was teased. She had told us that as a child her elder brother had bullied her mercilessly, and it seemed to me that she unconsciously recreated this past pattern in her present. She would react strongly if, say, we three South Africans spoke or joked in Afrikaans. Boredom in the cab would then have us do it later deliberately to annoy her, because we knew she would react. This exclusion through language emphasised the exclusion she felt within the group and her distance from support and empathy. Not seeing this, we thought her reactions were unnecessarily strong.

There cannot be victimisers without victims, and I was becoming aware that Bronwyn, in her relationships with men, was inclined to play the role of the victim, and in that way attract this negative attention towards herself. James, I knew, had always needed to dominate the women around him. Robbie too would use his caustic wit liberally, and for my part I also found myself speaking the bully's lines in this ad-lib play we found ourselves in. That was the dynamic that was forming. Hierarchical, patriarchal. A care and friendliness tainted with occasional outbreaks of spite.

We three men also had being South African in common. Bronwyn and Juliet's alien accents became sources of entertainment to us.

"Say it, Bronwyn, say it," James would ask.

"No."

"Go on. Four more pawpaws."

"Okay, then. I bought foowa moowa poowa-poowas," she would say, exaggeratedly, at which we would laugh and repeat it to ourselves. "You lot! God, I wish I was travelling with other Kiwis."

"Juliet," I once asked, "don't you think it's dangerous as a doctor to pronounce oral and aural in exactly the same way?"

And so on. One end of the seesaw would be pushed up sharply, unexpectedly, to provoke the person sitting at the other. In this way frustrations were released, but often not without someone being scalded by their steam. The tensions that existed after two months of each other's company never emerged in outright malice or violence, though. Generally we were getting on well, everyone pulling their weight and gravitating towards what they were best at doing.

★

We camped that night in a grove of trees that hid us from the road. Our introduction to the country, and the fact that of the people we had met very few could speak English and several were openly unfriendly, had made me nervous of Tanzania. Loud shouts from a village down the road added to my unease. Before collapsing into bed, tired after a twelve hour day that had taken us 450 kilometres, James and I turned the injector pump anticlockwise to retard the timing in the hope that this would reform the truck's sluggish behaviour.

We sensed no improvement the next day as we rose early and hit the road again. The old wheel wobble remained to haunt us as well, causing the truck to shudder wildly at speeds over fifty kilometres per hour. After an hour we climbed a steep hill to Iringa, an industrial town cluttered with small shacks whose crudely painted labels advertised them as a Restaurant or Hair Salon or New Technical Manufacturing Services. There was also a company premises with the proud label Thrust and Engulf – Alcohol Distributors. While James spent a patient two hours at the post office trying to telephone Abs Simba, a contact we had in Dar es Salaam, I swapped the front wheels in an attempt to assuage the shake, and siphoned diesel into the main tank, a distasteful job which had somehow become one of my unspoken responsibilities.

James hadn't managed to get hold of Abs, but we found the shake had almost completely disappeared as we continued east.

On the Michelin maps picturesque stretches of road are indicated by a green line running parallel to the road. We had noticed that the two hundred kilometres from Iringa were marked in this way, but that didn't prepare us for the beauty we were to witness.

The road wound steadily downwards, descending gradually from the plateau on the edge of the Rift Valley to the distant shores of the Indian Ocean. For a long section it ran alongside the Great Ruaha River. The mountain slopes leading down to the river were covered in forests of baobab trees, standing thick, grey, inverted: elephantine sentinels of the place. The horizon behind us was banded purple by uneven, brooding mountains. To our right, high overhead, spirals of vultures wheeled slowly, their curved wings supported by the rising heat of the day. Ahead a distant storm brought alive a glorious arcing rainbow, welcoming us forward. The people seemed to fit the place too. Ornately jewelled and colourfully dressed, with countless beads around their ankles, wrists and necks, and suspended from their lobes, their exotic looks enhanced and blended in with the beauty of their surroundings.

They were friendlier too, waving and smiling as we passed. My reservations about the country were quickly drowned under the sensational impact of that afternoon's drive. We left the valley, intoxicated by what we had seen. And so much more was yet to come.

★

We hadn't driven two hundred metres past the gatepost announcing the entrance to Mikumi National Park when Bronwyn shrieked, "Oh my God! Look! Giraffes! And there! Buffaloes! I just looove Tanzania!"

We drove on slowly. Wildebeest grazed quietly with zebra metres away from the road. A herd of elephant, with two small, cute babies in tow, crossed the road ahead of us. Impala leapt away startled, then stopped to look quizzically before darting off again.

"This is the best wildlife I've ever seen," said Robbie, "and it's all for free!" And then, "Over there! Those are wild dog!" A pack of four trotted in single file across the road just ahead of us. Heads down, glancing up now and then to catch sight of the splash of white on the tail of the dog in front of them, they were obviously on the trail of some fleeing quarry.

"Let's see where they're going," said James, turning off the road. We followed slowly from a distance for a few hundred metres, forging a path through the veld, before leaving them to their hunt.

"Wow! You can't believe how lucky that is. There are only about two thousand left in the wild. They've been wiped out recently by canine distemper and rabies," enthused Robbie, still staring at the area of bushveld into which the dogs had disappeared.

"This is the most incredible park," said James. "What say we camp here tonight?"

"Yes! Brilliant idea!" Bronwyn affirmed eagerly.

When Robbie agreed as well, Juliet and I had no option but to go along with the idea. We decided against a fire, much as we would have liked one, lest it be spotted from the road. After a pasta supper cooked on the gas stove in the back, we sat outside, talking softly. Clouds covered the sky, holding us in darkness.

"What's that rustling noise?" asked Juliet, an edge of fear in her voice.

"I didn't hear anything," I replied. "Probably just the wind."

"No, I'm sure I heard something. Just over there." She pointed towards the darkness in front of us.

"Why don't you hook up the spotlight to the cigarette lighter in the cab," suggested James. "It's in the library, on the bottom shelf."

Juliet retrieved the spotlight and plugged it in. She trained its beam on the source of the sound. "Oh my God!" she screamed.

The light reflected glassily off sixteen eyes. Ten metres away eight hyena squatted in a close group, their simian faces sharp and menacing. They moved uneasily, troubled by the light. We moved even more uneasily, fearful in the knowledge that they had been sitting there, watching, smelling the sweat of us. After a few minutes they slunk off, their mottled fur blending into the dark veld.

"So, who's sleeping in the tents tonight?" Robbie broke the tense silence.

"It's the back of the truck for me," claimed Juliet hastily.

I climbed onto the roof to see if we could remove the bicycles, tyres and tools that lay cluttered there and erect one of the tents in their place. Not five hundred metres off a lion roared. Bronwyn shrieked as a stone thrown by Robbie landed near to where she had gone for a leak.

With the hyena gone our courage came trickling back and we decided to sleep four of us in the false security offered by the thin walls of the tents.

I slept lightly and arose early the next morning. A herd of zebra walked slowly past the tents, their dark, bristly manes flicking as they shuddered against the day's first flies. A light rain had fallen during the night. Heavy drops still clung to the stems of grass where they had collected. I heard a car go by, the engine's pitch deepening as it passed. This then turned into the unmistakable sound of a vehicle reversing and I watched terrified as an army jeep weaved backwards down the road towards us. It swung off the tar and headed directly for us. Two other vehicles followed. Soon we were surrounded by twelve Tanzanian soldiers. Images of jail flashed across my mind.

"What are you doing here?" demanded the officer in charge.

"Well, we were driving through last night," I said, scrambling for an excuse, "when our lights shorted out and we were forced to stop here."

"You know it's illegal to camp in a national park?"

"Oh yes. We didn't want to camp here at all. We had planned to camp on the other side of the park. It's dangerous to camp like this. We were terrified the whole night."

He demanded all our passports and stood flicking through them officiously, a thin drizzle wetting their pages. It fast became apparent that we weren't going to get them back for nothing. Robbie tried to soften the soldiers' attitude, asking them about their work. Their role was to control poaching in the area.

"We shoot poachers on sight," the leader said, meaningfully.

James, who had been digging some money out of the safe in the back, then motioned to him that they should have a private talk. A few minutes later they reappeared from behind the truck. "He says it's okay," said James. "We can go. Let's pack up and get the hell out of here."

We hurriedly bundled the tents, which were wet from the rain that had fallen and blackened by the carbon remains of an old veld fire, into the back of the truck and left. "He wanted $50, and various other things as well, like my shoes and my watch," said James, "but I managed to beat him down to $10. Not bad for such a great camping spot!"

*

We had another wildlife experience later that morning. We bought eggs for breakfast at a small town called Morogoro and had a fry-up on the side of the road. James went on 'badza patrol' as we euphemistically called our ablutions, *badza* being the Shona word for a hoe, and returned to occupy the small chair next to me.

"Hey, James, what's that small red thing on your neck?" I asked.

"It's a tick! Oh my God, there are more of them. I'm covered!"

"You're a cesspit, James," said Robbie.

"I am! I am!" James agreed, frantically removing the microscopic creatures from his most secret parts where they appeared to have burrowed for warmth.

"Aaagh!" he wailed. "There are seven on my scrotum! Paulus, won't you check if there are any where I can't see?"

We both survived the trauma and drove into Dar es Salaam, the Tanzanian capital, early that afternoon. It was a busy, noisy place, rundown and unkempt but with a liveliness we found exciting. We got lost trying to find the post office where we had letters waiting at the *poste restante* counter, and had to thread our way carefully through narrow, potholed streets and alleyways, stopping every now and then to guide low-slung telephone wires over the roof. The historical and present Arabic influence was immediately apparent in the onion-domed mosques we passed and the robed and fezzed people walking down the humid streets.

After leaving a message for our contact Abs with hoteliers who said they knew him, we headed north out of town to the Silver Sands campsite the American Ross had recommended. We drove along the Bagamoyo road, the old slave route. Bagamoyo means 'lay down your hearts'. Over the centuries the despair of tens of thousands had been wept into the earth of this road, as their freedom was wrenched from them in exchange for bondage in Arabia and the New World.

Silver Sands campsite was bordered by a three metre high fence, patrolled by guards armed with AK-47 rifles. We were told later that they received a $10 bonus for every intruder they shot. We parked next to six overland trucks whose passengers were all on Zanzibar. Several of the drivers had remained behind to service the trucks, and we began for the first time to hear positive things about Zaire.

"The roads are abominable, but you can get through," two Australian women who had just led a Dragoman group through told us. "There are some horrendous potholes. You'll have to dig and push a bit. The bridges are pretty scary but you guys look light enough to be safe. It can get quite expensive if you get stung for a few heavy bribes. Try not to stop if you don't have to. When are you planning to get there?"

"We're not too sure. Probably some time in September."

"You'll have to hurry. It starts to rain about then. Those roads become rivers and you could struggle like hell."

Their confidence cheered me up considerably. I went for a swim in the Indian Ocean thinking that we might be in the Atlantic in a few months' time after all.

Sitting around the fire that evening, talk turned to Zaire.

"So what do you think we do if someone holds us up and tells us to hand over all our cash?" I asked, anxiety invoking in me the cold image of gun barrels pointed by nervous, malevolent hands.

"We'll keep all the money hidden, and maybe just hand over a bit," said Robbie. "Tell them we're travelling using credit cards."

"They'll never find it hidden beneath the seat there," agreed Bronwyn. "And there's not much else in the truck worth taking anyway."

"We'll just act dumb, pretend we don't understand. Talk Afrikaans or something," Robbie continued. "And be as obstinate as possible about handing anything over."

"Shit, I don't know how easy it'll be refusing someone who's pointing a gun in your face," I worried.

"In the end everything comes down to physical force," James joined in. "You've got to have as a last resort the ability to beat the shit out of someone. Ultimately we're physical creatures. Force is the lowest common denominator. And the more you have, the more you can afford to rely on more civilised methods of resolving conflict."

"That's quite a thing to say as a lawyer," I commented. "It sounds like you're advocating anarchy."

"Not at all. What I'm saying is that sometimes you just don't have the time or the opportunity to wait for the law. If some thug comes up to mug you, immediately he's setting the terms of the interaction. You can let him run off with your wallet and hope that he gets caught, but you can also respond on his level. And if you're able to use physical force more effectively than him, you can look after your interests better.

"It's like the SAS. In situations where the law is powerless, like in a hijacking, they're called in and can act above the law, kill out of hand if necessary. They're the ultimate security for the country, for when people refuse to abide by the rules civilisation has drawn up.

"And there are even more subtle dilemmas ahead of us," James went on. "I've been thinking a lot lately about the subjectivity of ideas and values. What I mean by that is if I think X and you think Y, and the two are mutually incompatible, when do I have the right to override your ideas on things?"

"You mean like whether we pay bribes or not?" Bronwyn asked.

"Sort of. But I was thinking more of ideological conflicts. Like when we get to Islamic countries like Algeria. To what extent do we conform to their cultural expectations? Especially women. How much should where we are determine our behaviour? Acting like we're used to could well cause conflict. But to conform to others' expectations might well mean sacrificing our principles."

We talked late into the night, the soft waves offering a murmuring backdrop to our philosophising. The flickering heat of the camp fire played over the fronts of our bodies, encouraging a drowsiness and security, and emphasising what contrast there might be in the less familiar worlds to come.

*

The next day was spent exploring Dar. We went down to the fish market. A steady stream of dhows were docking and offloading their catches: red roman, tuna, stumpnose, yellowfin, squid, barracuda, and enormous blue crayfish weighing over three kilograms. We nibbled throughout the day. Fried octopus was on sale at the fish market. On every corner stood vendors offering the milk of green coconuts, whose heads they would chop off with a single scythe of the long knives they were continually sharpening. Oranges, their skins peeled in a second, falling off in a single, curved helix, were held out to us with smile. The smell of roasting peanuts mixed with that of the sea in the air.

I was struck by how friendly the people we met were. In all our exchanges there was never the slightest feeling that anyone was trying to get from us more than they thought what they were offering was worth. Avarice seemed to be completely absent. It was a very different atmosphere to the one I'd experienced in Kenya two years before and I wondered if there wasn't an unacknowledged benefit to Julius Nyerere's socialist idealism. His uncompromising implementation of Marxist ideology might have been an economic disaster, but the society did seem to have less of the unfeeling competitiveness you find in more capitalistic countries.

We managed to contact Abs, and met him for dinner and dancing at Casanova's, a restaurant-cum-nightclub frequented by ex-pats and the wealthier Tanzanians. We all drank too much that night and the next morning, after leaving the truck at Abs's family's sanitary towel factory, boarded the Flying Horse ferry for Zanzibar feeling quite green about the gills.

*

Zanzibar, the spice island, shimmered white above the deep blue of the sea as the ferry chugged steadily towards it. We stepped off at the quay into air heavy with the sweet smell of cloves. Dust rose faintly from the narrow streets that ran between white-walled buildings which reflected the bright rays of the sun. There was a strong sense of antiquity. It couldn't have been much different when Livingstone came here, or Stanley, in the days when it had been in the control of sultans and slave traders – men like Tippu Tip – when it had been the centre of this part of the world, the focal point of the trade in spices and slaves.

As we walked through its labyrinthine streets over the next six days, the island seemed endlessly exotic. Thin alleyways wound their way below houses three storeys high and leaning in over the street, swayed by the vertical additions later generations had tacked on precariously. Huge, ornately-carved and brass-studded doors of oak and teak squatted stolidly at the top of stone steps. Thin wires and washing lines stretched between walls so old they had become the home of ferns perched just below their red-tiled roofs. Single-sailed wooden dhows tacked across the bay, silhouetted against an expansive setting sun. I was filled with the mystique of the place, its alien forms and ancient ways.

The people thronged in the busy main thoroughfares, walking or cycling. White-robed men in Islamic hats, some with callused feet broadened by a lifetime's barefoot walking, moved past small children darting between the legs around them. Veiled women, garbed in black, walked in silence, their cast-down eyes holding their censorship. Colour flooded the streets in a stream of bright dresses and shawls, in multi-hued scarves and jewellery, and wide smiles in dark faces.

Evenings were spent in the Jamituri Gardens, sampling foods sold by the light of primus lamps and candles. We ate thin kebabs there, and fried octopus, rice, fish, beans spiced with cloves, sugar cane pieces and juice, cassava, peanut brittle, ice cream and fruit salad, and small round doughnuts. We walked from table to table of this moving feast while the lights of stars winked as though in answer to the lights of the small ships and boats that bobbed in the waters of the harbour. The mood was friendly, jocular, and centred around the local people's needs and customs, with tourists like us joining in. The markets had none of the artifice that excessive tourism spawns. The general attitude seemed to be one unique to island cultures: friendly, relaxed, easygoing. Zanzibaris complain of Dar es Salaam being "too fast".

★

We were staying in cheap rooms at a small beach-front hotel called Bububu Beach Bungalows. The beach was covered in fairly coarse sand, and lined with very tall and thin, slightly crooked palms. Our exploring took us to the old fort, the slave caves, Livingstone's house, the sultan's palace and the national museum. We all bought batiks and kikois, and Robbie haggled for two days for an ancient wooden chest.

We visited tailors and James was kitted out with a flowing white robe while Robbie and I had matching harlequin trousers made for us. The markets were filled with exotic fruits: mangoes like volley balls, coconuts and passion fruit, and unbelievably large, fourteen-inch-long bananas I later found out were actually plantains.

A dusty, bouncy taxi ride brought us to Makunduchi on the far side of the island, to see the annual festival, where palm leaves are flailed in aggressive combat in a symbolic release of the pent-up frustrations of the past year. There we met the crew of The Beast and joined them in the feasting and dancing that followed.

★

On our last day we planned to hire mopeds and ride out to the beaches on the east coast. We had left a $10 deposit the previous day with Zameer, the proprietor of Al-Ridha Transport and Hire Services ("We hire at v. reasonable rates"). We arrived a little late to find that Zameer had let someone else have one of the mopeds – which were hired out at $25 per day – which we had reserved the day before. There followed a scene in grave contrast to the rest of our stay on Zanzibar.

"I do have another motorbike you can hire, but it will cost $30," said Zameer.

"We were only twenty minutes late," said James. "You should have kept the moped for us. So it's only fair that we get the motorbike for the $25 we would have paid."

"The price for the motorbike is $30," Zameer stressed, stubbornly.

Robbie then joined in the dispute, which quickly declined into acrimony, neither party willing to compromise. With tempers flaring and blood beginning to boil, we decided to cancel the whole thing and have nothing to do with Zameer or his mopeds. We asked for our deposit back.

"You can't have it," he said stonily.

Where before there had been acrimony there was now active hatred. James, Bronwyn and I, sick of the situation, decided to cut our losses and leave. Robbie, who by this stage was consumed by fury, stayed on. Like a bull terrier clamped to an intruder's arm, he refused to let go. His blue eyes blazed in anger.

He told Zameer that he was a thief, an embarrassment to his faith; that he'd better pray that night for forgiveness for what he'd done. He then told two moped-seeking Germans that Zameer was a thief, and then three Americans. He told Zameer again that he was a stinking crook, and that he was going to stand outside his shop the whole day. In fact he was going to write to *Africa on a Shoestring* about him. Zameer said he could tell the BBC for all he cared, and the slander continued.

Somehow amidst the ensuing confusion Juliet, who had stood watching silently, playing good cop to Robbie's very bad, managed to sweet-talk Zameer and recover half our deposit, which brought the whole bitter scene to a close.

*

Juliet had decided to remain on Zanzibar after we left and then to fly out from Dar es Salaam. We had a farewell dinner at the Sea View Restaurant and said our goodbyes the next morning, making plans to meet up in London in five months' time. Bronwyn and I had come across a plinth in one of the gardens near a crossroads on which the distances to other towns had been engraved: Bwelo 12 miles, Chuaka 20½, Fumba 13¾, and London 8064. It seemed an awfully long time and a long way to go before we would see Jules again.

Nevertheless, and despite a turbulent, listing ferry crossing which caused half the passengers to be seasick, we felt rested and relaxed when we arrived back at Dar es

Salaam. It felt good to be reunited with the truck too, and we returned to Silver Sands where we braaied a huge red roman for supper, our thoughts turning to Kenya.

Top: Rhodes Memorial, Cape Town
Bottom: The Mulanjes, Malawi

Top: The two-wheel-drive bus, Dar es Salaam
Bottom: James with his tailor, Zanzibar

Top: London 8064 miles
Bottom: Masai, Kenya

Top: 'The Beast' and its crew, Nairobi
Bottom: Andrew and Derek join us, Nairobi

Top: Bujagali Falls, Uganda
Bottom: Some had horns even larger

Top: "You are now leaving Uganda and entering Zaire"
Bottom: Silverback gorilla, Zaire

Top: Bog-hole, near Epulu
Bottom: Derek, a pygmy, James and Rob

Top: Another day, another obstacle
Bottom: A sturdy bridge

Chapter Eight

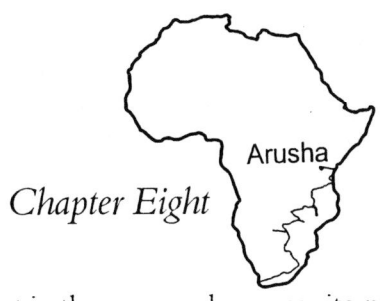

After a night spent out in the open under mosquito nets, we left Dar es Salaam on the old Bagamoyo road, moving slowly along its rough, potholed surface. Just after Bagamoyo we had to ferry across a minor river. The ferry was a rusting, hand-driven contraption. We drove carefully up its lopsided ramp onto the deck. Several women walked on after us, one with a baby strapped to her back. The ancient ferryman strained at the winch, hauling it round as the ferry inched its way across the slow-moving water. We paid a mere Sh200, about $0.36, for his back-breaking service.

The day had started with an argument. We were a few miles down the road from the camp, having made an early start.

"So how much did we end up paying for the camping?" I asked Robbie.

"Well, nothing as it turns out. I looked for that guy last night but couldn't find him. And then this morning I forgot all about it."

"So we haven't paid then?"

"Hey, don't get stressed about it. They're the ones who were slack. It's their lookout! I did go out looking for them."

"Shit, Robbie, we can't just run off like this. We must turn around and go back. We've got to pay what we owe them."

"Oh come on, don't be so neurotic. They won't even notice."

James joined in. "I agree with Paul. They've given us a good service and we should pay them for it. I vote we turn around."

"It's just not worth the hassle, James. We've come a good ten kays by now," said Bronwyn who was driving. "Let's just leave it."

Split into two factions, the argument was just beginning to become heated when we saw the bulldog-faced shape of The Beast travelling towards us, heading, as it turned out, for Silver Sands.

At James's and my urging, Rob gave them the money to hand over to the camp owners.

A second argument began two hours later. Driving through a small village, we noticed an entrepreneur who had rigged up a grinding stone to the frame of a bicycle and was sharpening blades, pedalling furiously. James stopped and retrieved our blunt panga from the back for him to sharpen. Two Masai warriors stood nearby. They had a regal bearing, emphasised by their height which was well over six foot, and they wore dramatically colourful clothes and jewellery. Their purple cloaks and long, braided hair, their elongated and beaded earlobes and their fine facial features gave them a graceful, feminine beauty. They stood out among the other villagers like peacocks among chickens. But when Robbie moved to take a photograph of James they glided swiftly out of shot, evidently anxious not to be captured on film.

Shortly afterwards, back on the road again, we stopped to give a lift to another Masai warrior who hailed us with one of the two large knobkerries he was carrying. We had taken out the fifth seat, a jerrycan wedged between the two other seats, after Juliet left, and indicated to him that he could stand in the doorway. He obviously did not even consider the idea and sat down on top of James, forcing him to balance precariously in the gap between the two seats. He then spoke to us, loudly and at length, apparently assured that anyone of any worth would be able to speak his language. After it became obvious that we did not understand him, he started pointing at various objects, cassette tapes and bracelets on our wrists, indicating that he wanted them. James mimed that we would give them to him in exchange for his photograph, at which he became extremely agitated and all negotiation ceased. If I looked towards him he stared back at me boldly, with a greater expression of self-assuredness than I have ever seen.

When we dropped him off, James again indicated that he wished to take his photo, but the Masai again refused vehemently.

"I'll take it while he's not looking," said James. "What he doesn't know can't hurt him."

"No, James, don't!" I said firmly. "You've got to respect his wishes. Just 'cause his culture's different, doesn't mean we should impose ours on him."

"Oh, come on, Paul! What harm will it do him? He won't even know I've done it!"

"That doesn't matter, and he might well hear the shutter click anyway." I felt strongly the need not to affront the man's grave dignity and prevented the photo being taken. We drove off engaged in a loud argument over the ethics of the whole business. Eventually I halted the argument without resolution by climbing out of the cab and onto the roof. I thought about the man we'd given a lift to. I'd never before encountered such confidence, such a strong sense of self. As Robbie had said, it was in some ways like having a roan antelope in the cab with us.

★

"Here, I'll siphon the diesel this time," offered Bronwyn as we broke camp and prepared to leave. "There's no reason why you men should always do it. What's the technique then? I've just got to suck as hard as I can, haven't I?"

Unfortunately the thick hosepipe we had originally used for siphoning, and which did require prodigious efforts of sucking to generate a vacuum into which the diesel would flow, had been lost, and we had only been able to find a much thinner pipe as a replacement. We forgot to warn Bronwyn about the radically different physics of the new hose.

"Here we go then," she said, extravagantly wiping the hose with a cloth and then bracing herself before sucking mightily on its end. Litres of diesel flooded down her throat. She coughed and spluttered. "Oh my God! I'm drowning! Weugh! You bastards! I can't believe you told me to suck so hard. God, it's disgusting! Urgh, I can taste it when I burp!"

It was then, amid the laughter, that James came up with the idea of standing on the upper fuel tank and sucking diesel upwards until it filled the pipe before jamming his finger over the end to hold the vacuum, jumping down and inserting that end into the main tank below. Although it required more effort to suck the fuel against gravity up the length of the pipe, a day without the constant resurgence of diesel gas made it well worth it.

The drive through northern Tanzania took us past expansive fields of sisal, their sharp leaves pointing skywards in long green, uniform rows. We were heading for Mombasa, Kenya's major port, where we were to stay with family of a friend of mine. As ever, our choice of route centred largely around the location of the game parks. We planned to head back into Tanzania from Mombasa to visit the Ngorongoro Crater and the Serengeti. Beyond that we still had not decided.

Six kilometres short of the border post at Lunga-Lunga the gasping coughs of our dying engine came back to haunt us. James and I conducted the now well-rehearsed ritual of removing the engine cover, loosening the injector leads, making sure each had a constant flow of fuel being bled out, tightening them and hoping the engine would catch. This time it did and we were moving again.

Once in Kenya the countryside changed, becoming flatter and more grassy. The engine's idiosyncrasy remained, though, and we came to another spluttering, fuel-starved halt. Frustrated, we went through the procedure again. Each time it took about half an hour to complete, as we had to unlock the back, set up the ladder and climb in, take out the toolbox and locate the 9/16 spanner, then open the cowling, loosen and bleed the leads before finally tightening them again, hoping the engine would catch. This time we left the engine cover off, as though daring the ghost to revisit us again.

Superstition held, and we made it to Tiwi Beach campsite just south of Mombasa, slightly deafened by the direct noise of the engine and with the smell of scorched oil strong in our nostrils.

The warm waters of the Indian Ocean offered us an escape from our worries. We had to wear shoes as we swam for protection against the purple spines of the sea urchins that littered the ocean floor. Later that night we met a Dutchman, an energetic, enthusiastic man, who had just come through Zaire in a Mercedes Unimog. He spent some time with us, poring over maps of the region, offering advice like buying extra jerrycans to trade and ignoring all roadblocks in the Central African Republic. As he spoke, I felt my remaining misgivings about Zaire dissipate under the vivid brush strokes his confident words painted.

The truck broke down again the next day, just short of the Likoni ferry that would take us to Mombasa Island. We felt desperate, and vowed to find the source of the problem in Mombasa, no matter what the cost. For now, though, we were set on finding the home of Roger and Carol Jessop, parents of a squash team-mate of mine, Adam, who had said that they would happily put up four strangers for a while. Five actually. Sandy Young, a friend from university, would be joining us for the second half of the journey to London.

"Hell, I'm looking forward to seeing Sandy again," I was telling Bronwyn and Robbie. "You'll really like her."

"I'm just glad it's another woman joining us," said Bronwyn, "someone I can relate to."

I too felt the need for empathy. We had been travelling for over ten weeks now and although the relationships between us had been unstrained, I missed the closeness of people who knew me well, with whom I could easily be myself. Sandy and I had become close friends while studying together, and her joining us would, I knew, fortify me for the long passage still to come.

The map showing how to get to the Jessop's house, drawn for us by Adam months before in Cape Town, was easy to follow, and we arrived to an openly warm welcome, mountains of post, and Sandy who had flown in the previous day. She had come laden with books we had requested in letters, a new neon camping light for the truck and an excited delight at realising a dream, at stepping off a cliff to free fall into the unknown.

"I'm just so thrilled to be here!" she gushed. "The Jessops have been absolutely wonderful to me. And I'm so relieved to see you all. I had no idea exactly when you'd be arriving."

"We almost didn't arrive," I told her. "We've been having a nightmare with the truck. The engine keeps on stalling. But we'll get it fixed in Mombasa tomorrow."

"Then we'll be ready for the less tame part of the trip. The jungles of Zaire, or the mountains of Ethiopia – whichever way we decide to go!" said James.

"I can't wait! If it carries on the way it's started, it's going to be everything I've dreamt of."

Sandy's obvious delight reinvigorated our own passion for what we were doing, and we spent the evening regaling her with our adventures of the weeks that had passed and imagining what more there would be in the weeks to come.

But underneath the excitement of post and reunions and having a home for a while, there sat in us a travel weariness, a loneliness only exacerbated by the letters we received and the all too transient telephone calls home. Robbie in particular was missing Bridget. There was little comfort from strangers after seven years so close, and with each mile we stretched from Cape Town, he felt the void more keenly.

The letters also brought news about friends we hoped to team up with for the second half of the journey. Derek Hume had left Johannesburg a month after us on his motorbike and evidently was hot on our heels. Our old friend Andrew Birrell, we read disconcertingly, had abandoned his trip and turned his Land-Rover back towards Cape Town.

*

We headed into Mombasa early the next day, the others to explore the town, James and I to dig down to the root of the infernal fuel problem. At a workshop called Dieselcraft we had the internal filter of the injector pump cleaned, thinking that might be where the blockage lay. As ever when working on the truck, we noticed other things that were wrong, and created additional complications ourselves. The alternator bracket had snapped again. We managed to buy two spares and have one fitted, and were replacing the injector pump when we broke the seal on top of its governor-housing. Diesel seeped steadily onto the road below us as we drove back with the uncomfortable thoughts that we might well have achieved less than nothing in the day. We mixed up some Araldite, an adhesive which we had been told sticks to metal 'like shit to a blanket,' smeared it over the broken governor-housing and went to bed with fingers crossed.

The Araldite seemed to hold and we decided to have a day off from repairing the truck. At high tide in the afternoon, after a morning spent wandering through the streets of Mombasa's Old Town and visiting Fort Jesus, we accompanied the Jessops on a traditional family outing to the seventeen metre Mtwepa bridge. We all plucked up the courage to jump off and fall screaming into the salty water below, except for Bronwyn, whose fear of heights no amount of peer group pressure could quell.

Back at the house, one of the dinner guests peered under the truck and noticed something which scuppered our plans to depart the next morning: the upper two leaves of the front left springs had snapped in half. We hauled out the pieces of chopped-up sleeper we kept for such a purpose, rested the chassis on them, and set about replacing the springs right there and then, using, for the most part, a large hammer and crowbars. The job took us into the next afternoon, and we decided to leave the following morning, more than a bit weary by now of repairs to the truck.

We said goodbye to the Jessops, and gave them, as small thanks for their wonderful hospitality, a book we had bought at a bookstore in town. As it turned out, not only was the book second-hand but, as the inscription inside showed, it was the very book Carol and Roger had given to friends the previous Christmas.

"What goes around comes around!" laughed Carol.

We left with the warmest of feelings towards these people who had been so kind to five strangers.

*

"How you can take the Bible to be the word of God I just can't understand." It hadn't taken long for James's atheism, impelled by his need to explain everything in strictly rational terms, to seek out Sandy's religious convictions as a target against which he could direct his argumentative arrows.

"Firstly, it contradicts itself. The moral tone of the Old Testament differs radically from that of the New. An eye for an eye suddenly becomes turn the other cheek. An angry God who hardened Pharaoh's heart suddenly becomes forgiving. Surely a God who is immortal and omniscient wouldn't do moral flick-flacks. To me the writings in the Bible are obviously a record of their time's social morality, with suitable threats for those who don't abide by them.

"And then to state Christianity is the only true faith..."

"Hang on, James!" Sandy interjected. "You're just taking pot-shots here at a Christianity that is literal and potentially closed-minded. My Christian beliefs are not necessarily exclusive of other beliefs."

"But that's what Christianity is all about!" James continued, his voice rising. "To be a Christian you have to believe that Jesus Christ appeared on earth as the son of God, to save our souls, and if you don't you'll be damned for eternity. And if you were brought up a Moslem in Tehran or happened to be born in 1,000 BC, then that's just tough shit, because there's no way to heaven but through him!"

"Hell, James, don't get so aggressive, man!" interposed Robbie, reacting to James's attack on what was his faith as well, but unwilling to join the theological fray.

"No, it's okay," Sandy continued. "It's good to have one's beliefs challenged. There is of course a danger in taking the writings of the Bible too literally. The concept of heaven, for example, is not so much a place as a state of being. It is union with God. The anguish of hell is the pain of separation from God."

"But how can this God so indiscriminately advantage some people over others? If I was born Jewish the odds of me accepting Christ as my personal saviour are a hell of a lot smaller than if I was born Roman Catholic. And what if I died at two months, without even the chance of understanding Christianity, let alone accepting it?"

"I know you might perceive it as something of a cop-out, but there are certain issues I cannot offer complete answers to – the early deaths of children, the extreme suffering some people endure. All I can say is that I have faith that there are reasons for this, that it forms part of God's plan for us."

"Faith. That's the problem for me," I joined in. "It's not something you can just have. I'd be lying to myself if I tried to pretend all of a sudden that I believe in Jesus Christ. I don't. And I don't think I ever will."

"And that there's some kind of over-arching plan, I'll never believe," said James. "We're here by chance, the random coming together of molecules over billions of years of evolution. And when we die, we die."

The discussions continued, earnest and at times impassioned, spiralling round through philosophy and genetics, and back to religion, James speaking as heretic in the on-going war of mind against faith.

Sandy's joining the trip had given a renewed impetus not only to our conversations, but to our enthusiasm for the journey itself. Romanced by the thought of what lay before her, she infected us all with her excitement. We were all pleased to be moving again, looping via Tanzania to Nairobi and from there west into the jungle. We weren't to know then that she would be with us for only another eight days.

*

On the Nairobi road just out of Mombasa we approached a roadblock, marked by two flat plates, one on each side of the road and about fifteen metres apart, from which protruded an array of spikes three inches long. James, who was the best driver of us all, somehow failed to negotiate the chicane. The truck jolted as its left front tyre rolled over the plate and James was forced to pull over and watch in horror as it deflated rapidly before us.

While we were replacing the wheel with our spare, two young men came up to us and asked for a lift. They said their names were Chris and Ian and that they were trying to get to Nairobi, having run into bad luck in Mombasa. Each was dressed in a kikoi and sandals and had curly blonde hair and a goatee beard. Their possessions were in small cloth knapsacks slung over their shoulders. Most of their possessions, that is. Chris was carrying as well a huge, ornately-carved wooden chest which he said he had been carrying around for the past two years and in which he kept his valuables: passport, money, and a large stash of dope.

They told us they had also been to the University of Cape Town. One summer's day they had decided to put a decisive end to the tedium of lectures and head north. After a series of vaguely remembered escapades and robberies, they found themselves penniless on the beaches of Mombasa. Undeterred, they had convinced Ian's father to wire to them money he thought would bring them home. A short spending spree and a robbery later, they were again penniless on the beach. They had then hit upon the idea of approaching the British consul for emergency aid, as one of them had a British passport. They were on their way to Nairobi to collect the plane ticket the consulate had purchased, to be paid for in London. They were hoping to cash it in and use the proceeds to extend their stay. They loved Kenya, they told us. As we were turning left at Voi, to head back into Tanzania, we dropped them off and wished them luck. It wasn't the last we were to see of this strange pair.

While removing the punctured wheel, James had noticed that the wheel bearings were loose and needed to be replaced. The truck was becoming a Hydra. Resolving one problem seemed to reveal or cause several more. As the engine coughed and died again ten kilometres out of Voi, a silent scream shook my brain. Grimly we prepared for the ritual, performed the bleeding, and drove on. Five minutes later we had to do it again. And two minutes after that. The next time, fed up, we decided to stop for the night.

Apart from the presents he received, James had the worst start to a birthday of his life. We repaired the puncture, bled the fuel line, and managed to get ten kilometres further before slowing to a powerless halt. We then discovered that we'd lost our main set of keys, possibly at the night's campsite, and that our fifteen litre tub of hand cleaner had spilt, covering the floor of the truck in a gelatinous pink ooze.

James had the theory that air might be entering the fuel system from the overflow pipes, so we spent two hours diverting these into the main tank, bled the engine, and set off back to where we had camped. We managed to travel for one kilometre. Put-put-put. Phut.

I go for a short walk to ease my frustrations. I sit down on a rock beneath the fierce afternoon sun, staring idly at the corpse of a beetle in the sand below me. It jerks as if alive but it is only ants carrying it away. I'm hating the truck, these interminable repairs. I'm hating being a mechanic. My despondency asks how we'll ever cope further west, where there are no workshops or Bedford spares, and when we'll be driving twice as far in as much time over terrain far less sympathetic to our ageing truck's rheumatic joints and unsteady heart. This growing uncertainty compounds the creeping insecurity in me.

James was busy removing the engine cover. "This is a fucking nightmare!" he cried, shaking his head as he looked at me with anguish. "I think we should stop buggering around, and go right back to basics. We'll set up a gravity feed again and bypass most of this bloody fuel line. At least that'll tell us where the problem is."

We set about rigging up our elaborate chemistry experiment, while Bronwyn and Sandy played their guitars and sang. Robbie called out that he had found the keys. Perhaps our luck had changed. An hour later we were moving again, the five of us squeezed in beside the jerrycans and tubes of the gravity feed apparatus, our mood lightening with every unhalting kilometre. The steady sound of the engine filled me with delight, leaving me inured to the fumes rising from the diesel that slopped from the jerrycans into the cab.

The road took us through Tsavo National Park, Kenya's largest game reserve. There was almost no other traffic. Game abounded on either side of the road: northern species, related to but distinct from their southern cousins, which we half-recognised, like mistakenly identifying a friend in a foreign city. We saw red hartebeest, looking so much like tsessebe; Thompson's gazelle leaping like springboks; waterbuck without the characteristic white circle on their hindquarters, and the lesser kudu, a pretty animal far smaller than the kudu we knew from home.

Back in Tanzania again, we stocked up with beer bought from a roadside store and were soon filled with the same buoyant jubilation we had felt on our drive into Maun two long months before. Suddenly, in front of us, rising out of a band of cloud was the snow-capped summit of Kilimanjaro, broad, immense. We drove towards it through the yellow evening light, exultant, giddy with excitement. The sound of Toto's 'Africa' filled the cab and we sang along and laughed, in love with where we were.

It was dark by the time we started searching for somewhere to camp, just past Moshi. The area was densely populated, and we drove for almost an hour without finding anywhere suitable. Frustrated, James turned down a road running through a maize farm, causing me to worry that we might be caught trespassing. A few more lucky turns later we found ourselves driving down a lane lined with jacarandas at the end of which sat an abandoned farmhouse. It was a perfect site. We sat around a fire, surrounded by red bougainvillaea. The night was alive with the crackle of flames and the calls of insects. Before us, majestic, magnetic, stood Kilimanjaro, shawled in mist, its white peak rising up to touch a near-full moon. The day had turned around.

★

Arusha is the tourist capital of Tanzania, base for the thousands of safaris that head each week into the Serengeti National Park and the Ngorongoro Crater. While Robbie walked into town to find out about safari excursions, James and I started dissecting the lift pump, the next suspect in our line-up of possible culprits. Bronwyn had bumped into an old university friend of hers who was on an overland truck heading south and was engaged in animated discussion, overjoyed to have a sympathetic, and New Zealand, ear to talk to.

We dismantled the gravity feed, stripping the fuel filter housing and snapping a fuel lead in the process, and reassembled the lift pump. An American from one of the overland trucks parked at the camp chatted to us as we set about what we hoped would be a final cure for the truck's fuel ills. James worked swiftly and energetically, anxious to put an end to the problem, talking animatedly as he levered and tightened the various parts. After a day's work under the truck, the tell-tale bubbles emerging from the lift pump told us we'd accomplished nothing. James leapt up, cursing, put on his shoes and sprinted off on a run. The American, who had watched and listened fascinated for most of the afternoon, stared after him as he disappeared down the road. "Is he on speed?" he asked, in all seriousness.

I decided to go for a jog also, to burn off the frustration still in me from the battle with the truck, and wound my way along thin, hard-packed paths up over the foothills of Mount Meru. I ran through small villages perched on the steep hills and past slow-moving herds of lowing cattle being rounded up by small boys flicking long sticks and whistling. Immediately I felt more peaceful, more at ease in such uncomplicated, elemental surroundings. It was an incongruous sight that I saw then as I descended into a huge field at the upper end of the marshy valley floor. An evangelical churchman was striding up and down a raised platform before a hushed crowd of a thousand people. He bellowed from froth-flecked lips words of salvation and God's fury, his voice amplified hugely by the massive speakers that straddled the stage.

★

Back at the camp, Robbie was winding into a tight coil the two ropes hanging from the branch of an overhanging jacaranda tree, from which was suspended a small wooden aeroplane onto which Bronwyn had climbed. Released, she would spin dizzily as the ropes unwound, accelerating, and then twisted up once more.

"Stop it, Robbie!" she shouted, launching into a string of profanities.

"Hell, not if you talk like that," he replied. "You New Zealand girls are worse than sailors."

"Fuck you, Robson! Now stop it, I'm about to do a helicopter chunder!"

"It'll serve you right for such disgusting language," said Robbie superciliously.

Bronwyn still shocked us with her uncensored, earthy speech. It was natural in her, unaffected, but still not what we were used to, and our old habits judged her for it.

Leaving the truck behind for a couple of days was a definite motivating factor in our decision to take a two day package tour with Roy's Safaris to Tarangire, a smaller park to the south west of Arusha, and the Ngorongoro Crater. Robbie had been keen to visit the Serengeti as well, on a week-long safari, but we dissuaded him, restricted as we were by our time and money constraints.

We passed through the front gate of Tarangire, flanked by two huge, sun-bleached elephant skulls, just as the last of the morning dew was evaporating off the grass. The view we had, looking through the open roof of a Land-Rover, was spectacular. Vast herds of wildebeest, impala, zebra, buffalo and Thompson's gazelle stood quietly or ran skittishly as we approached. The earth was dry, covered in brittle yellow stalks of grass and acacia trees whose canopies cast small pools of shade, offering respite from the heat. The long cactus arms of euphorbia candelabra stretched upwards like a garrison in mass surrender. Elephants walked steadfastly by, young ones trotting to keep up with the tails in front of them which their trunks were curled around. A tiny dik-dik looked up frightened and ran, blending into the short grass around it.

"God, I hate zoos!" I exclaimed. "Seeing animals like this makes me sick to think of how we lock them up in cages just so we can gawk at them. They should all be shut down."

"I disagree completely," James objected. "It's fine for you to say that – you have access to animals in the wild. But what about kids growing up in a place like London? The only opportunity they'll have of seeing live animals is in a zoo. The benefit they derive from seeing the animals easily outweighs what suffering the animals might endure. And anyway, most modern zoos look after their animals pretty well nowadays."

"You haven't been to Paris zoo in the winter, then, and seen camels and lions almost freezing to death. I've never seen such unhappy creatures. To me that kind of suffering is inexcusable. Those kids can see the animals on TV. Apart from the work they do conserving endangered species, what zoos supply is a cruel and outdated entertainment."

"Rubbish! There's no comparison between seeing animals in the flesh and in a TV image. Just look at children in a zoo. They love it! The understanding and excitement they get easily compensates for the suffering of a few animals. And who's to say whether their lives in the wild would involve less suffering, or if they would have lives outside the zoo at all?"

The argument continued heated amongst us as we sat down to a picnic lunch, James staunchly defending his position that human experience should be valued above that of animals.

"We forget too easily that we're animals ourselves," I said. "We speak of humans and 'the animals', forgetting that we're animals as well, just more evolved ones."

"And that's debatable in itself," added Bronwyn.

After lunch our guides, Burrha and Martin, drove us to the Ngorongoro Crater, in the north-eastern corner of Tanzania, an ancient volcanic crater, its fires cold now, whose bowl has become home to numerous species of game, confined there by its steep walls, and whose lives form the pattern of a self-contained and complex ecosystem. The road leading to the crater, which lies due west of the Serengeti, is rough and corrugated, covered in a fine, infiltrating dust. I felt glad it was not our truck, sitting gutted and immobile in Arusha 200 kilometres away, that was having to buck and twist its way up the ascent to the crater's edge.

We slept the night at Simba campsite on the western rim of the crater, and woke to witness the most glorious sunrise I had ever seen. Twenty kilometres across the mouth of this long-dead volcano, clouds were pouring over the edge in a colossal waterfall, billowing and churning before dispersing on the rocks of warmer air below. About 600 metres down, thin ribbons of mist hung above the reawakening ground, clinging on to the morning cold. The disk of the sun rose from out of the clouds, flooding the sky in orange and red and streaking with pink the avalanching vapour that continued to pour beneath it. In the flat basin of the crater's floor lakes began to sparkle and we could dimly see the moving forms of the life that had as their home the veld of this cauldron sanctuary.

Descending into the crater, down hairpin bends, we passed Masai herdsman driving their cattle towards the water they share with the wild game. We had met other Masai the previous day, men with handsome angular features, dressed brightly in blankets of checked red and blue; young women, shaven-headed, demure, garlanded in beads and with large wooden bungs in the lobes of their ears; and a couple of old crones who had pestered us for money while we refuelled, their stubbled grey heads and hunched shoulders giving them the appearance of Marabou storks. The pride and independence which has so characterised the Masai seemed to be fraying at the edges. The road to the crater held pockets of tribespeople who were more elaborately dressed than others, charging tourists to take their photograph.

The plains of Ngorongoro were as full of game as had been promised. Herds of buck and antelope walked slowly towards the water of its lakes, elephants ambled twenty metres away from the car. Hippos stared at us over their raised nostrils, ears wiggling. A lone rhinoceros grazed stolidly, lifting its head occasionally to sniff the air. But there was something missing. The animals seemed more domestic than wild. An old male lion slept peacefully while we watched, not three metres away. On the other side of him, in a gawking arc, were five safari vehicles. James, William Brown, bet he could leap out, smack it on the bum, and get back in before it knew what was happening, and I had to restrain him from proving it one way or the other, his insensitive bravado angering me.

Even though there was something of a zoo about seeing the animals there, in contrast to the other places we had been, it had been exhilarating to be that close to massing herds, and we returned to Arusha with their gamey smells and milling voices still fresh in our minds.

*

Back at Masai Camp in Arusha, we decided to rebuild the gravity feed, and look into the fuel problem while waiting for visas in Nairobi. A German at the camp confirmed that

Zaire was traversable with patience but had bad news about the countries that lay after the jungle.

"The Route d'Hoggar through Algeria is still closed. You have to go round the bulge if you want to get to Europe. And that might not be possible either, the way you want to do it, from what I've heard. It is okay if you go from north to south, the way I came. But you cannot go the other way. The Moroccans won't give permits to anyone coming from Mauritania. You would have to put your vehicle on a ship perhaps."

This news worried me. Not being able to cross Algeria would add 5,000 kilometres to the trip. And we'd miss out on seeing the famed Hoggar mountains in the central Sahara.

"Oh well, on the bright side, at least we'll get to visit places like Ougadougou, and Timbuktu," said James. "And I'm sure there will be a way through to Morocco. We'll make a plan one way or another. Let's get through the jungle first. One challenge at a time."

We left Arusha with a sense of confidence. Parked at the campsite was a battered, rusty Volkswagen Beetle with Cape Town licence plates. Scrawled on the back was the bold statement "Cape Town to Cairo or Bust." If that little thing could make it across Africa, then so could we.

Chapter Nine

We arrived in Nairobi having covered 600 fume-filled kilometres with diesel sloshing and spilling from the jerrycans of the gravity feed. Ma Roche's campsite had been recommended to us, and we made our way across town towards it, driving slowly through busy streets filled with cars both new and decrepit, and countless packed *matatus* – minibus taxis that were brightly coloured, ablaze with slogans and paintings of animals, and that seemed to follow their own, somewhat unorthodox highway code.

Parked at the campsite was an incongruous sight indeed. A bright red double-decker London bus filled most of the yard. At thirty-one it was two years younger than our truck, but had seen a fair bit more of the world. Its clock showed it had covered over 3,000,000 kilometres in its globetrotting lifetime, setting off, on the first trip of its reincarnation, from London to Seoul for the 1988 Olympic Games, and not stopping ever since. On this leg it had given a lift to a group of Danes who had had it shipped to Cape Town. We manoeuvred our truck into the lee of its imposing compatriot.

The camp was full, and we spent the evening chatting to an English couple who were cycling around East Africa, and a French teenager who had arrived in Kenya without even a sleeping bag, and who curled up next to the dying fire for a cold night's sleep.

The following day we began work on the mechanical and bureaucratic mountains that had to be shifted before we could continue west. While James and I took the truck to a breakers yard where we hoped to get spares and advice, the others went to find out about visas for Central Africa. At the yard we bought half a dozen spare leaves for the suspension. While they were being searched for along the endless corridors of racks filled with the nameless parts of dead trucks, we discussed the spluttering fuel problem.

"We need to tackle it methodically," James stressed. "Let's start at the main tank and follow the flow of fuel all the way through to the engine, isolating each section as we go. There might even be a blockage in the fuel tank itself. There's probably a little filter here where this pipe comes out," he said pointing to the thin lift pipe that emerged from the top of the tank. "We might as well check it out now, while we're waiting."

He soon had the bolt undone. I shone the torch into the tank, through the new aperture but could see nothing except the dim line marking the level of diesel. James meanwhile was trying to peer through the L-shaped pipe we had removed.

"What's this?" he asked, and blew as hard as he could into its short end. With a loud pop a small ball of muck which had been wedged in the elbow joint of the pipe shot out, arcing twenty metres across the car park to land on the windscreen of a Mercedes-Benz. We'd found the problem. We'd exorcised our ghost. Elated, we drove back to the others, eager to share the good news.

It was immediately apparent that the news that they were bearing was not good. Sandy looked pale and shaken. The South African consulate had asked her to phone home. She heard from her family that her mother had a brain tumour, and might have only a few months to live. Grief for her mother welled up in her. And, to an extent, for the end of this journey she had had her heart set on. She had booked her flight already and was leaving the next day.

We ate a subdued supper that night at the Everest Hotel, with the crew of The Beast whom we'd met up with again at the traveller's meeting point, the Thorntree Café, that evening. The next morning we took Sandy to Jomo Kenyatta airport to bid her farewell. We returned, our hearts heavier with the loss of her caring nature and enthusiasm, to consider what to do next.

There had been two messages for us wedged under the elastic netting of the Thorntree Café's noticeboard. Derek Hume had arrived in Nairobi on his motorbike and was keen to join up with us through Zaire at least. Andrew Birrell, contrary to what we had heard, had also arrived and would be returning from an excursion to Lamu in ten days' time. Although the three women on The Beast were due to fly back to South Africa, Richard and Greg were considering also driving on to London, provided Greg didn't die of the malaria he was suffering from.

I felt relieved that we had various options of teaming up with others for the second half of the trip. Bronwyn, however, was uncertain. She had become depressed by Sandy's departure. The two had quickly become close, and the loss of this companionship weighed down on her.

"It's all very well for you," she pointed out, "but these other people we're considering going with are all men. South African men. There's no way I can cross the rest of Africa with a bunch of guys. All my closest friends are women. I'll go mad without female company for four months."

"Oh, come on, Bronwyn," said James. "What's your hassle? It's only a short time."

"There's just no way I'll go if I'm the only woman."

Later, in private, James and I discussed the situation. "I'll be pissed off if she pulls out," I said. "It'll be bloody expensive for just the three of us to go the rest of the way by ourselves."

"I don't know. It might be a blessing in disguise," James replied darkly. "She's been irritating me unbelievably lately. I reckon it'd be worth the cost."

We decided to advertise for a fifth person, preferably female, and put up small posters at the campsite and the Thorntree Café, but with little hope of attracting anyone, let alone an adventurous, financially stable woman, at such short notice.

*

After two months on our heels, Derek finally caught up with us the next day. He and I had known each other superficially at university, having raced wooden toboggans together down the eighty concrete steps leading up to Jameson Hall in the annual Rag races. As then, it became apparent now that Derek had his own way of doing things. He told us how in two months he had used his sleeping bag twice, the rest of the time living in the luxurious care of people he hadn't known until a few hours before. In Lilongwe he had knocked on the door of the long-suffering Markhams. In Lusaka he'd woken up the South African consul. Riding into Dar es Salaam, he'd followed the first white man he'd seen and asked for a bed for the night.

He was brazen, and his vitality did something to restore us, fresh air to replace that which had escaped with Sandy's leaving, deflating us. I thought that Derek would be a good person to have with us if we got into trouble. I couldn't help but think also that he might be the one who got us into the trouble in the first place.

We also heard from him more about Andrew's ill-fated trip. His Land-Rover's four man crew had split up in Tanzania, the other three going their way and Andrew his. Derek told us of Andrew's stubbornness, of how he had treated the vehicle and trip as his own, and the other three as passengers, and how he had brooked no discussion about dates and routes.

Of course there are ever two parties to a conflict and later we were to hear of the other side, of vindictiveness and malice, factions being formed and three turning on one, riling, baiting, each side tearing the other down. The pressures of travelling make people's colours glow more brightly, or darkly; and I wondered what the months ahead would show us of ourselves, and whether the pressures on our group might not split us apart too, like a nut in the slow fulcrum squeeze of the nutcracker.

Derek, in his inimitable fashion, was ensconced in the garden flat of the Church family whom he'd met the day before, on their farm near Karen. He said we'd been invited to camp in their paddock if we liked. We were eager to move out of the cramped conditions at Ma Roche's and accepted. On the way out there the truck overheated. The water pump had broken, and we added replacing this to the list of necessary repairs and maintenance: replacing the two wheel bearings we'd noticed were loose, replacing the oil and fuel filters, changing the oil, greasing the nipples and tightening every bolt we could find.

After installing the new water pump, before putting the radiator back on, we started the engine to make sure the pump was working. Thin plumes of steam rose out of the air inlet as we watched.

"Oh Christ!" moaned James. "I think we've burnt a hole in the cylinder head gasket. Nothing else would produce steam like that."

I felt sick in my stomach. "Oh, shit. How serious is that?"

"It's a massive job. We'll have to take the cylinder head off and replace the gasket. It'll take days to sort out. If at all. There's so much that can go wrong."

But this time fate smiled on us. A couple of hours' nervous diagnosis proved that the gasket was undamaged, and the truck seemed to be running more sweetly than ever.

★

Over the next four days we continued our search for spare parts and our run of the embassy gauntlet. Fortunately none of us was on a British passport as the British embassy was refusing to supply the letters of recommendation needed before applying for Zairean visas, saying it was far too dangerous to enter. British subjects were also being warned against entering Nigeria.

Robbie and Derek returned from the South African embassy bearing trophies. Derek had T-shirts with a blue and green ethnic design and the logo "Progress through Co-operation" which he handed out. James refused one, saying he would never wear anything distributed by the Nationalist government, which irritated Robbie. Derek and Robbie had been left alone in the office of the ambassador's secretary for a while and Robbie had seized the opportunity to open one drawer, remove several sheets of headed notepaper, open another, take out the official consulate stamp, and stamp each sheet of paper.

"What on earth for?" I asked.

"Oh, just in case," he said. "You never know."

They had also organised fake employment cards through the camera shop opposite the Thorntree Café who were operating the scam, profiting from the fact that Kenyan residents paid one tenth of the fees of non-residents at the national parks. We had all become teachers at the Mombasa Academy.

We had an indeterminate amount of time ahead of us to kick our heels while waiting for visas for the Central

African Republic and decided to spend two more days servicing the truck and then visit the Masai Mara and Mount Kenya. Susie and Tony Church, whose farm we were camped on, ran horse safaris in the Mara and kindly said we could stay at one of their camps, Kampi ya Farasi, just outside the boundary of the reserve.

★

As we descended from the highlands to the flat, dusty plains of the Rift Valley below, a deafening clatter announced that we had a hole in our exhaust. Yet again a search through the spares in the back turned a previously nameless piece of metal into the very part we needed. Praising the foresight of Dave, the mechanic on the truck's first journey, James and I set about repairing the hole with Derek's help. The delay meant we arrived late that night at our first camp near warm springs called Maji Moto.

The springs were set in barren veld, littered with the dung of the neighbourhood cows whose hoofprints lined the muddy banks along the thin stream. The water was lukewarm and we followed it upstream to its source, a small gravel-bottomed pool in a nondescript patch of dry grass. A cold breeze was blowing and I prostrated myself in the shallow waters of the spring, trying to keep as much of my body as possible within the relaxing warmth of the flowing water, wondering what myths early people must have attributed to such a strange phenomenon.

The next day we found ourselves on the outskirts of the Masai Mara, struggling to determine which of the dozens of tracks cutting their way through the savannah grass would lead us to the horse camp. We picked up a brightly dressed woman who seemed to be signalling for a lift, hoping she would be able to help. As we knew little Swahili and she no English, communication was difficult, but she nodded and pointed when we said 'Kampi ya Farasi', so we followed her directions. We arrived at the camp wondering where it was she wanted a lift to. It soon became apparent that our destination was hers. We explained as best we could that we didn't want to purchase her services, at which she appeared quite upset. We then had to take her some way back along the road. We dropped her off next to a soccer match that was being played in front of an enthusiastic crowd. The game was wild and aggressive. Not two hundred metres away other wild game grazed peacefully.

The horse camp itself was perched on a steep bank above a bend in the Mara River. It was simple, consisting of a few acacia trees and no buildings, suiting us ideally. Two Masai appeared, William and Joseph, offering to be our askaris, guards for the night. They stabbed their spears into the ground and sat down next to the fire, protecting us against the hyena and lion whose howls and grunts jarred the still night air.

★

The dew on the grass rubbed onto my bare legs and the early morning air was sharp with the acrid smell of blackjacks and khakibos. Movement alerted me to a small family of impala who were watching me, their delicate brown ears twitching, nostrils sniffing the air. My anxieties about the future – *How will we get through West Africa to Europe? Will the already-apparent tension on board get worse?* – were forgotten, their discord quieted by the music of the present. I returned to the camp. A hundred metres from it was a herd of fifty or so elephants moving, in their slow-motion rolling gait, like huge grey ships on a sea of grass, crossing from one shady port to the next, babies sheltered in their midst and age-darkened adults on the perimeters, guarding the convoy.

Following close behind, doubled over and treading quietly, were James, Robbie and Bronwyn. A guide from Buffalo Safaris saw them and drove across, furious. He berated them, saying a tourist had been killed by an elephant only last week, and threatened to report them to the park authorities.

"What an arsehole!" exclaimed James as the ranger drove away. "Some people just have to flaunt whatever power they have."

"I agree with everything he said," I rejoined. "That was a bloody stupid thing to do."

"But we were ten metres away! Anyway he couldn't have reported us. We aren't even in the national park out here."

After a lazy breakfast of porridge and scones, we went on a game drive. Because there are no fences around the Masai Mara, the reserve itself is a geographical region only, and its animals roam freely well beyond its borders. William was our guide and took us on a route which greatly added to the number of diverse species of African wildlife we had seen. Topi, small yellow-legged, iron-flanked antelope, stood proudly atop termite mounds. A spotted eagle owl stared at us from behind the leaves of a riverside willow, and two secretary birds stepped lankily across a field, their quill-decked heads bobbing jerkily after their insect victims. We came across a herd of a hundred buffalo standing in the road and had another minor altercation. I was at the wheel and refused to drive through them until Bronwyn, who was sitting on the front bumper, climbed inside. She became angry with me, saying I was being paternalistic. I said she was *naïve*. Only when we were all inside did I drive on through their muscled ranks.

We saw a leopard too, sunning itself in a low anthill, but our enjoyment was diminished by the fact that it was surrounded by four Land-Rovers, telephoto lenses extended and trigger-fingers contorting. Returning to the camp, I spotted a warthog skull, well preserved and with its tusks intact. We fastened it to the bow of the truck as a figurehead.

Back at the camp, we found one of William's family's cows stuck fast in the thick mud at the side of the river, as though it had tried to migrate across it like the strings of wildebeest we had seen earlier in the day. Hauling and pushing, we manhandled it up a steep hippo track with hardly any assistance from its exhausted limbs, and left it next to the fire, covered by Rob's army poncho and staring dully at the earth in front of it.

*

Derek had begun to fit in with the group. He was ceaselessly busy about the camp, and always willing to help others out. Their pasts united by their common army experiences, he and Rob were warming to each other, the beginning of what was to become a close friendship. Bronwyn's initially strong misgivings about his joining us were dissolving, to a large extent because Derek treated her with chivalry whereas we other three did not.

The teasing and criticism Bronwyn received, the isolation of her difference, were weighing heavily on her. She had been away from her close friends for over a year now and was missing their supportive, female company. Sandy's departure had heightened the remoteness she felt. That night she spoke of her difficulties, in plain terms. "I get on best with Robbie," she said at one point, "and then Paul, but I have a problem with James." We were shocked at first, and a bit hurt. It was the first time any of us had spoken forthrightly about what was troubling them. It had the effect of prompting more honest discussion. James agreed that he put Bronwyn down too often and we all acknowledged the need to show more tolerance and understanding. The pressures of living together so intimately were beginning to build.

*

We drove into the Masai Mara proper the next morning, entering through Musiara Gate where our teacher status ensured we paid next to nothing in entrance fees. We surmounted a long rise and looked down into the valley below. It was difficult to believe what we were seeing. From horizon to horizon the savannah was covered in teeming animal life. Long black lines of game, mostly wildebeest, zebra and buffalo, were strung across the plains, impelled by the ancient momentum of the migration instinct.

Descending into the midst of this vanguard of the annual northward march, our approach cleared a band of grass as we parted the sea of dense, black herds. All around us were snorting, rearing zebra, skittish Thompson's gazelle in their hundreds, and line upon line of wildebeest, plodding one behind the other and suddenly breaking into wild, bullocking charges, their shaggy, heavy heads careering drunkenly as they turned and bucked on their tough, spindly legs. The profusion of life filled us with awe. Over a hundred thousand animals were visible across the expanses of the yellow plains.

We turned towards the Mara River, hoping to see the herds crossing its muddy waters. They weren't, but that they had recently was all too apparent. The river was littered with drowned carcasses, misshapen and rigid in their death. Circling above and feeding in this charnel house were vultures, ugly in their undertaker black, picking the white bones clean; and Marabou storks, uglier still, their pointed beaks and sparse feathers soiled by the blood of their carrion feast.

After a picnic lunch on the roof of the truck we drove to the small town of Talek just outside the reserve. There we met a Masai named Robin who assured us he would take us to see lion and cheetah. Robin was an entertaining guide and slipped between perfect Cockney and Australian accents, which were all the more amusing coming from a long-lobed, blanketed Masai. He was as good as his word and we saw five lionesses, their stomachs turgid from a recent kill, escaping the day's heat in the shade of a acacia, and a cheetah who was eating a Thompson's gazelle ram, whiskers bloody and stomach visibly distending, while vultures circled high overhead.

We drove out of the park under the most beautiful of evening skies. In the east black thunderclouds darkened the air, backdrop to a vibrant rainbow that reached up out of the earth in front of them, like a banded assegaai hurled down by some African god. A steady breeze rippled across the flat plains that reached out forever on all sides. The gentle touch of the evening softened as we neared the night, turning the yellow of the grass into a vivid gold and bringing out in the leaves of the bushes and trees that lined the watercourses a deep kikuyu green. To the west the setting sun, sending shards of silver between the clouds behind which it partially hid, was like that of the first day of creation. Everything was new, fresh, pristine. I was filled with a sense of grace. The splendour of that evening will resonate in me forever.

★

After camping the night near Talek, we returned to Nairobi, going via the towns of Aitong and Narok where we all bought Masai blankets. Driving into Narok, we saw a sign outside St Paul's School. The sign proudly displayed the school's name, crest, and its motto: "Strive and Exel."

Back in Karen, we ate at a roadside restaurant. The menu was in Swahili so we pointed at the first item of the four on the list. When two bowls of boiled tripe were set down before James and me, the others hastily changed their order to the third item, which contained the reassuring word *nyama* – meat. We also had *vetkoek*, or doughnuts, and milk, the bill for the five of us coming to $3.

The days of freedom we had had in the African wilds made me loath to spend more time than we had to in Nairobi. The wait for visas was becoming increasingly frustrating, and although it did give us time to prepare the truck properly for what lay ahead, I was becoming impatient to leave East Africa and enter the shadowed worlds of the centre and west.

Chapter Ten

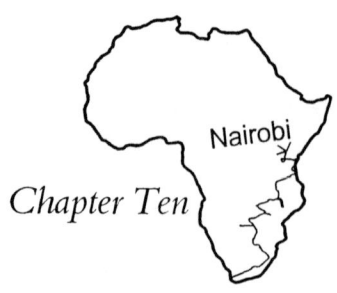

With our fuel problem resolved, the odds were that the most likely future breakdowns would be due to suspension problems, so we spent our first morning back in Karen replacing all the bushes and pins in the springs, as well as the rear shackles. Conscious that we were about to move out of the former British colonies, places where Bedford mechanics and spares were easily found, we sought to make the most of our time there. In the next few weeks whatever was broken by the more arduous roads ahead we would have to repair ourselves.

Derek had ridden in to fetch our passports from the Nigerian Embassy. He met the crew of The Beast in town. They were in a sombre mood. Greg, still weak from his bout of malaria, had been mugged by eight gangsters. He'd lost all his travellers cheques and $100 in cash. But far worse than that, they'd made off with his passport. As the South African bureaucratic machinery would require at least two weeks to issue a new one, it put paid to thoughts of our groups joining up in convoy through Zaire. Already well behind schedule, we couldn't afford to spend those weeks, and then more waiting for visas, sitting idly in Nairobi.

The next day, over lunch at the Jacaranda Café, we decided that as a farewell we would all go to Mount Kenya together for three days. It was a pleasant change to ride in The Beast and to hear different music and topics of conversation. It had always been refreshing to come across the other five, as our twin journeys intertwined, sharing stories about the places we had seen. Our two groups easily accommodated each other.

At Nanyuki we crossed the equator, for what would be the first of five crossings on our zigzag course north. We drove on to the start of the Siriman Trail, one of the main routes up Mount Kenya, camping near the entrance gate of Mount Kenya Park, at an altitude of 8,400 feet. The glade in which we pitched our tents was beautiful. Our pegs slid easily into the thick grass which was lush and green from the regular afternoon downpours. Lichen-bearded yellow-woods circled the camp. In the morning, before they became shrouded in mist, Mount Kenya's twin snow-capped peaks stood over us like sentinels, second only to Kilimanjaro in their height above the African earth. Below us was a salt pan. Eland and zebra appeared in the mornings and evenings to lick there, moving serenely through the shadows and mist.

Our days consisted of long walks along the rivers and through the forest, cricket games on the lawn and reading or writing in the enchanting peacefulness of the place. The presence of the mountain set up strong weather patterns. Mornings were sunny and cloudless. The heavy dew of the night evaporated quickly. At about midday the wind would begin to strengthen, dark clouds would gather and quickly take over the sky, letting loose a deluge lasting for a few hours before the sky would clear again, letting in a tranquil evening, with mist hanging in wisps in the upper boughs of the trees and vapour rising slowly from the rain-soaked grass.

Evenings we spent sitting around a fire rekindled with the aid of litres of paraffin poured over wet wood, chatting and playing games. For the five of us whose overland journey was continuing, there was a strong sense of our relaxation there being a calm before the storm. We had no doubts that the second part of the journey would be far more arduous than the first. The fact that the truck was in as good a condition as we could get it, the engine running sweetly, the fuel problem resolved and the suspension geared for the pounding ahead, filled us with a quiet optimism. Our emotions continued to fluctuate in accord with the state of the truck. There was also in us a sense of pride. We were carrying on where others weren't.

The sores that James and I had been plagued by since hiking in the Mulanjes exactly two months before were continuing to fester. As none of the others had the same problem, we suspected the Lariam we were on. I had a cold sore as well, for the first time ever, and felt self-conscious about it.

"Don't let it bother you Paulus," James counselled caringly. "It's just a part of being human."

We took the decision to stop taking the pills. It was a relief not to be swallowing drugs every Saturday, and we dismissed the threat of malaria casually, thinking that we would just be careful, covering up in the mornings and evenings, and that we hadn't seen that many mosquitoes anyway. Just as in the depths of illness our imaginations cannot rise above the distress signals of the body to envisage how it would feel to be well, so in good health illness is beyond imagining. Young and fit, we felt little of our own mortality as we stuffed the remaining pills into the backs of our lockers.

Following our success in the Masai Mara, Robbie and Derek decided to pay Kenyan resident prices for our three day stay on the mountain. Undeterred by the fact that there were only four faked employment cards among nine of us, that neither of our overland vehicles had Kenyan licence plates, and that the side of our truck was decorated with a large map of Africa across which snaked a red line directly to Mount Kenya, six of the group, led by Robbie and

Derek, entered the warden's hut. I hid in The Beast with Lucy and Alison. We three agreed that it was preferable to pay the money than incur the stress that was no doubt mounting inside the hut.

Richard soon joined us to confirm that the scene inside was one of out and out deception and belligerence. Eventually the officials, confronted by a resolute and angry insistence on our Kenyan residency, caved in to the bullying. The group emerged triumphant forty-five minutes later, waving at us the seventy-four separate receipts – relics of the days before sharp inflation – which had been individually stamped and punched by the warden. I felt ashamed that we had taken advantage of the park officials, intimidating them into submission, but at the same time, knowing the limitations of our budget, I felt glad that we had saved the R1,200 – $360.

*

The Church's farm in Karen welcomed us back. It had become like a second home after these long weeks in Nairobi. The next morning was spent at Nakumatt supermarket, shopping for provisions to take us through to Nigeria. We manoeuvred a convoy of trolleys towards the till, laden with huge sacks of flour, sugar and rice, hundreds of tins, bags of pasta, four new enamel mugs, and countless other goods for camping and eating, feeling like adventurers of old, about to embark on a long sea voyage. The till slip, which came to Sh25,000, was almost three metres long.

Lunch was taken at the cheap Jacaranda Café where we met up with the other three members of Andrew's fractured group, Glen, John and Ray. They were planning to backpack northwards into Egypt. Needing to lighten their loads, they sold us their supplies of what proved to be tasteless dehydrated vegetable packs and, far more beneficial to us, a portable shower to replace the one we'd lost.

There had been only one reply to our advertisements for a fifth to join us. We met Barbara, a young, cigarette-smoking American, for lunch, but it soon became evident, and even Bronwyn had to agree, that she was not the ideal travelling companion. She would struggle to raise the funds, and her obvious insularity – she thought the rest of Africa was just like Kenya – and abrasive manner made her entirely unsuitable. It would be just the five of us – four South African men and her, as Bronwyn put it – driving to England. Bronwyn's silence announced her misgivings.

James stayed behind with Derek to find out about our visas for the Central African Republic, while the rest of us headed back to the farm. Halfway there, we ran out of fuel. As we hadn't filled up yet for the journey west, we had to jog along the road to the nearest petrol station and buy twenty-five litres of diesel. Running out of diesel means you have to bleed the fuel system to remove all the air that has been sucked into it. James and I had done it countless times to restart the truck after the fuel blockage caused it to falter, and I removed the engine cover confidently, directing Bronwyn to press the starter motor while I loosened the injector leads. I cocked up the operation completely and repeatedly, eventually draining both the batteries. As we sat stranded on the side of the road I was filled with a vast frustration towards myself, a sense of incompetence at being unable to do what James did so easily. I roared in my rage, hitting the steering wheel to ease my frustrations. My outburst scared Bronwyn, who had not seen me angry before. We sat waiting for James and Derek to come past.

As they clambered off Derek's bike, I appraised them of the situation. Without hesitating, Derek stepped into the middle of the road with his arms raised, forcing an army truck to stop. He then directed its driver to park as close to our truck as possible so that we could link jumper cables from their battery to ours. This done, James quickly bled the engine and we were mobile again. I returned to the farm on the back of Derek's bike in order to be in time to receive a telephone call from my parents. The joy I felt in the wind rushing by as we sped past the other traffic and in our having again surmounted obstacles in our way, was tinged with a sense of inadequacy. On the trip, I was beginning to find, my strengths were not required, and my weaknesses were being exposed.

★

After an enjoyable night eating, drinking and dancing at The Carnivore restaurant, we awoke to our last day in Nairobi. During the night a horse had chewed some of Bronwyn's clothes which she had hung up to dry.

"I can't believe it!" she cried. "The stupid animal. This was my favourite shirt."

"That gross pixie thing?" asked Robbie. "He's done you a favour, Bronski. That was probably the most obnoxious shirt in existence."

"I know you guys hated it, like all my clothes, but I loved it. And I've so few clothes as it is." Finding no sympathy, only laughter, from the rest of us, Bronwyn clamped her distress and helped pack the truck.

Driving through Karen, we met the two South African hitch-hikers we'd given a lift to out of Mombasa. They were dressed in the same sandals and kikois, with slightly longer beards, and were now wheeling in front of them two cheap mountain bikes, acquired with the cash from the black market sale of the air ticket they'd been given by the British consul. They were, they said, going to cycle to

England, wooden chest and all. They would leave in three days' time.

We wished them luck and left them, shaking our heads, aghast at what they planned to do. Many months later I was to hear the next chapter of their African adventure from a friend, Jacques Penderis, who was backpacking to Egypt and who arrived in Nairobi ten days after we left. They had sold their mountain bikes by then and were planning to both get to London by a rather convoluted method. While Ian entertained himself by building a raft and floating down several of Kenya's larger rivers, Chris would hitch-hike north to London where he would raise sufficient money to fly Ian over.

They had even gone so far as to work out a cunning and easy way of making this money. By chance the Kenyan five shilling piece is exactly the same size and shape as the British fifty pence piece, but is worth less than a tenth of the value. The scam was to enter a casino laden with five shilling coins and to emerge with an equal, or hopefully even larger, number of fifty pence ones. Last seen, Chris was moving from tent to tent at Ma Roche's, swapping cash for coins, his wooden chest fast becoming a treasure trove for those heptagonal pieces of silver...

★

Last minute shopping involved buying extra jerrycans to trade with and three pairs of gumboots for the mud. James and I decided to return to the industrial area to get a few more spares. Driving back along the Uhuru freeway, we were in the middle lane as signs had indicated that the left lane was closed ahead for repairs. A Toyota to our left realised this late and swung sharply in front of us. Unfortunately it caught the edge of our inflexible steel bumper which ripped open a jagged, metre-long, ten centimetre-wide rent from the rear door to the boot. Scarcely noticing the impact had happened, we pulled over to assess the damage.

The driver, terrified at what his boss would say, tried feebly to make out that it was our fault. James pointed out that it was patently obvious that it wasn't but offered to accompany the man to his boss to help soften the blow. Fortunately the boss viewed the whole affair reasonably, although at that stage he hadn't yet seen his brutally can-opened car.

We continued on to lunch at the Trattoria where we said a sad farewell to the crew of The Beast, who had all decided to return to South Africa, to home and "to porcelain" as Alison said. As most were planning to spend time working in England, we agreed to meet on 16th December in London. It seemed a long way away, both in time and space.

After a visit to the AFEW Giraffe Centre in Karen, where we fed pellets to orphaned Rothschild giraffes, amazed at their chameleon-like tongues which curled around the pellets in our hands, at their size close-up like that, and at the graceful way they moved, we left Nairobi. It was now late in August, almost three and a half months since we'd departed from Johannesburg. We were halfway in time, but had almost two thirds of the distance still to cover, over far more difficult terrain. The holiday part of the trip was coming to a close.

Andrew Birrell had teamed up with us. He was going to accompany us to Uganda and then turn his Land-Rover around for a solitary run back to Cape Town. We drove in convoy westwards, aiming to stop first at Lake Nakuru, whose caustic soda waters are home to great colonies of flamingos. Just outside Nairobi we passed an ambiguous road sign. "Toll funds used to repair roads," it said.

The police attempted to exact further funds from us, stopping us for speeding as we were lumbering up a hill.

"What?" asked Robbie, incredulous. "There's no way we were speeding! We wish we could! Our top speed is fifty kilometres per hour. Come on, jump in and we'll show you. We'll take you as fast as we can."

Accepting the limitations of our ageing truck with an almost insulting readiness, they let us continue on our way.

Large vehicles weren't allowed into the Lake Nakuru Reserve, so we parked the truck at Backpacker's Camp near the entrance and all piled into Andrew's Land-Rover. We drove to the top of Baboon Cliffs and looked down. Fringing the lake, in a thick band of pink, were flamingos in their millions. Like a second beach, they packed together around the entire circumference of the lake. The guide book called it 'the world's greatest ornithological spectacle' and it was hard to imagine a more magnificent profusion of birdlife. Individual birds broke off from the crowded mass looking top-heavy as they flew, while others rejoined it, extending their thin red legs as they came down to land. The colony vibrated continually like a living thing as birds bent their curved necks and heavy bills down to the water and then lifted them again.

Walking amongst the reeds at the water's edge, or kneeling in the grass to rest, secure in this park with hardly any predators, were hundreds of waterbuck. Again I was entranced by the dramatic beauty of the life that thrives in the abundant lakes and plains of the Great Rift Valley, Africa's nurturing heart.

★

The next morning James and I stayed behind to change tyres. The second-hand road tyres we had bought cheaply in South Africa had reached the end of their lives. Nylon showed through where stones had ripped chunks of rubber from their retreaded surfaces. I was concerned about the vehicle's roadworthiness once we got to the less accommodating countries of Europe, and so we decided to leave our two new tyres off and to use instead the old off-road tyres, which had already crossed the continent once, until they too gave out. We were just finishing the job, jumping with all our weight on the long wheel spanner extension to tighten the wheel nuts, when the others returned, talking excitedly about a five metre python they had seen.

After buying diesel at Nakuru service station, where James and I sold the old road tyres we'd replaced, for $6 each, an excellent buyer's price judging by the wide smile on the face of the man who rolled them away, we continued west towards Uganda.

Because they are on the equator, and at such an altitude, the Kenyan highlands have very mild weather throughout the year. There is no winter to speak of, only two rainy seasons, one short and one long. We passed through the town of Eldoret where the signs welcoming visitors proclaimed, "The best climate in the world." Taking advantage of the temperate climate were extensive pine forests, undulating across the hills that stepped down towards the valley floor below us. Derek, who had ridden on ahead in his role as *voorloper*, found a camping site half a mile off the road, next to a flowing river. We pitched camp in a clearing among the towering pines and sat down to a dinner of braaied eland and zebra meat which Andrew supplied, untroubled by the light rain broken into a mist about us by the branches of the pines.

Chapter Eleven

Rain was pouring from the sky when we noticed that the battery warning light was on. Our alternator bracket had snapped for the fourth time. We tried to install Andrew's spare alternator but our truck's system rejected the transplant. Anxious to preserve our batteries, we continued with the windscreen wipers turned off, squinting between the runnels that streamed down the twin panes of the windscreen. Ahead of us Derek was soaked through despite his waterproofs, but the tropical climate made it warm enough to put up with the wet.

The border crossing at Malaba, Kenya's western border with Uganda, was trouble-free if rather tedious. In an attempt to stamp out corruption, the Ugandan authorities required that the road tax be paid at a local bank which then issued a receipt. These receipts were then sent to the customs officials at their offices a kilometre away. They were sent en masse every now and then, and we had to wait three hours for ours to appear.

While we were waiting, Derek bought Cokes for all of us, at the cost of Sh500 each. He then noticed a local man buying a Coke for only Sh250, and turned on the youngster who had sold us ours.

"What do you think you're up to?" he demanded, prodding the back-pedalling kid in the ribs. "Are you trying to rip me off, hey?" The glare of Derek's gaze soon reminded the Coke seller of the change he had forgotten to give him. He hastily pulled money out of his pocket and counted out Sh1,000. Derek returned satisfied.

Like the waters of the rivers themselves, we were drawn towards any waterfalls we passed near, and all agreed readily to drive from the border to the Bujagali Falls near Jinja. Our route there took us through a changing landscape of tropical jungle, rice paddies, banana plantations, cane fields and grasslands.

A lawn of bright green stretched out to the rock-lined river's edge. We took off our shoes and walked across the soft grass, stepping onto the black, time-smoothed rocks. The evening air lay thick and warm around us as we waded into the waters of the Nile. Its source, Lake Victoria, so long the grail of African exploration, lay five kilometres upstream. As twilight set in, bats began to flit above us, their swift, soft-flapping passage losing them into the gloom. A full moon hung above the falls, climbing into the approach of night. Its light drowned out the minor stars and reflected fluorescent off the tumbling rapids, water, like us, that was headed for the Mediterranean.

The morning light prises open my eyes. I look up and see five or six mosquitoes suspended on the underside of the tent above me. Their bodies, on delicate thin legs, are turgid, bloated. Angry, I move against them. I kill two, staining my fingers red with my own blood. Briefly I wonder about the wisdom of having stopped taking Lariam, but push such thoughts aside as I unzip the tent and crawl out to engage the day.

The warm morning lured us into the water for a swim. Robbie dove in ahead of me, his stocky frame lean now after the weeks of healthy living. Invigorated, we drove on towards Kampala. The signs of Uganda's tragic past were manifest. Few of the houses or shops were painted. The corpses of tanks lay abandoned next to the road. The vehicles we passed were rundown. But there was also an air of hope. The people we saw were all quick to smile and wave, and Kampala's new and refurbished buildings were witness to the economic regeneration that was taking place under president Museveni's pragmatic leadership. We headed first to the post office, to collect *poste restante*.

There occurred one of those fractal events whose chance, domino-like impact can so broadly shape the future before it. A man walking down Kampala Road happened to see a young boy taking a green backpack off the bonnet of a Land-Rover against which a man dressed in a multi-coloured rugby jersey was leaning. He shouted at the boy who dropped the bag and fled. The man picked the bag up and returned it to Derek, behind whose oblivious back all this had happened. In the bag Derek kept his money and travellers cheques, his carnet and his passport. The loss of it would have meant several weeks' delay in trying to get a new passport from Kenya, the nearest country with a South African consulate. There was no way he would have been able to continue the trip with us.

We camped at the Backpacker's Hostel. Robbie was sick with stomach troubles, and we decided to go to bed early. Despite the tropical heat and humidity of the past week, which had increased as we descended from the highlands, the sores on my and James's legs were at last beginning to heal. We were relieved, and felt fit for what lay ahead.

The next day was spent exploring Kampala and on repairs. James and I took the truck to the garage of Robbie Rodrigues, a forthcoming and friendly Portuguese ex-pat. While helping us restore the alternator and set the tappets, he told us about the country's barbaric past under the merciless rule of Amin and then Obote and of the hope beginning to grow again, as the economy slowly regained its health, as persecuted Asians returned to what had been their homes; and as a growing number of tourists began adding Uganda to their East African itinerary. The stories he told us of the atrocities committed in the past, especially under Amin, of massacred villages, houses piled high with skulls, and people tortured and bludgeoned to death, were sickening. Winston Churchill called Uganda "the pearl of Africa." In those dark days it was a pearl cast before swine.

We were halfway through the repairs, with the truck's innards lying all around us, when a booming explosion, followed by excited shrieks and shouts, erupted in the street outside. We rushed out of the garage. A huge tower of flames and black smoke rose up from a paint shop three buildings away, punching the sky like an angry fist. Every now and then a barrel of thinners or the petrol tank of a car trapped in the yard would explode, enraging the fire. As it spread, the bitter thought came that our overland journey might end here, a gutted wreck in a Kampalan street.

People were thronging to watch. They would crowd forward and then disperse wildly under the angry sjambok lashes of the teenaged policemen who maintained a harsh order. The fire department, which had returned to service only the year before, arrived but failed to control the fire initially. The water they pumped in settled below the volatile fluids that were burning, spreading the flames and destruction. Vehicles caught by the groping arms of the blaze continued to explode, and our anxiety to rise. Eventually, as we were hurriedly trying to reassemble the engine in case we had to drive out, foam was brought in from Entebbe airport and the fire extinguished.

The Great Wall Café lured us into its cheap but clean interior for supper that night. Chicken and chips featured prominently on the menu and we knew, having asked the locals, that the normal price for the meal was Sh1,700. So when the waitress told us we'd be paying Sh2,500, we got up indignantly to leave. However Derek went to the manager and complained fiercely.

"This is ridiculous! You're charging us tourist prices, aren't you? This is discrimination. We know what the normal price is."

The manager quickly relented and we paid the local price.

We discussed how we planned to spend our time in Uganda. Our list included visiting the Murchison Falls, hiking in the Ruwenzoris, seeing the chimpanzees of Queen Elizabeth Park, and relaxing at Lake Victoria. After lengthy debate, swayed by the need to increase our pace, which we were all beginning to feel, we decided to forsake all these plans and drive instead to the Zaire border, and visit the gorillas there. It was a pity to have to leave so much of the country unexplored, but the vast regions coloured in green and yellow on our map, dense jungle and untrammelled sand, reminded us that the roads that lay ahead would be not only longer, but far harder than those we had been on already.

Driving home, we experienced Kampala gridlock at the Entebbe turning circle. For an hour we watched as cars headed in both directions in the same lane, bounced over pavements, squeezed between roadside trees, and ramped down the embankments. Amazingly, an air of calm prevailed. There was hardly any hooting or shouting. Drivers sat concentrating like chess players, sizing up lines and gaps, and the nerves of the other drivers. We found out that it was an everyday event.

Andrew had decided to see more of Uganda, and so we said goodbye to him the next day and set off towards Zaire. As we drove west the suburbs of Kampala soon gave way to hilly countryside flanked in the many colours of their crops, huts replaced houses, and cattle not cars filled the road, often forcing us to stop.

The cows in Western Uganda have the largest horns in the universe. Some were more than a metre long and fifteen centimetres in diameter at the base, so heavy that the poor, prized creature wearing them could hardly lift up its head under their weight. Their owners flicked patiently at them – their pride and wealth – with long sticks as they moved slowly along, their huge, almost grotesque horned heads bending over massive necks to pull at the sweet grass that was growing at the side of the road.

After a night disturbed by the drunken ravings of three men smashed on an evidently potent local brew, which we were offered but declined, we set off for what would be our last day in Uganda. That evening we would be camped in Zaire. Inside myself I was urgent to get there, to confront what I feared, to get through it. I had felt it growing in me, this urgency, from as early on as Malawi. The name itself, Zaire, had by now assumed in my mind the colours of shadow, cast by my own fears and affirmed by the stories of other travellers and the literature of the West. It had been there a long time, this image of Zaire, part of my thoughts. It dwelt in the nether reaches of my mind, fearsome yet enticing, unknown but in some instinctive way familiar.

*

The countryside on the way to Kisoro, the border town, reminded me of images of Asia. The road rose up and down through hills covered in groves of bamboo with stems twenty centimetres thick, or blanketed in different-coloured crops, every square metre cultivated, even on the steepest slopes. The terraced hills sank down to still, blue lakes. People worked the fields busily. Hoes rose and fell. Cattle plodded heavily before wooden ploughs. The atmosphere was peaceful, industrious.

The hills we could see ten miles to the south were in Rwanda. In less than a year they would be stained red with blood in the most concentrated and brutal spate of bloodletting humanity has ever seen. In sixteen weeks over half a million corpses, mostly hacked to death – sometimes even by their loved ones forced to do this – would litter their slopes, and more than a million refugees would be flooding the borders, fleeing from the horror or from guilt. The bodies of tens of thousands of murdered people, disposed of in the Kangera River, would rot and swell as they were carried along its turbulent waters to the mordant calm of Lake Victoria, one hundred miles away. There, behind us, from among the misshapen and dismembered corpses hauled from the lake by volunteers, a man would find three babies skewered on a spear. Makeshift asylums would start to fill with people turned insane by what they had seen or what they had done.

Two years later, two years of cholera and hunger and terror, the human tide would reverse and flow back towards the uncertainty of its source, like a single large shapeless creature, directed by the will or caprice of stronger armed men.

And all the while, for the most part, the rest of the world would look on. In the first weeks of the killing, France, squarely to blame for not opposing the genocide they discovered was planned, would compound their complicity, in their neo-colonial narrowness and bigotry, by actively supporting the slaughterers, because they spoke French. The arbitrary lines ruled in haste by a scrambling Europe still cut Africa to its heart. The colonial powers in Rwanda followed a policy of ruling through division, favouring one tribe over the other, fostering ancient enmities and fomenting the hostility and paranoia that underlay this bloody chapter in Rwanda's history. Central Africa, the last part of the colonial cake to be seized, and the first abandoned, where colonial masters took from but never gave to, bears scars that break open and fester and seem never to heal.

*

At Kisoro we replaced the diesel we'd used since Kampala. What little fuel we did expect to find in Zaire we were sure would be expensive. Parked at the campsite was a Mercedes overland truck called The Pig. We shared a bonfire with its passengers and got some advice from its Australian driver, Steve. He warned that in the towns of Rutshuru and Bondo especially, officials would demand that we had insurance. If unable to provide any, we would have to purchase theirs for $200 or so.

The next morning Rob and James entered the local administration offices in the town and asked if they could borrow a typewriter. Rob took out from his blue folder some stationery carefully purloined from his bank four months before for just such a purpose and began inexpertly to type:

Policy number: 670 2342.

This serves to confirm that the following vehicle, Bedford 773 BLC, has been comprehensively insured to the sum of United States dollars $5.000-00 or the equivalent, for the period ending 31 December1 1993. Such cover will be validf for claims arising in Botswana,Cameroon, Central African Republic, Burkina Fasso, Algeria, Malawi, Niger, Nigeria, Tanzania, Morocco, Uganda, Zaire, as well as countries belonging to the European Community.

Vehicle Details:

Make   : Bedford
Registration Number   : 773 BLC

> *Year of Manufacture* : *1961*
> *Colour* : *Yellow*
> *5Chassis Number* : *RML 3/26585*
> *Engine Number* : *A 50630 RW*

A.E. Neuman, authorised signatory.

For good measure he then produced a compliments slip and banged away on that too.

"Dear Mr Hoard," he typed, *"we wish you well on your journey to London. Regards, Alfred E. Neuman."*

Leaving Uganda proved unproblematic. We set foot for the first time on Zairean soil. Zaire has had a bitter and exploited past. In the seventeenth and eighteenth centuries slave traders rampaged through its heart, taking its shackled people through its forests or down its rivers for the last time before herding them into the cramped and squalid confines of the slave ships bound for the Americas.

In the nineteenth century it became the obsession of a single man, King Leopold II of Belgium. Through political chicanery and duplicity he annexed for Belgium a swathe of Africa eighty times its size, almost as large as the whole of Western Europe. And then proceeded to bleed the country of its raw wealth, felling its forests, slaughtering its elephants for their tusks, and tying its people through taxation to supply rubber to feed the Western world's growing demand.

Independence brought in a different dictator, Mobutu Sese Seko, an autocrat whose method of quelling dissent was to imprison or assassinate opponents and to enfeeble the country's economy to such an extent that survival and not revolution became its people's first priority. Mobutu, or, to give his full name – Mobutu Sese Seko Kuku

Ngbendu Wa Za Banga (*All-powerful warrior who because of his endurance and inflexible will to win, will go from conquest to conquest, leaving fire in his wake*) – set himself up as a paramount chief and proceeded to transfer the country's wealth into his own, living a life of regal splendour while the country disintegrated around him. Attempted coups were put down ruthlessly by his troops, with the tacit support of the US who saw his un-Marxist greed as a buffer to the perceived threat of communism in Africa.

By the time we arrived the country was in a state of anarchy, with Mobutu in hiding in France and his soldiers marauding in search of the pay they hadn't received for two years. We entered the immigration and customs building prepared for a fight. We emerged having met the friendliest border official we'd come across so far. He warned us to be careful in the country, not to stop if we didn't have to. "There is no law here," he said, "but there are many lawless people."

"Well, fancy that! That was a lot easier than I expected," remarked Rob as we returned to the truck. "They didn't even ask us for the road tax I've been told we were meant to pay. That's $65 we've saved!"

We hoped this was a good omen and were optimistic as we lifted the rusty boom and drove past a sign saying "You are now leaving Uganda and entering Zaire." I was on the roof, chatting to six backpackers who had been hitch-hiking in Kisoro, on their way to see the gorillas, and did not notice the three men watching us from a stationary white sedan on the side of the road.

We hadn't gone a kilometre when a soldier armed with a machine-gun stepped into the road and ordered us to stop. We did so obediently. He asked to see our papers and we handed several photocopied sheets to him. He then asked for our actual carnet which we also handed over after some deliberation. He said we needed insurance. All this was conducted in French, with me grasping into the background of my memory for the words I'd learnt in a one year university course four years before. We handed over our freshly forged insurance letter. It left him unimpressed.

"*Non, non,*" he said, shaking his head under his round green helmet, "*vous avez besoin d'insurance du Zaire.*" We needed his insurance. And it would cost $100.

"But we are only going to see the gorillas, it is only twenty kilometres there and back. It is crazy to pay so much for such a short journey," I argued brokenly.

"If you kill a child here or at the other end of the country it makes no difference," he replied.

"Tell him there's bugger all chance we'll run some kid over driving twenty kilometres!" shouted James. The official remained adamant. The tension mounted and got worse when he was joined by his accomplice, a man with cold eyes dressed in civilian clothing.

Rob was in a rage, frustrated by his inability to communicate. He tried gesticulating and speaking in slow, three word sentences but was met by implacable stares. He grew steadily more furious, his blue eyes blazing, and was just about to seize the barrel of the rifle with his one hand and wrench our papers away with the other. Fortunately, before he could do so, James came up with a strategy, which he explained to us in Afrikaans. We would tell them that we couldn't afford the insurance and would return to the border and walk from there to see the gorillas. Of course what we planned to do was drive up the road, perform a quick U-turn and then come flying through at speed.

The officials tried to say we had already driven on Zairean roads and would therefore have to pay the insurance anyway, but, as we started turning the truck around, realised they were beaten and said we could drive to the gorillas. Provided, they added for appearances' sake, we drove carefully.

We continued down the narrow road, pleased at having got away victorious. Suddenly we came upon the white car that had been at the border. It was stopped on the left of the road. Two men were standing behind it, heads over the open boot. A large box and a discarded tyre blocked the right hand side of the road. The set-up seemed odd, false, or perhaps it was just our nerves. Under James's instruction, Rob jumped out of the truck, shoved the box out of the way, and we carried on, unsure of what we might have just avoided, but with our sense of unease sharpened by these experiences.

*

We had been warned that there could be a few days' wait to see the gorillas, but we discovered that a group who had booked hadn't arrived and we'd be able to hike into the rainforest the next morning, to meet one of the two families in the park, who made up twenty of the three hundred and fifty mountain gorillas still alive in the wild.

The gorillas are visited every day by the wardens, regardless of whether there are tourists or not, as part of the habituation process. The wardens took us on a two hour walk, mainly past cultivated fields, to where they had been the day before. I was surprised when one of the guides stopped a local villager, seemingly to ask if he knew where the gorillas were today. My romanticised view had been that we would find the gorillas in a small, shady clearing in the forest, and watch them pluck berries from the trees they lived in.

Instead they were rampaging through the mielie fields grown by nearby villagers, tearing down and eating the immature white cobs as they moved. The villagers tried unsuccessfully to defend their crops. Threatened by the government with death should any of the gorillas be killed, they hurled stones at them, trying to scare them off. At this provocation the leader of the family, a huge silverback standing 1.6 metres tall, with a chest girth the same, would scream and charge on two legs down towards those who had antagonised him, accelerating at an alarming speed. Through their constant habituation, the gorillas had learnt to discern between harmless tourists and hostile villagers. They ignored us altogether, and would brush past us as they moved on in their search for food.

There were eight in the family, the silverback, a younger male, three mature females and three adolescents whose fur stuck up in uneven tufts. Their eyes were brown, small and shrewd, and seemed to display great caring for the others in the family. They all moved together, waiting patiently for stragglers to catch up. Being so close to them was wonderful. Given the politics of the countries they inhabit, I thought that the odds were against there being any mountain gorillas left in the wild by the end of my life.

Leaving the park that afternoon, we met the group whose place we had taken. There were fourteen of them, mostly women, and they called themselves The Tarts. They had driven their truck, a Bedford slightly younger than ours with a huge pair of sunglasses painted on its front, down from London, travelling via the bulge of Africa, and we chatted excitedly about the journeys we were sharing. They confirmed the stories we had heard about the insurance salesman at Rutshuru. They'd been forced to part with $100 and an old car stereo. They had met a group who had avoided him by driving through at night, though. We decided to do that too.

★

Our initial experience of Zairean roads had matched our expectations. They were narrow, potholed and we twice had to cross over bridges made of large logs thrown across a stream. We were surprised, then, to find a brand new tar road heading north towards Rutshuru. It was about the best road we'd had come across so far, built by the Chinese we discovered, and we raced down it as the day's light began to fade. It was dark when we reached Rutshuru. We had decided that even if someone tried to stop us we would just drive on. There was nervous excitement in the cab as we moved between the town's unlit buildings. We emerged at the other side unmolested. Excited by our good fortune, the quality of the road, and the beauty of the night, we decided to carry on. We sped onwards, our headlights, one yellow one white, strobing the vegetation in a manic, wild-eyed glare. Shouting happily above the music, we scythed our way through the central African night.

Suddenly across the road in front of us was a boom. Derek was stopped next to it, and lifted it as we approached.

"Go, go!" he shouted. With the warnings of the customs official at the border still in our heads, and unwilling to meet a similar extortion racket to that in Rutshuru, we hurried through. A man carrying a torch came running towards us from a nearby building. His angry shouts carried to us as we accelerated down the road, the thudding of the engine an empathic echo to the pounding in my chest.

Rob was looking at the map. "Hey, we're actually in a game park! That was the south gate of Virunga National Park." His words were soon given dramatic confirmation. With Derek riding just ahead of us, we rounded a corner to find a large hippopotamus standing in the road. Terrified, it started running away, its short pink legs moving frantically in our headlights. Derek, who had been right on top of it coming around the corner, braked hard and came to a skidding halt only inches behind its lumbering rear. We stopped to see if he was okay and to ease our jangled nerves. Derek was fine but our nerves were not allowed a rest. Lights reflecting intermittently off the low clouds behind us told us we were being followed.

We set off. The tar road had ended and we watched through the dust kicked up by our wheels as our pursuer drew inexorably closer. We were passed, chugging along at fifty kilometres per hour, by a Mercedes truck which drew away from us steadily. Soon after, our lights revealed a second boom barring the road. Derek was again at one end, struggling with a huge chain looped over it. The truck driver was talking animatedly to a group of military figures and pointing towards us. They made Derek stop his attempts to lift the boom, pointing machine-guns at him, and signalled to us to pull over.

"*Passeports, passeports!*" they shouted, followed by a torrent of French I couldn't understand. Rob was in a belligerent mood, demanding that they let us proceed as we hadn't done anything. We resolved to try to settle things diplomatically but he continued to seethe as we handed over photocopies of our passports. By this stage we had determined who was in charge. 'Le chef', as the other men called him, was a short, ugly man with a scarred face and uncompromising, bullet-like eyes. He said we would discuss the issue in the morning, but in the meantime we would have to spend the night at Rwindi Camp. We were told it was too dangerous to camp and that we would have to stay at the hotel.

"It is $70 for a double room, and $50 for a single," the hotel manager told us.

"There's no way we're going to pay that," said James. Seeing us laugh at him, the man graciously revised his pricing.

"Okay, I'll let all five of you stay in one room for $70."

"Listen," said James, "we don't want to pay a cent. We don't even want to be here." And so we camped.

I spent an uneasy night and woke early, prompted by my innards which had evidently been churning as I slept. It was still dark as I picked up the badza and wended my way into the bush. Squatting down, I felt a red hot sting all over my rear, and leapt up stifling my shrieks, thinking I had sat on poison ivy. I'd actually sat on a colony of red army ants, some of which I had to prise off my softer parts, which their jaws were locked onto. It was a bad start to a day that got steadily worse.

We went to see the chief at 9.00 as we'd been told, but he'd gone to Rutshuru. He returned at 10.00 and said we'd have to pay a $100 fine for illegally entering the park. For the rest of the day we tried to get him change his mind.

"We were scared by all the stories of lawlessness we have heard, even from the customs official at the border," I said. "Okay, so we made a mistake, but no harm's been done."

"*Cent dollars*," he said coldly, and turned back to his writing.

"We've already had to pay $300 for insurance at the border and then at Rutshuru," I tried, hoping to invoke some sympathy. He ignored me.

"You're making the bad name of Zaire a whole lot worse!" shouted Rob, fuming, and we left.

We returned now and then to try some other tactic. We said we were prepared to pay $50 as a compromise. We even offered him a bottle of Highveld whiskey. He held out for his $100, confident that we couldn't leave without our papers.

The day was spent performing minor repairs on the truck, befriending the soldiers, who seemed to hate 'le chef' as well, and looking at other ways of breaking the impasse. We moved the truck directly in front of the hotel, which we had discovered was surprisingly modern and well-stocked, and inhabited by a number of French and Belgian tourists who had flown in. Our hope was that the hotel manager could bring some pressure to bear on the chief to remove this eyesore which was tarnishing his hotel's image. We told some of the Belgian guests how we were being held to ransom, gaining their sympathy.

As a pleasant diversion we played with a pet baby chimpanzee one of the guests had. If we approached, it would leap into our arms and hug us around our necks, sucking our fingers. I gave some local children a geography lesson, using the map on the side of the truck to pick out the countries of Africa.

All the while our frustration was mounting. As the sun sank lower, so did our spirits. We hated the chief with a passion by now, and the thought of giving in to him. At five o'clock we saw him leave the park driving south.

"Let's just go," said Rob. "Derek and I have checked things out and we could bypass the boom by driving through the veld over there to the road."

"I'm keen," said Bronwyn, "I'm sick to death of hanging around here. Let's go!"

"I reckon we could get away with it," agreed James. "It's worth the risk anyway just to not have to pay that bastard."

Hearing this I felt my stomach contract. "Wait, wait, wait," I urged. "There are a dozen soldiers down at the boom. They've got machine-guns and Land Cruisers. We can only go at fifty kays an hour so there's no way we'll outrun them. And all it takes is for one of them to lose his head and start shooting. It's not worth the risk."

The others looked towards me, the weak link in their chain.

"We don't have to if you don't want to, Paulus," said Derek. "But I've been chatting to those guys and they're fine. There's no way they'll come after us."

"They might be friendly enough, but they're all shit-scared of the chief, so I reckon they'd chase us, and who knows what might happen when everyone becomes excited in the middle of a car chase."

"You've been watching too many American movies," said Rob.

"I'm just not prepared to stay here another night," said Bronwyn emphatically.

"Look, I know the rest of you guys are all keen to go, but I just don't think it's worth the risk. Not for $20 each. I won't do it."

We sat in an uncomfortable silence.

"Okay, here's another plan then," offered Derek. "You guys go and I'll stay behind. If I'm here they won't chase you, and I'll then try to make a getaway if I can."

"Hell, Derek, that's not really fair on you," I said.

"No, don't worry, I'll be fine. Just leave the hundred bucks with me in case things get nasty. I tell you, the slightest gap and I'll be out of here."

"Well, I suppose if you're sure, Derek. Jeez, I dunno. Ag, what the hell, let's go."

We climbed into the truck. James was behind the wheel. We waved to Derek sitting alone next to his bike, and started forward.

Chapter Twelve

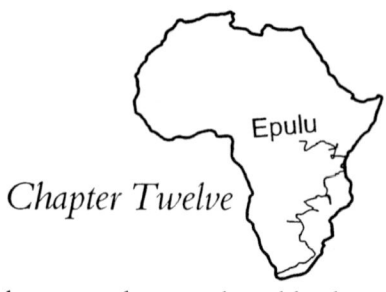

The truck bounced across the rough veld, the steering wheel kicking in James's hands. The noise of its engine shattered the quiet of the evening. There was no subtlety in our escape. Shrubs and bushes were flattened beneath the wheels as we accelerated forward. Rocking violently at full speed we dived down into a sandy ditch and up onto the road. Everything was happening in slow motion, with the adrenaline clarity extreme excitement brings. A thick cloud of dust billowed out behind us. I stood in the door-well, staring back into it, wondering if it would suddenly resolve into the shape of a pursuing Land Cruiser, with guns pointing.

As our distance from Rwindi Camp increased, kilometre by dusty kilometre, my fears shifted to the road ahead. Would we find another boom at the north gate? Were they waiting for us, alerted by radio of the approach of a truck full renegades, desperadoes? We raced onward, braced for the unknown. There was another boom, but it was raised and we tore past the small hut next to it, elated. We drove on for another fifty kilometres, into a thickening gloom, before pulling over to camp, and wait for Derek.

Despite the fear I had felt, and despite knowing that even a small risk for that amount of money was irresponsible, I was pleased that we hadn't let ourselves be bullied into submitting. The chief had thought we were at his mercy but we had proved otherwise. The air of anarchy we'd breathed since entering the country was beginning to infect us. We were learning the rules of the place and starting to play by them.

The excitement of the escape still bubbled in us. While Rob and Bronwyn prepared supper, James and I rigged up the truck's speakers on our table outside. The hundreds of people who had gathered to watch us joined in as we started dancing to Juluka, releasing the stress of the day. James added to the festivities by making hydrogen balloons out of condoms filled with the gas released by the caustic soda, water and tin foil he mixed in a Coke bottle. We tied the balloons to sticks and exploded them over candles, to the delight of the crowd. In the erupting balls of jagged flame that blinded the night we celebrated being free. Our temporary incarceration gave our liberation a sweeter taste. But there was still no sign of Derek. It had been dark now for almost two hours.

"That must be him!" I shouted, hearing the sound of an approaching engine. A single headlight silhouetted the roadside trees. It grew larger and then was extinguished, fading to orange as it dulled. Derek swung off his bike and removed his helmet, a wide grin on his face.

"Derek! What happened?" asked Bronwyn. Questions rained from all sides. "Why were you so long? Did you escape? Did you end up paying?"

"Hang on, hang on. I'll tell you. Jeez, I'm starving. Is there any supper left?" While he ate, Derek told us what had happened after we left.

"As soon as you guys started the engine these little kids who were there took off down the road shouting like mad. They told the soldiers what had happened and they came up immediately. There was no way I could have got away. Anyway, they took me down to the hut at gunpoint as a prisoner until that bloody chief of theirs got back. But these guys have got no idea, hey. I even grabbed one of their guns while they weren't looking and you should have seen this guy's eyes – like saucers! I just said 'No, no, don't worry, I'm just having a look,' and he calmed down a bit. The barrel was stuffed with mud. I doubt it'd have worked anyway. We carried on waiting and I got chatting to them. We started getting on quite well. I offered them $50 to let me go. Hell, they were tempted, hey, but in the end too scared of the chief."

"Did he come back in the end?"

"Ja, he got back after a while and seemed quite pissed off that you guys had gapped it. He was still acting *hardegat* though and demanding the hundred US. By this stage it was getting dark and I was a bit worried about driving through the park on my bike so I tried to negotiate a deal. I offered him fifty but he stuck out for the hundred. So I asked if he was going to give me a receipt. That bothered him. He said 'No receipt, no receipt' – the bastard could speak English after all – and so we settled on fifty. Shit, I tell you, handing the money over to him was one of the hardest things I have ever done. I've spent the whole drive out here wondering if there was any other way I could have played it."

"No, Derek, hell man, that's brilliant! We couldn't have hoped for better. And the main thing is we've all come out of it all right," I said.

"I tell you, I nearly didn't, hey. As I was leaving the camp out of the corner of my eye I saw these eyes on the side of the road reflecting in my headlight. The next thing I see it's a lioness, crouched low, ready to spring! It came bounding at me and I just hit the gas and put my head down. It was a close thing. I've never cacked myself so much in my life!"

★

We went to bed, exhausted by the excitement of the day. The drizzle that had been falling was turning into a substantial rain so Derek and I decided to risk the diesel fumes and sleep in the truck. The next morning we woke early, bundled the sodden tents into the back, had a cup of tea and set off, hoping to make Beni almost two hundred kilometres away.

The Ruwenzoris, the Mountains of the Moon, towered to our right, their peaks covered in cloud, as we negotiated the rocky, potholed road that wound through hills covered in villages of round, thatched huts and occasional pockets of jungle not yet levelled. It was obvious trucks like ours were a less common sight here. Small children ran along the road behind us, calling *"Mzungu! Mzungu!"* Whiteys!

We stopped late in the morning for a skottelbraai breakfast and drove solidly from there until we reached Beni, a small town in the middle of nowhere, at five in the evening. We followed signs saying 'Camping' to an incongruous campsite. A relic from colonial days, it had obviously once been a quality restaurant. Now, though, the buildings were dilapidated. Flaps of ceiling hung loosely over tables that hadn't hosted guests for decades. Water stains discoloured the walls, and windows in the buildings were smashed. The furniture on the long, open veranda sagged under the weight of time.

The garden, by contrast, was immaculate. Smooth lawns with neatly trimmed edges sloped down to a small stream. Strelitzias, like blue and orange cranes' heads, rose up above beds of lilac agapanthus. Hydrangeas, whorls of blue and pink, surrounded a frangipani with flame-red blossoms. Bougainvillaea bushes draped themselves over the low wall on the property's rim. We were approached by the caretaker, who tended the garden. He was a gentle old man, with large, callused hands, dressed in a pair of weathered blue overalls. It seemed as though he had been there forever, continuing to care for his garden while things fell apart all around him.

He could speak neither English nor French, and we had difficulty determining how much it cost to camp there. He then drew a 2 and a 5 in the sand, and nodded when we showed him 2,500,000 zaires in notes. "*Ndio, ndio,*" he said. "Yes, yes."

Rampant hyperinflation had ravaged Zaire's fragile economy in recent years, destroying savings overnight. Two years before, $1 was worth 470 zaires. We had exchanged ours for 7,000,000. The inflation would have been worse, but the people had rejected the 5,000,000 zaire notes the dictator Mobutu printed to pacify his unpaid soldiers. This left the 1,000,000 zaire note, equivalent to fifteen US cents, as the highest denomination bill, and a wheelbarrow more useful than a wallet. We were surprised at the cheap cost of the campsite but thought it was a reflection of the poverty of the place. We pitched the tents in an old outbuilding whose roof, though riddled with holes, still offered some protection from the rain that was drumming incessantly down.

*

We awoke to a warm, steamy morning, and were soon engaged in a vitriolic argument. The two owners of the property arrived and told us camping fees were actually $2.50 per person. They said there were additional costs of $5 and $2.50 for the truck and motorbike as well. Derek and Rob started arguing with them.

"If we had known it was that much we would never have camped here. We'd have camped on the side of the road somewhere. Here's the 12,500,000 zaires we were told it costs. That's all we're prepared to give," said Derek. The two men were unhappy but before they could express this they were sidelined. Frustration and resentment, whose sharp prods had been felt for weeks over the way in which we dealt with local people and parted with our money, now ripped through the covers of restraint.

James turned on Derek and Rob. "Why do you have to be so fucking hard the whole time? I think we should pay them $10, as a compromise. It's obvious to anyone, even a blind man, that a simple mistake was made here."

"Ja," Derek retorted, "but it was their mistake, not ours and I don't see why we should have to pay for it."

"Why? 'Cause it's the fucking decent thing to do, man! Christ, you two are behaving like fascists! You distrust everyone we meet, you grind them into the ground with this hard bargaining. I find this hard-nosed army mentality bloody sickening. I want us to treat people with respect, like human beings."

"Jesus, James," joined in Rob, angrily. "Don't give us this pontificating crap! We've treated everyone we've met fairly. If you want to go around dishing your money out to every hand you see, you can. But I'm not a mobile charity. And I don't appreciate these insults."

The bitterness continued to flow. I sided with James, but tacitly. I disliked the suspicion with which Derek especially, and Rob as well, treated anyone we met. Everyone was a potential fraudster, a thief, and this initial contact soured for me many meetings we had. And if we did part with a little more money than we could have, what of it? It was so little anyway and worth it for the friendly relations we'd have. Fear of confrontation prevented me from expressing my frustrations directly. I would speak to James, his agreement assured, but pushed my anger with Rob and Derek down, not letting it speak my mind. I left James to be spokesman for us both in this. I would speak out and support him, but not as openly, as honestly. He was in the trenches, gun blazing, and I was mostly behind the lines, firing only occasionally, when covered by him.

We ended up paying the $10, but not through common consent. Rob capitulated only to stem the flow of James's invective. "Oh, go on then, pay it. Let's just get out of here."

Derek acquiesced as well, begrudgingly. Bronwyn had watched the whole episode silently. Her attitude to money was almost innocent. Money was useful, because of what she could do with it, but she didn't value it in itself. She would worry about not having enough, but spend what she did have easily, generously. When she haggled it was for the fun of it, not the cents she could save. The emotions of the arguments struck no chord in her: money was not something she could become passionate about.

As we left the camp we were like stones thrown together in a rushing stream, under attrition. Differences were becoming more marked. Our forced intimacy and reliance on one another was inching our different value systems towards collision. Like slow-moving tectonic plates, their momentum threatened to press up between us mountain range divisions.

*

The road was beginning to deteriorate. It was pockmarked with shallow, water-filled potholes. James gritted his teeth whenever a tyre bounced into one, haunted by visions of the truck's buckling suspension. He suffered especially when Bronwyn drove. He would sit in the back seat, tense, staring at the road in front, flinching audibly before each small impact. The potholes were everywhere, and avoiding one often led directly to steering into another.

"Christ, Bronwyn! Didn't you see that hole?" James asked, exasperation breaking through. "Please be careful. This truck's thirty-two years old, you know."

Bronwyn, smarting under the rebuke, said nothing. An uncomfortable silence followed. Shortly afterwards we stopped and Rob took over the driving. James and I climbed onto the roof. The countryside was wilder now, the brown of cultivated land turning into the deep, vital green of jungle.

"God, I just can't handle it when she drives like that! She's so cavalier about it as well," James complained above the noise emerging from the exhaust pipe to his left. "She's not the one who has to fix the damn thing when it breaks."

"I know how you feel. I'm sick of bloody motor mechanics. And God, the grating when she changes from third to second! It goes right through me. Do you think she could be damaging the gearbox?"

This is how our frustration spoke. Bronwyn's driving itself did not warrant it. Her driving had become the focus for a deeper frustration. The scapegoat for her as scapegoat. Bronwyn's unapologetic difference from us, and our inability to bridge the gap in communication between us, to empathise with her, set her apart. Cut off from her usual structures of support, the outsider both in background and in gender, she was the one most easy to criticise. And would draw such criticism to her, in lieu perhaps, of a more caring interaction. Contained as we were within the cab, the collision of personalities brought about by the jolting of the truck was aggravating the small burns of friction that had been rubbed along our nerves.

In trying to avoid a pothole I managed to steer the truck into a ditch. The grass verge was not as firm as I had thought, and we slid ignominiously off the road, coming to rest at an angle. The two wheels that were off the road spun freely. There were no trees near enough for us to tie the winch to. The inevitable crowd of onlookers watched us in our plight as we considered what we could possibly do.

Fortunately a solution appeared behind us, in the shape of a huge Mercedes truck. It was burdened with a load of dried fish swelling high above its sides and held down by a brown tarpaulin. Sitting on the tarpaulin were fifteen passengers. Five more sat inside. The truck would easily provide the inertia we needed to winch ourselves out. Redirecting the winch cable from the front of the truck where it emerged to the back took a few minutes, but we were able to haul ourselves out easily, the wheels and winch turning in tandem as we slowly regained the road.

Derek meanwhile had been busy swapping the old clothes and other goods we had put into the beer crate he had attached to the back of his bike for food and money. He drove up alongside us, and passed peanuts and bananas to Rob who stood catching them in the door-well. We found out later that he had sold three jerrycans for 15,000,000 zaires each, almost three times what we had paid for them in Nairobi. Derek had also sold an empty Blue Band margarine tin for 500,000 zaires, and an old grease can for 1,000,000.

The road stretched ahead of us, a thin brown ribbon closed in on both sides by an ever-thickening jungle. Hardwood trees towered hugely above us, gathered thickly together and covered in swarming creepers, in the close profusion of life that marks the beginning of the Ituri rainforest. Even the roadside daisies were giant. Their yellow flowers bent into the road from stems that stretched three metres into the air, higher than the roof of the truck. I found the carcass of a Goliath beetle. Its heavy round body covered the palm of my hand.

Hemmed in on both sides by this impenetrable mass of ferns and shrubs and trees, the road was wide enough only for a single truck. On the few occasions that we did meet an oncoming vehicle, it meant one of the two reversing to a place in the road that was wide enough to accommodate both. Cresting a hill, we found a Leyland truck broken down. Derek sat on his bike next to it, waiting for us. Evidently the truck's engine had failed while climbing the hill and it had been dragged back down by its weight, its engine-assisted brakes unable to halt its descent. It had jackknifed, its back plunging into the dense vegetation of the jungle. The cab sat squarely in the centre of the road, facing forward. The broken angle it lay at made it look like a creature whose neck had been snapped.

"Think we can pull them out?" I asked James.

"We'll have to try," he replied. "We don't have much option. It looks bloody heavy though. I'll turn the truck around so we can use the forward gears. I don't want to use the winch in case it gets ripped out of its mountings."

James performed a U-turn and together we looped the massive chain we carried over the tow hook on the back bumper. I tied the other end to the front of the Leyland truck, threading the locking bolt through the large, U-shaped shackle at its end. The driver explained that he wouldn't be able to help move the truck out of the way as he couldn't get his engine started. James climbed into the cab, fired the engine and engaged four-wheel drive. The wheels rolled slowly up the incline. Metal clanged as the links in the chain shifted and tightened. He increased the revs. The engine screamed and the wheels slipped spasmodically on the sand of the road as they strove to move forward against the inert weight behind them. The violence of straining machinery filled the air with tension, tightening our nerves, until James killed the engine, aborting the attempt.

"We'll only burn out the clutch if we try any harder," he said as he climbed down from the cab. "We're going to have to find another way forward."

We began to examine the vegetation on the side of the road more closely.

"I reckon we'll be able to dig a way around," said Rob.

"It'll take a while," James agreed, "but we should be able to. Luckily our truck's not too wide."

I climbed onto the roof and handed down the spades and picks we kept there. We dug and hacked at the soil and undergrowth for two hours, cutting through vines and creepers and the thick roots that burrowed beneath the soil. Turning and reversing repeatedly, James managed to steer around the white cab of the stricken truck. We were on our way again, sweating under the exertions of our digging and the increasing humidity of our descent into the rainforest.

*

We stopped at a small village just short of Komanda. While Bronwyn went off to make use of their toilet, Rob decided to exercise his selling skills. The eyes of several young men who had gathered around widened in desire as Rob took out from his locker the neon green sunglasses he had bought at Clicks for R3 – $0.90. Rob tantalised them with this passport to coolness. He let them all try them on. He held his hands wide and praised their looks. He put them on himself. "How much you give me?" he asked. "Good quality, good quality," he added. And, gently bending the ear pieces, "Look, see how strong they are. Just like Ray Bans. How much? 5,000,000? Are you mad? These are worth at least 40,000,000." As Rob made his pitch I translated the gist into French. Figures were drawn in the sand with sticks as the elaborate mime and haggling continued.

The young men laughed at Rob's antics, but could not divert their gaze from the glasses. In this unsophisticated place they shone as a talisman of the rich and exalted West.

Eventually an agreement was reached. "14,000,000? For these? No, no, no," said Rob, shaking his head and looking hurt. "Give me 18,000,000. Special price. Just for you."

The deal was done. Behind his hard-done-by look Rob was delighted, enlivened by the challenge of haggling he derived from all such transactions. As the eighteen notes were being counted out into Rob's open palm, Bronwyn returned, standing uncertainly on the periphery. I noticed something wrong.

"What's the matter, Bron? Oh my God! What's that? You haven't..."

"I fell in the shit!" she wailed. "Help! I'm knee deep in turd!"

Bronwyn's left leg was covered to the knee in a viscous layer of inch-deep brown ooze. She was holding in her hand an object bearing only a faint resemblance to a sandal she had bought on Zanzibar.

"I went to the new one, but it's not ready yet so I had to use the old one." She was speaking more animatedly now, as James poured water and washing liquid into a bucket to clean her with. Bronwyn's non-stop description seemed to distance her from the horror of it all.

"As I was about to sit, the bloody floor caved in. Whoosh!" she said, hands slicing the air. "Down I went, into the depths of hell! I managed to crawl out but didn't know what to do. I tried to use twigs to get it off but they kept on breaking. You can't believe how sticky this stuff is. I wanted to die. I kept thinking, 'Oh my God, oh my God, I can't go back! They won't want me near them like this.' I almost had to live in the forest like a pygmy."

While Bronwyn stood with her foot in the bucket, James scrubbed her leg. Rob had given up his attempts at suppressing his laughter, and let it come bursting out. It was infectious and we all started to laugh, both at the tragedy of it and with relief that it hadn't been us.

"Right, let's get going again," said Rob when Bronwyn was clean. "It's onto the roof for you, Bronski. There's no way you're coming into the cab after that."

"Come on, Bron. I'll keep you company," I said. "Just stay downwind of me."

*

We stopped at a small village called Bawanza. The people in the village said we could camp in their church, a single-roomed brick building with a tin roof. Two thirds of one wall had fallen in. As we carried our mattresses in through this opening, moving aside low wooden benches for space, a large crowd gathered to watch. The inside walls of the church were covered in Biblical scenes. A crudely painted white Christ stared past me at the people outside.

The church adjoined a soccer field. We tried to organise a game, but the only ball in the village was punctured. We then asked some of the women if they would cook for us the food they normally eat. In return for this we would give them clothes. The meal they served us was of beans and boiled green bananas. The beans were large and pink, fairly edible, if rather tasteless. The bananas were tough, slightly bitter, and difficult to swallow. They weighed down the bottom of my stomach like lead shot. Not wanting to disappoint the expectant faces watching us, I forced down the three bananas allotted to me. Seeing this, Bronwyn snuck two of hers onto my plate, but no amount of good manners could get me to contemplate eating them. I smiled at the women, thanking them for the meal, and thinking how hard it must be to eat such food every day.

We all showered under water heated over a small charcoal fire. Fireflies flickered over the soccer field like fairies.

I awoke to the sound of a rooster crowing. We packed and left early, after donating 10,000,000 zaires to the church at James's behest. Driving further into the jungle we started seeing more pygmies. They had flat features and were hirsute. Some of the men carried bows and quivers full of arrows. There appeared to be a fair amount of miscegenation between the pygmies and other tribes as we saw people with similar looks but who stood taller than the pygmies whose height seemed to average well below five foot.

At Mambasa we were stopped at a boom. A young official politely asked if we had paid our $65 road tax. We replied in Afrikaans. Confused, he went off to consult his boss. We lifted the boom and drove through.

We had had eight long days of almost continuous driving since leaving Kampala, covering 1,100 kilometres by the time we reached Station de Capture d'Epulu, a national park and home of the jungle-dwelling okapi. Driving into the campsite, with its expansive green lawns, and the wide Epulu River tumbling past, churning white over a series of small rapids near the bank, was like emerging into an oasis from under the dense blanket of trees that had loomed over us the past three days. We decided to spend the next day there as well, and enjoy the tranquillity of the place.

Michel, an articulate, English-speaking official, came down to chat to us. He said that the price per night for camping had unfortunately been increased the previous week, from $1 to $5. After protracted negotiations with Rob, he reluctantly agreed to contravene the rules he diligently wanted to uphold and let us stay at the old price. Rob gave him a jerrycan as thanks. He then took us to see the okapi, who were in a sanctuary run by the Zairese Institute of Nature Conservation in conjunction with the American-funded Okapi Preservation Fund.

The okapi is a strange-looking creature. Its closest relative is the giraffe, and in its longish neck and triangular head something of the giraffe can be seen. But the shapes of many other animals can be seen in the okapi too. Its rear is striped like a zebra's, its torso shaped and coloured like a bay horse. Its ears reminded me, of all things, of a rhino's, and the way it walks, with lowered hindquarters, is much like the gait of the hyena. Three of these rare animals roamed the fenced-off sanctuary, their long tongues curling around leaves as they ate. Before we left Cape Town I hadn't even known of their existence.

★

Bronwyn was cleaning her sandal at the river's edge. Rob walked up to her and grabbed it. "You're not going to wear this again, are you?" he asked.

"Of course I am! There'll be nothing wrong with it once I've cleaned it," she replied.

"Come on, it's disgusting! Just think where it's been."

"My foot's also been there and I'm not going to chop it off. Now give it back. Come on, Robbie, give it back!"

Rob held the sandal out of her reach. He then seemed to relent. He threw it, but well over her head. It landed in the river. Bronwyn could have retrieved it but watched helpless instead as it floated downstream, gathering speed.

"Look what you've done now! How could you, Robbie? Those were my favourite sandals. That was just fucking mean!" she shouted.

"Oh come on, Bronwyn, it was foul"

"I had cleaned it! You just don't care how I feel, do you?"

"Of course I do. You're just taking it too seriously."

The sandal still hadn't sunk. It bobbed over a small series of rapids fifty metres downstream. I ran down the bank and dived in to retrieve it but it sank just as I got to it. I walked back up to tell Bronwyn.

"I can't believe you always mess me around like this, Robbie," she was saying. "You're so insensitive."

"I'm sorry, Bronwyn. I didn't mean for your shoe to get lost," replied Rob, not too apologetic. "Anyway, I've probably saved you from getting hookworm or something. Come on, let's forget about it and go for a walk in the forest."

They went off together down a thin path between the trees, like brother and sister. Elsewhere, in some other, more pernicious jungle, a fat boy's spectacles were being ground beneath a heel.

I love this jungle, its abundance of life, its vitality stretching further than the imagination can follow. The trees soar upward, ironwood, yellow-wood, fig and ebony, all reaching out to the life-giving light. Tall, pale, branchless trunks erupt suddenly into the network of leaves and branches that forms the canopy of green above me. Parasitic strangler figs wrap themselves snake-like around the largest of the trees, in a slow, deadly embrace. Below, the ground is thick with ferns, shrubs, vines, elephant ears. The trees stand one hundred feet tall. Everything is massive, and ancient. It warms me to think that this is how it has always been, this vast, primeval giant, lightly slumbering in the basin of Africa's heart.

The next morning we invited Alan Root, a film maker who lived across the road, to a breakfast of pancakes. He was a freelance producer, at present creating a wildlife documentary for ITV. His body testified to the dangerous nature of his work. His right forefinger was missing, the result of a puff-adder bite; two huge depressions on either side of his right calf marked the calling card of an irate hippo; and the gouge mark on his left thigh was from a gorilla bite, received while filming a charge scene for *Gorillas in the Mist*.

He invited us over to his house, which served also as a studio and menagerie. His car was parked next to it. It was the perfect vehicle for his neighbourhood's roads. Called a Steyr Pinzgauer, it was a six-wheel drive vehicle, with an independent axle for each of the six wheels. We had seen it drive past the previous day, riding smoothly as its insect legs rose and fell. Alan was filming the behaviour of two rare creatures whose habits had not been observed before – the aquatic chevrotain, a small buck like a duiker, and the aquatic genet.

"The chevrotain," he was saying, "is an amazing little thing. It's nocturnal, and if frightened it will jump into a river and swim, with just its nostrils above the water, like a hippo. It'll stay like that for as long as it needs to. The genet is also fascinating to watch. It catches fish by gently patting the water, attracting them to the surface. It's also nocturnal. I'm the first white person ever to have seen one. Which makes you lot the second. I've been filming them over there." He pointed to a large glass-walled enclosure, across which a small artificial river ran.

"I've got some other pretty little animals I've been filming too," he continued. "That one there with the bandit's mask, is a civet, which isn't actually a feline. Nor is the genet, by the way. And those cute chaps over there, that look like bushbabies, are called potto."

He showed us snakes too, among them the bothrap thalmus, so rare it doesn't have a common name, with thin red lines running the length of its body; gaboon vipers, so well camouflaged they had to move before they stood out above the dead leaves they lay on; a water snake; a cobra; and a horned rhinoceros viper. A palm nut vulture, its breast and neck features white like a fish eagle's, sat in a palm above us, plucking the small yellow seeds from under its leaves.

★

"Where are you headed from here?" he asked as he walked with us back to the road.

"We want to drive to Kisangani and get onto a river barge there and float down the Congo to Lisala, before heading north to Bangui," James replied.

"Haven't you heard?" Alan asked. "You can't get to Kisangani at the moment. A forty ton truck demolished one of the major river bridges between it and here. We're pretty much cut off until it's repaired. And God knows when that will be. The only trade that's happening now is by trucks stopping at either bank, offloading their cargoes and having it paddled across in pirogues."

"Shit!" said James, with feeling. "The river trip was one of the things I was most looking forward to. The guys who came down said it was one of the highlights of their trip."

Back at Epulu we studied the map. The only viable alternative was to take the little-used northern route, cutting north-east through the rainforest via Isiro to the border with the Central African Republic at Bangassou. Despite the difficulties that this route would hold, evidenced by the thin lines represented on the map – tracks, not road – I was secretly quite relieved. Among the horror stories we'd been told about Zaire were a number tales of barge cranes dropping trucks into the river, and the owners being charged a fortune to have their submerged vehicles retrieved. At least now we'd have to rely only on ourselves.

★

Back at Epulu we were approached by Michel who asked us if we would mind giving the chief warden of the camp, Masimbuka, a lift to Buta, just over 900 kilometres away. We agreed, but not without some reservations at the thought of having the company of a stranger for what would probably be a number of days. Especially one who spoke no English. I personally thought it would be interesting having him along, both to find out more about the inner workings of this strange country, and to practise my French. He put his luggage, a small suitcase and a briefcase, into the back and took his seat in the cab.

Leaving Epulu, we were asked to sign the visitor's book. James leafed back through the years. There, on the page dated 18th February, 1992, was the entry "Douglas Moody-Stuart, Woking, Surrey, British Telecom Bedford, 773 BLC." Almost twenty months before our truck had been in the exact same spot, but going the opposite way.

Chapter Thirteen

Masimbuka sat in one of the back seats, not speaking much, watching the road. He was a short man, under five and a half foot, and was dressed in stone-washed denim jacket and jeans and a blue peak cap. He had been noticeably reserved since our departure, though out of aloofness or shyness I wasn't sure. I asked him what the road ahead was like. *"Très mal, très mal,"* he replied. Very bad, very bad. *"Beaucoup de trous. Les grandes trous."* Lots of holes. Bogholes.

He was soon proven right. Seven kilometres took five hours to cover. After six and a half kilometres we came across our first boghole. Bogholes start off life as small, muddy depressions, usually in the wetter sections of the road. Trucks that get stuck are freed from the mud by copious digging. As each truck passes through, the hole gets deeper, and the more likely it becomes that the next truck will get stuck as well. Our first boghole did not look too daunting. There were two Mercedes trucks waiting on the other side, however, and we had to wait an hour as the first one plunged through, pulling a trailer behind it, and then returned to tow the second one across as well.

I drove the truck through in second gear in four-wheel drive, pleased with the ease of the crossing. My elation was short-lived. A few hundred metres down the road a yawning abyss of a boghole awaited. It was all of three and a half metres deep. Fractionally wider than a truck, its walls were scored by the bumpers and wheels of past trucks that had scraped their way through. The bottom was covered in a foot of viscous red mud. Two heavily burdened trucks were waiting to attempt a crossing, one of them the Mercedes we had used as an anchor to haul ourselves out of the ditch three days before. Half a dozen men were at the bottom of the hole, preparing it. While some scraped away the loose mud, flinging it onto the growing mounds that lined the hole, others spread diesel along the bottom which they then lit to dry out the mud.

The prospect of waiting for the two trucks to cross did not appeal to us. Confident that we would be able to cross without getting stuck, I approached the drivers and managed to persuade them to let us through first, saying that once we were on the other side we'd be able to help them out. I suggested James do the driving.

After the other trucks had moved out of the way, he climbed in behind the wheel and accelerated down the steep runway to the hole. The truck slid on the slippery surface of the descent, all traction drained into its mud. James fought to steer the truck away from the vertical banks of the passageway, the steering wheel twisting and jolting under his hands. The smell of mud and diesel smoke filled the cab as we slewed our way forward, the wheels torn from their path by the inert strength of the mud. Just past halfway we foundered. The sharp edge of the front bumper had gouged its way through the red earth lining the hole. The back wheels were banked deep in churned-up mud. James engaged reverse gear and accelerated. The rear wheels spun haplessly.

"We're going to have to use the winch," he said, grimly. "We'd be here all day if we tried to dig it out. We'll have to thread it back out the front. I'll let some cable out. Take up the slack at the back."

I put on the gloves we kept to protect our hands from the sharp strands of the cable, and pulled out a few metres, until I felt all the slack taken up. The cable had actually snagged, however, and the winch spindle continued to spin for a while, until James stopped it. The unwound cable had become tangled under the truck. We managed to release it after twenty minutes spent crawling around in the mud, tugging free the long coils of wedged cable. We emerged, caked in clayey mud, looking like trench soldiers from the Somme, and took the cable out through the front of the truck, and forty metres up the road.

Rob and I tied it around a young ironwood tree close to the edge of the road. James engaged the winch. The cable grew taut. With a mighty crash the tree was uprooted. We untied the cable and dragged it further into the forest. An old stump, more than a metre in diameter looked a solid enough anchor. We looped the cable over it. It too was ripped out of the ground, its wrenched roots spraying soil over everything around it. Further in we found a large yellow-wood. Its huge body easily braced the pull of the winch. With the winch turning, and all four wheels driving as well, our yellow truck crawled slowly out of the hole, like a swamp creature from the primordial ooze.

We sat watching or helped as the men of the other truck dug and levelled the bottom of the pit. We looked nervously at the huge bulk of the Mercedes, piled high under its cargo of fish, aware of our promise to pull it through. "How much does it weigh?" I asked the driver.

"*Dix tonnes, dix tonnes,*" he emphasised. "Only ten tons." The truck and its fish weighed at least twenty tons, we were sure. After two hours the hole was ready. A lot deeper, but significantly flatter. The truck accelerated forward and lurched over the edge of the hole, its cargo pressing it remorselessly into the soft mud. It slithered, it slid, it bullocked and bumped, engine screaming and wheels churning, coming eventually to a gasping halt, its tyres sunk deep and front end squashed against the side. The driver signalled that we should try to pull his truck out.

"We'd better use reverse gear as it's the lowest," James stressed, "if we're to have any hope of pulling it out."

"But the chains aren't long enough," I questioned. "Aren't we going to have to use the winch?"

"No. We'll use the winch cable, but what we'll do is just tie it around the front tow bar to take the tension off the winch mountings."

Our truck sat above the Mercedes, David about to haul a dead Goliath uphill. James tried to reverse. The turning force of the wheels, arrested by the banked inertia of the truck, caused them to spin violently, slipping over the packed mud of the road, and wearing shallow grooves in its surface. If our clutch wore out we would be unable to replace it. James killed the engine and clambered down.

"We can't do it," I told the driver. "Your truck's too heavy. We're scared we'll ruin our clutch."

"You must try again! Maybe this time it will work," he exhorted.

"No ways. We said we'd try, and we've done that. Our truck's just too small."

We freed our cable and turned the truck around to continue. We felt bad about abandoning them but the health of our old truck and the thousands of miles ahead made us unwilling to risk serious mechanical damage.

The road improved as we approached Nia Nia, the junction where we would have continued west towards Kisangani but were now forced to turn north, into the remoter regions of the country. There were no more bogholes, although water-filled potholes continued to abound. Rounding a corner, we found Derek standing next to his bike, near a large puddle. He had fallen taking the corner too quickly and was swathed in a layer of brown mud. He had been quite badly winded by the fall but was putting on a brave face. A strange knocking noise was emanating from the bike's engine, and we decided to wheel the bike into the back of the truck, using as a ramp the long sand ladders we'd thought we'd only need in the desert. Derek would overhaul it when we stopped for the night.

At Nia Nia we again encountered a roadblock. There had been similar roadblocks at all the major towns so far. They were all alike, consisting of a bamboo pole lowered across the road beside a small palm frond-roofed hut. Usually a number of soldiers sat around, their uniforms a mismatch of different styles following a camouflage theme, with guns, mostly AK-47s, slung casually over their shoulders, the barrels protected from dust by bungs of toilet paper soaked in palm oil and stuffed down the barrels.

A few words from Masimbuka saw us through. On the far side of the town we had a near accident. A green pickup came flying around a corner and we were saved from a head-on collision only by the rally-driver reflexes of the other driver and James, who swung off the narrow road into the grass verges on either side. For the most part, on the roads behind us, there hadn't been a verge to pull onto. Yet again the flicked coin of luck had landed heads up for us.

We camped soon after, near a pygmy village along a river in which we washed off our accumulated layers of mud. We had managed 120 kilometres since the boghole and were all in high spirits after the excitement of the day. A pygmy man passed our camp. He was dressed in a loincloth and carried a small bow and arrow. We asked if we could take his photograph and he indicated he wanted something in return. We offered him a choice from the supply of second-hand clothes we had. He happily took a pair of smart evening pants, previously owned by Giselle Gemmill, a fashionable society lady who lived near James in Balgowan, and who, at four foot eleven, was only marginally taller than the pygmy.

*

Derek had stripped his bike and put it back together again. Although the mysterious knocking sound could still be heard, it was quieter now and he felt confident about continuing. We set off early the next day, blissfully unaware that come evening we would be a mere sixty kilometres away. The road continued as before, filled with ruts and potholes. Swarms of butterflies, blue and green and yellow, floated amongst the long stems of grass at the roadside, or drank at the edge of the muddy puddles that had formed in the potholes. A few times a thick rope of army ants, each ant dark red and the size of the top joint of my baby finger, lay across the road. An inch high and two inches wide, this living rope writhed ceaselessly as the ants moved, running over each other in response to the unquestionable urge of their social duty.

The mood on board was light. The further we ventured into the jungle, the freer Bronwyn's spirits seemed to become. Whereas before she had been prone to depression each time we neared a large city, now the wildness of the jungle, its scents of danger and excitement, uplifted her. There was a greater sense of unity amongst us, stimulated by the past week of working together against the elements. More so than before we felt part of a team as, after the day's driving and digging, we set about the chores of chopping and cooking and setting up tents before sleeping off the exhaustion of the day. We were drawn together too by the shared thrill of the exotic, enthralled by the alien nature of the jungle, its formidable depths and ancient feel. We reached our first boghole of the day at nine in the morning.

Held fast in its clutches was a huge articulated Fiat truck, far too heavy for us to pull out. The road was quite wide at this point, and we noticed narrow tracks running through the soft mud to the left. Evidently a smaller vehicle had used this alternative route some time before. Not wanting to wait the hours it would require for the other truck to get out of the hole, we decided to chance the detour. We did not get far, sinking deep into the gelatinous, wet mud. We would have to winch ourselves out. I climbed into the cab, engaged the winch and slowly let twenty metres of cable out, gently accelerating in reverse gear to turn the spindle. I climbed out and went to help decide which tree we should anchor to. Behind us, the truck's engine caught and stalled.

Like a mother recognising the sound of her baby crying, James noticed immediately. The truck had never stalled while idling.

"What's up?" he wondered, walking quickly towards the cab. "We can't have run out of diesel." He leapt up the stairs and looked in. "Oh, Jesus! Paul you forgot to put the truck into neutral! It's been idling in reverse! It must have stalled when the cable ran out."

With heavy hearts we stepped through the mud to look underneath. It was far worse than I had dared imagine. Sixty metres of inch-thick cable was enmeshed in the undercarriage, wedged firmly into every crevice. Around the spindle of the winch itself loops of cable were tangled and twisted. Jammed in between the side of the spindle and the thick iron frame of the chassis were several coils of graunched cable, bent and distorted by the massive force of the five and a half litre engine driving its lowest gear that had squashed them there.

I felt desperately unhappy. There seemed no way we'd be able to untangle the untidy mess of spaghettied steel. We'd be stuck in that hole forever. If the knot was jammed tight enough to stall the truck in reverse, we'd never be able to undo it with our hands. Stricken, sick with despair and self-recrimination, I felt like crying.

"Come on, then," urged James, "get the crowbars out! Let's see what we can do."

James and I crawled into the mud under the truck. The activity, the hope that I might be able to remedy my mistake, brought me out of my dejection.

"Let's first clear away as many of these loose coils as we can," I suggested, "so that we can see what's going on. We'll have to find where they start and feed it around from there."

For an hour James and I forced loops of cable up over the spindle, prising apart twists that held lengths nearer the free end of the cable under others nearer the attached end. Rob and Bronwyn took up the resultant slack, pulling the freed cable into the road. We were left with ten coils wrapped tightly around the spindle. From here, though, another five or so loops had slipped over the spindle's edge and were wedged between the winch and the chassis. It was this knot that had stalled the engine. We tried to prise it loose, hindered by the inaccessible position it had been forced into. The long metal bars on which the truck's yellow box sat were in the shape of a capital I. The winch sat about three inches from this bar and it was into this gap, and from there into the hollow of the bar itself, that the cable had been forced. After half an hour, tired and bloodied by the sharp strands that had snapped loose from the cable, we had made no progress.

"We're going to have to cut the cable," said James, resignedly. "We'll probably lose about forty metres. If we can thread the longer bit back on to the spindle, that is."

"Before we do that, let's just try using the engine," I urged, desperate. "Perhaps if we turn it the other way it'll loosen this mess up."

"Okay, there's nothing to lose. I'll turn it just half a revolution. Try and lever this bit here out. Shout to Bronwyn if I must stop."

As the engine turned the cable tightened, seeming to knot even further. A coil, pulled over the edge of the spindle by the pressure, sheared off the brake pads of the winch's brake, something we fortunately didn't use. Suddenly one of the stuck coils was jerked loose. I screamed at Bronwyn to stop. After another half hour of turning and tugging the full length of the cable was free, and I was reprieved. After reconnecting the end of the cable, which had been torn off, we emerged with relief, plastered ochre with mud. We winched ourselves out of the boghole easily enough and continued down the deteriorating road.

*

At midday we reached the grand-daddy of all bogholes. It lived in a shallow valley, and stretched for about a kilometre. The first part was the worst, a three metre-deep, hundred metre-long chasm filled with a viscous, light-brown mud. The jungle crowded in close on both sides. There was no way around. In the hole were two trucks, which sat facing each other. A huge, overladen Fiat lay deep in the mud at our end of the hole. At the opposite end was an articulated Mercedes wedged skew where it had run aground. Behind the Mercedes was its trailer and a Gelanderwagen waiting to cross. Further back, stuck in a different hole, was another truck. Parked off the road just ahead of us were two more Fiats waiting their turn to enter the gaping maw once the present occupants had escaped.

The boghole began at the bottom of a long hill. We walked down to see what was being done to empty it. Along the side of the hole, in the metre-wide passage between it and the jungle, soft mud was piled high, the by-product of trucks extricated previously. The mud sucked at our feet and we soon removed our gumboots, preferring to walk barefoot. We sank into it halfway up our calves as we struggled forward to talk to the men busy working in the hole. Everywhere was the smell of rotting vegetation and diesel. People were all around, digging mud out from behind the wheels of the truck or watching from the side. They sat patiently. Many were passengers from the stuck or waiting trucks. They seemed to accept delays like this as a way of life.

The roofs of the trucks lay level with our feet. We could easily have stepped onto their cargoes which were covered by weathered and patched tarpaulins and festooned with jerrycans of all shapes and sizes and small bags of personal belongings. This was the Zaire I had been told about but had been unable to imagine. That such blighted roads existed was beyond any image travellers' words had conjured in my mind. And that people could accept such bizarre adversity, confront it, step by step, and assimilate it into their everyday lives filled me with incredulity.

James had started talking to a group of men working to free the Mercedes. We learnt from them that the stuck Fiat had no starter motor and would have to be towed out. This was what the driver of the Mercedes had tried to do, before it too had got stuck. Most of the effort was now being put into liberating the Mercedes, to reverse it back in the direction from which it had come, to a position where it could obtain sufficient purchase to haul the stuck Fiat free. This seemed unlikely. The truck could not even find purchase to get itself out. The hour of digging that we watched, and the subsequent revving of the engine, pushing and reversing moved it only a few inches back towards the edge of the hole.

Rob had walked on past the boghole and returned now, shaking his head. "We're going to be here forever! There's another two trucks stuck back there. And three more waiting. The road goes on like this for at least a kay. It's one huge boghole! I didn't get to the end but it was shocking the whole way along. There's no way around anywhere! Good thing we bought all those tins."

The men working to free the Mercedes were among its passengers. They dug energetically at the mud in shifts, hard payment for their passage. They were Liberians and spoke English with an American twang. They told us of the unrest and civil war they were leaving behind in their troubled country. They were on their way to Nairobi where they hoped to find work. All four were big, strong men. Mud rained down over the edge of the pit as they worked to free the truck. By sundown there was no improvement. The boghole's victims remained clenched between its jaws. Work was stopped for the day. After supper we went to bed, wondering how long we would be stuck here, fifth in the queue and with such slow progress being made. A week did not seem unlikely.

I was drifting off to sleep when I was disturbed by the sound of a motor racing down the road towards us. A pickup filled with drunk soldiers stopped next to our fire. The drivers and passengers who had been sitting around it fled into the enveloping night. It became apparent that the soldiers' destination was Isiro, over a hundred kilometres beyond the hole, and that they wanted to get there tonight. Their aggression, and the arrogance their guns gave them, terrified me. They exulted in the power of their guns. Potential brutality hung heavy in the air. They rounded up the drivers of the two Fiats waiting before the hole and said that they should haul out the stuck Fiat. Manual labourers would be needed too, to dig the truck out. Most of the nearby villagers had melted away as the soldiers arrived. A gunshot ripped the night. The soldiers beat a man who seemed unwilling to work. The villagers came drifting back to dig.

We were told to help remove the truck. "We will tie the three trucks together and pull it out," ordered the leader, a huge man dressed in camouflage fatigues with a thick leather belt and a black beret. I thought we should comply, fearful of what they might do. Masimbuka was also scared, and counselled obedience.

"Forget it!" said James to me. "We'll help out in the morning, but not now. This is stupid. We can hardly see a thing. Let's just head back to the tents." Rob and Derek agreed. We drifted out of the confusion and back up the hill to the camp. They didn't come after us.

The night was filled with the rumbling sounds of straining diesel engines and the shouting of human voices. At around midnight more people were forced to join the work crew, and beaten for signs of demurral. As an eerie backdrop to the noise came the incessant, banshee scream of a tree hyrax, sounding for all the world like the anguished cries of a man being lashed. I slept uneasily. Each time I awoke I could still hear the grumbling of stubborn, stuck trucks.

I woke shortly before dawn, prompted by my guts which had been churning as I slept. I hurried up the road to relieve myself. I then walked down the hill to see what the night's efforts had brought. Less than nothing. There were now five trucks in the first hole. A second Mercedes truck had been brought through from beyond the next boghole and was now wedged firmly behind the articulated Merc on the far side. On our side there were now three Fiats all stuck fast. The soldiers' tempers were the worse for a sleepless night. They strode about arrogantly, proud in their mixed uniforms, their dark glasses hiding eyes yellowed and bleary from alcohol and lack of sleep. They held the confidence of their machine-guns loosely in their hands. We watched helpless as they beat a small man they accused of not working hard enough. Earlier James had seen a man flailed with a rope for the same crime.

While the end two Fiats were being dug out, another truck, a Mercedes, arrived. We decided to assist the attempt to extract the original Fiat. Once the two Fiats had been dug and pushed out, we coupled the four waiting trucks together. The plan was to haul the powerless Fiat out backwards. I suggested we put our truck at the back of the chain, to minimise the stress on it. James climbed in behind the wheel. At a signal from one of the Liberians the four engines tried to accelerate in reverse. The Fiat, loaded down under its cargo of dried fish, tobacco and beans, and with no power of its own, did not budge. Engines screamed as they fought against its dead weight. Our truck was almost levitating as its wheels caught and spun, caught and spun, bouncing its body into the air. It was like seeing a child being hurt and having to watch. Eventually, thankfully, we stopped. The noise of voices reappeared from under that of the tortured engines. I ran to look at the truck. On the ground in front of each tyre was a small mound of melted rubber. Its acrid smell burnt the air.

The soldiers ordered the Fiat to be unloaded. While this was being done two more vehicles arrived, one on each side. Ten trucks and a trailer now faced or sat in the hole. Further down the road were four other vehicles. We were in a very Zairean traffic jam, one which had taken two days to assemble and would, it seemed likely, take as many weeks to resolve.

Chaining five trucks together, we were at last able to haul the Fiat out. At the same time the two Mercedes were extricated from the other end. By this stage, ironically, the soldiers now regarded us as their friends. We had helped remove the trucks and they forgave us our absenteeism of last night. Derek had noticed that one of them was wearing South African Defence Force-issue webbing. The soldier said he had completed a parabat training course in Bloemfontein, part of the Nationalist government's attempts to foster relations with the other pariahs of Africa. Derek had also been a parabat and they swapped stories. The suffering of war creates strange bonds. Three days earlier Derek had met a Zairean who had fought against the SADF in Angola. Though on opposite sides, this common experience had sparked a connection between them, and they had parted smiling, as friends.

There was another reason too why the soldiers were friendly towards us. Their two-wheel drive pickup would never make it through unassisted. Knowing this, Derek had pointed put that our truck had not only four-wheel drive but a winch as well, and suggested that they might be able to make use of it. They latched onto the idea and ordered us to tow them across. We agreed easily. It could take ages for the four trucks ahead of us in the queue to negotiate the hole.

We would drive across first, towing them when they got stuck. We made it through the initial hole comfortably, feeling a little guilty at having jumped the queue, but relieved to be moving again. The pickup set off after us. The driver evidently had vast experience of the conditions. Despite the fact that the ridge in the centre of the road rose higher than the car's clearance and huge mounds of mud were ploughed aside by the front of the twisting, bucking vehicle, he managed to ride it more than halfway across. We winched them out and continued. The scene repeated itself several times over the next 900 metres of waterlogged ditch and mud bank that passed for the road.

Near the end another stranded truck blocked our way. James tried to squeeze the truck past it. We tilted to the side as the right hand wheels slipped off the road into the ditch alongside it. Its nearly frictionless mud held us fast and we were forced to winch ourselves out before completing the final hundred metres of that ravaged and churned stretch of road.

Once across, the soldiers were jubilant. They went into the village in search of alcohol and said we should wait for them as they wanted us to travel in convoy with them to Isiro. We were only too happy to have nothing further to do with our new friends and drove off. More than twenty-four hours had passed since we first got to the boghole.

★

We stopped for lunch at a river where we swam and cleaned off the day's mud. While we were eating, an overloaded overland motorcyclist drew up. He was Ronald McCutcheon, a Scot who had left London only four months before. He had a breezy nature, laughing at the hardships he'd been through. Two days before he'd fallen twenty-three times, on one occasion having to unload his bike in order to lift it up again. He gave us warning of obstacles to come: bogholes, bridges, and another insurance salesman at Bondo. He also told us that the Hoggar Route through Algeria was open again. He'd been the first to cross it. This news elated us. Not only was it quicker than going round the bulge, but it meant we would be able to cross through the centre of the Sahara and see the spectacular Hoggar Mountains. Suddenly our plans to get to London in December seemed realistic again. We were in high spirits as we drove towards Isiro.

The road remained appalling, but decent compared to where we'd been that morning. So much of our appreciation of life is relative. This is the power of extreme experience. It calibrates the yardstick against which later experiences are measured.

In the early evening a storm began to build. The skyline to the north grew moody – dark and lightning-shot. Palm leaves were blown horizontal by the gale force wind. The rain began to fall in heavy drops that thudded onto the windscreen. Fortunately Derek had found a village where we could camp up ahead and had parked his bike next to the road where we could see it. The villagers said we could sleep in their church. We erected our tents inside it as the roof leaked badly. Again the people of Zaire, with so little to give, offered what they had. After our supper a woman came up to us and gave us hot palm nuts for dessert.

We reached Isiro the next day. It had obviously once been a well-to-do town. Ghosts of the past still haunted its streets. Huge red-brick churches sat empty and dilapidated. Telephone lines that have not carried a voice for decades hung drunkenly from bent poles. Street lights stood rusting, dark shadows at night. Patches of tar showed up through the dust. A railway carriage lay on its side next to tracks slowly disappearing beneath a blanket of plants and grass. Once-bright painted names could still be discerned on the façades of some of the buildings.

I wondered what lay behind the town's deterioration, what complex forces had led to this slow dissolution of Western influence in the place. Did it show a failure to learn from the West, or that the fruits of the West had been tasted and spat out as unpalatable to the Central African tongue? As we drove out of the town back into the dark and dense jungle from which it had been hewn, its images stayed with me, secretive, enigmatic.

Further on a man tried to sell us a five zaire note. Its current value was $0.00000071, but he asked 10,000,000 times that for this token of Zaire's ravaging 70,000 percent hyperinflation. It had been printed in 1977, and contained the same portrait of Mobutu Sese Seko as current notes. Then as now Mobutu's face stared past every person in the country he had raped. At one stage he was ranked among the world's five richest men, Zaire among its five poorest countries. His personal wealth alone could pay off Zaire's foreign debt. Malevolent despot for over thirty years, Mobutu owned Zaire with the same disdain as that of the region's leaders who had sold their people and enemies into slavery in exchange for wealth centuries before. A Weekly Mail profile on him had the entry "Profession: most successful thief in history."

We reached two more roadblocks, the first of which Masimbuka talked us through. The second proved more difficult. Masimbuka's authority seem to wane the further we ventured from Epulu. Frustrated at the negotiations, which hinged, again, on money for insurance which we were not prepared to buy, we eventually drove off, waving goodbye to the guards in the cheerful pretence that we had been allowed to do so. Masimbuka was horrified and for the next half hour peered out the door behind us.

After 200 kilometres of bad road, we camped at a small village. The Zairean people whose villages we stayed in were unfailingly generous. The simplicity of their lives, cut off from the globalisation of culture, from Internet linkups and jet travel, in no way hindered their basic humanity, and seemed indeed to foster it. Again we were offered a gift, this time a bowl of mushrooms which we added to our dinner of pasta with tinned pork and onion, tomato and garlic sauce. Bronwyn baked pumpkin scones, and after our daily shower we went to bed.

*

The next morning was overcast. After donating 8,000,000 zaires to the church we set off. Seven kilometres past Dingila we came across a truck that had stalled. As it had neither battery nor starter motor, the only way it could be started was by jacking up the rear of the chassis, looping a long rope around the rear axle, and then having a dozen men charge down the road holding the end of the rope. The revolutions of the axle would then kick-start the motor, like a giant lawnmower. It clearly didn't always work, and the tired men were relieved to accept our offer to pull-start them.

After we disconnected our chain and were walking back, Rob stopped to look under our truck. "Hey," he said, "look here! Half of a spring has fallen out."

"Let's see," said James, squinting underneath the wheel arch. "It's worse than that," he reported. "Three leaves are completely broken. We could carry on, try to get to a garage, or even Bangui, but it'll just put greater strain on the other leaves. The whole lot could snap!"

An image came to mind of the suspension of some of the other trucks we'd seen. They were literally held together by lengths of rope. Where pieces of several leaves had fallen out, bricks had been inserted to reduce the stress on the remaining leaves. Emotion cried out to keep going forward, not to lose momentum, but reason said we should repair the damage immediately, before it spread.

"What's in that town we just passed?" asked Rob. "Does Masimbuka know?"

I asked Masimbuka. "He says he thinks there is a garage there. And evidently these guys here," I said pointing to the other truck, "reckon there are *mzungus* living in the town."

"Well that's it then," affirmed James. "We'll turn back."

Top: No way across
Bottom: The main road from Cape Town to London

Top: The worst of days
Bottom: Myself, James, Bronwyn and Derek

Top: Cameroon 3, Zimbabwe 1!
Bottom: Uris, Sarah and Herbert

Top: Nigeria
Bottom: Agadez

Top: Beltran
Bottom: The Sahara

Top: Sand-buggy, the Sahara
Bottom: Assekrem

Top: Assekrem
Bottom: Our guide Ahmoud and a colleague

One year later, Bronwyn, Robbie, Sandy, Derek, myself and James (kneeling)

Chapter Fourteen

On the Michelin map Dingila is just a small dot. Its name is not even in the bold print of the larger towns. But we couldn't have found a better place to carry out repairs in all the 1,200 kilometres of Zaire we had traversed. The town centred around a huge cotton estate run by a French company called Codenord. By necessity the farm was completely self-sufficient. It maintained the hydroelectric generator on the river running through the town, and had extensive workshops in which its vehicles and machines could be repaired. The workshops also contained sophisticated equipment used to fashion spare parts that could not be bought locally. We approached one of the managers. He said we could use whatever equipment we needed, at no cost. We could also camp in his garden.

As the workshop had closed for the day, we parked the truck and set off to explore the town. Here too signs of past grandeur were everywhere. Large buildings, evidently once imposing but now rundown, flanked the wide empty street. Empty or jagged-toothed windows stared out, open now to the infiltrating dust. Paint flaked off the walls in large curls, like the leaves off dead maize plants. Bushes and grass grew wild in the alleys and on the pavements.

A faded sign identified one of the buildings as a hotel. We entered its dimly-lit hallway and found ourselves in an informal bar. We were able to buy several quarts of Primus beer, famous throughout Africa, though at an expensive price, unsurprising considering the efforts that must have been made to transport it there.

That afternoon Derek had bought the leg of a freshly killed goat hanging up for sale in a tree outside one of the villages. It had been stewing in the potjie for three hours and we sat down to a fine meal. The garden we were in was situated on top of a hill. Sitting there eating, we looked across an endless expanse of jungle, a green sea stretching to the horizon under black thunderclouds that gathered while we watched. Jagged lightning split the darkening sky. An electrical storm to the east danced and flashed continuously for two hours, its bolts illuminating the dark mass of forest below. No single other light shone. For as far as we could see the jungle swallowed into itself whatever signs there might have been of people making their living within it.

Relaxed by the beer and the unbridled beauty of the night, we began setting up camp.

Bronwyn again erected the tent we had let Masimbuka have as sleeping quarters. She had done it on the first night as a friendly gesture. He hadn't been too appreciative and seemed to expect it from then on.

"God, I can't wait till he goes!" said Bronwyn angrily. "If he said thanks I wouldn't mind but he just sits there like I'm his slave! It's as though he expects it 'cause I'm a woman."

"So why do you carry on then?" James asked. "Tell him to do it himself."

"I don't think he knows how," she replied, uncertainly. "And it's hard to get out of this now that it's started. Anyway it's only for a couple more days."

Masimbuka did have a lordly manner about him. On four occasions when we had stopped for lunch or at night the nearby villagers had approached and offered him the finest chair in the village to sit on. He had shown no surprise at this and would sit regally while we prepared the meal. I suspected that he would have liked to be able to help but couldn't see how to. His silent presence, and the exacerbating factor that no one but me could speak to him, was causing resentment to build up towards him. The company of "More Sambuka", as we had come to call him, was being tolerated more than it was being enjoyed.

Smoke curled thinly from the dying fire as we sat around it, writing letters and diaries. Rob got up to fetch the accounts book. Walking past Bronwyn, he glanced down at what she was writing. Sensing this, she quickly raised her diary to her chest, hugging it to her.

"Come on, Bronwyn, what have you got there?" asked Rob, tugging at a corner of the book.

"No, don't!" Bronwyn shrieked, leaping up from her chair, her glance flicking towards James and back. Rob moved towards her. "Come on, I want to see what you're writing about me. Let me have a look!"

"No!" she screamed, running into the gloom clutching the book tightly. "Don't ever read my diary. None of you!"

*

The next morning James and I drove down to the workshop to conduct the repairs. The spare leaves we had bought in Nairobi were all the long topmost leaf. We would be able to replace the three broken leaves from two long ones, and set about using the farm's equipment to do so. As we cut through the tempered steel with an angle grinder I shuddered at the thought of trying to use a hacksaw for the job. Again, using the huge press drill to make a hole for the anchor bolt, I realised that without electricity and tools we would have struggled to repair the truck.

Derek, who had spent the morning with Rob baking bread, came down to help us. We topped up the diff oil, greased the nipples and set the brakes, ending up as ever covered in oil and grease. After seven hours the truck's health was restored and we returned to a late lunch. I broke open one of the small loaves Derek and Rob had baked. The yeasty smell and warmth of the fresh bread was a cherished reminder of a luxury so easily accepted before. Masimbuka's popularity decreased even more when he ate far more than his share, Derek only half-joking as he suggested we drive off without him.

As we were packing up to leave, we were approached by two men selling wooden carvings. I bought a small stylised head whose glum looks pleased me. Rob bought several carvings to add to the extensive collection of African craftwork he had stowed away in the back of the truck or sent back with other travellers who were southward bound. Derek by contrast bought only a single small figure. "The only curios I'm buying on this trip are ones that can fit on my keyring," he told us. James delighted in buying an enormous wooden phallus.

After a twenty-four hour set-back we were back on the road. Twenty kilometres on we were stopped by a massive hardwood which had fallen across the road, its hold on the earth weakened by recent rains. Villagers had already begun dissecting it, hacking at the stubborn wood with an old axe. We helped to complete the third cut, which divided the tree into four huge sections. To winch out the centre piece, which weighed over a ton, we had to dig a hole beneath it, through which we threaded a thick chain. James started the engine. The winch cable grew taut, the links in the chain clanking as they tightened. Slowly the huge section of severed trunk slid across the road, yawing sideways as it was pulled, scoring deep lines into the dirt of the road. The onlookers from the village clapped and laughed. We handed out cigarettes as thanks for their help.

I climbed onto the roof to stow away the chain and the spades. The angle-iron hook we had welded onto one of the vertical bars of the roof-rack frame was empty.

"Hey, where's the third spade?" I asked. "I'm sure it was here when I fetched the other two."

"It must be somewhere," replied James. "Check on top. I'll look around here, underneath."

The spade was nowhere to be found. "One of these guys must have stolen it," said Rob. He picked up one of the other spades and turned to the crowd, pointing towards it. "Where is our spade, like this one?" he demanded. "Someone has taken it."

He received only a few murmurs and shakes of the head in response.

"Let's just abandon it," I suggested, "and get a move on. Someone's obviously run off with it. We won't get it back now."

"Oh no we will!" Rob stated bluntly. "I'm not leaving here till we do."

He addressed the crowd again. "You must find the spade. We wait here until you get it!"

The minutes passed, five, ten, fifteen. Most of the villagers remained where they had been, watching us. It seemed to me that we were wasting our time, that whoever had taken the spade had long since disappeared with it. Suddenly there was a commotion a hundred yards down the road. A group of five or so people were shouting at a roughly-dressed man, pushing him before them. One of the group carried our spade in his hand. While the cringing thief was verbally abused by the rest of the villagers, our spade was ceremoniously returned to us, along with profuse apologies. We left without seeing whether the man received any further punishment.

An hour further down the road we decided to stop for the night at an old abandoned coffee plantation. Evidently once a massive estate, it stood unused and dilapidated. The main house, a grand, stolid building which commanded a view over the thousands of acres of now fallow land, stood empty, its interior stripped of any objects of use. The families living on the premises welcomed us and showed us to one of the outhouses, on whose verandah we lay down the mattresses and erected the mosquito nets.

Masimbuka's home, Buta, lay 170 kilometres away. We left early, hoping to reach there by nightfall. Again we were over-optimistic in our hopes. We covered 130 kilometres in the day, each kilometre taking us into more and more surreal events, like successive scenes in a film by Fellini.

The road was deteriorating, eroded by recent rains. Potholes scarred its rutted surface. Huge bamboo groves, their stems forty foot long and as thick as my calf, had fallen across the road, their roots undermined by the subversive force of the rain. Twice in the morning we had to hack our way past, swinging our panga at the splintering stems of bamboo. The jungle closed in upon the road, great leaf-covered boughs reaching across over it, forming a canopy that fended off the light. For hundreds of kilometres now the sky had been occluded like this, cut down to a thin strip of blue. Our world had become these basic elements, the strip of blue mirroring that of the red road below, and on either side solid walls of green, the dense profusion of the jungle. Only when we came across one of the sporadic villages could we see more than a couple of metres off the road.

In a shallow boghole we found the truck we had pull-started two days ago. Derek was helping them extricate it. It had stalled, and as they had no starter motor it had to be pushed out of the hole. The passengers had unloaded the cargo of fish and coal from the back and were manhandling their transport forward. Their means of doing so was to jack up the back of the truck, wedge long planks under the rear wheels, and then lever the truck off the jack. Each effort gained them a foot. The hole was over fifty foot long. They had been there since the previous day. Being on the wrong side of the hole, we couldn't help by towing, but assisted with the final stint of digging and pushing. Once they were out we drove across, and pull-started them again. The weary and muddy passengers thanked us profusely.

We were soon forced to stop again. Two armed military figures waved us down and demanded a lift. They were aggressive and smelt of alcohol. It turned out their destination lay three kilometres further on where a large Hino truck was parked in the middle of the road. Derek was there already, trying to speak to the driver. We got out and went up to him. He said in French that he had run out of diesel and that we must give him some. I told the others.

"But that's crazy!" James exclaimed. "How could anyone set out from Buta with only enough diesel to get here? The next place selling fuel is Isiro, 300 kays away."

The driver stood next to his bumper, glaring at us.

"Well," I realised, "he obviously did it on purpose. All he has to do is block up the road and people will have to give him diesel."

"Sod him! Tell him we'll sell him some diesel at 7,000,000 a litre, but that's all," said James, becoming frustrated.

I told him this and he flew into a rage. He said he worked for Mobutu and that we had to give him diesel. We shouted back, demanding that he move. He had with him the two soldiers as well as four other passengers. Our two groups sized each other up. The driver stared at us through serpent eyes. It was obvious he was not going to back down.

"Do you reckon we can get round him?" Bronwyn asked. We examined the muddy bank to the side of the road. The surface looked soft and yielding. Just beyond the truck was a deep, perpendicular ditch, gouged by water running off the road. Immediately behind that lay the jungle, impenetrable, a green barrier of trees and mud and undergrowth. It would be difficult to pass. If we were able to get enough traction under our wheels, we would still struggle to regain the road before hitting the ditch.

"There's no way we're giving anything to this bastard," said Rob grimly. "I vote we try go round." We all agreed. The truck bogged down immediately it left the road, its left wheels sinking deep into the mud, its right side only two inches from the other vehicle. We tied the winch cable around a tree thirty metres down on the other side of the road and winched ourselves forward. The truck moved parallel to the road, the pull of the bank cancelling the sideward pull of the cable. We were heading straight for the ditch. The only way to get back onto the road would be to anchor the winch around a tree almost in line with the nose of our truck. But the other truck sat in the way.

I approached the driver and asked him to move his truck forward a metre or two.

"*Je refuse!*" he spat at me.

"*Pourquoi?*" I asked.

"*Je refuse!*" he spat again, his eyes malevolent. Derek went around to the front door, planning to release the handbrake so we could push the truck forward. The man jumped in front of him, locking the door. They stared at each other. Derek's eyes were like drill bits, boring hatred into the other man's gaze. The tension of suppressed violence stifled the air. I had a crowbar in my hand. I wanted to bring it smashing down on the man's head, to break his obnoxious face.

If it weren't for the armed soldiers, I don't know if we would have held our atavism in check. We returned to the truck and started cutting deep trenches in front of each wheel, to guide it into the road, our anger digging into the mud and flinging it into the jungle. Winching and digging, we managed to regain the road just inches short of the ditch. In our breaking of the impasse the tension came into flux. Unsure how the highwaymen would react, we drove away in haste.

After the frustrations of the morning, we decided not to stop for lunch. I sat on the stairs behind the driver's seat, watching the jungle flash by in a malachite stream of branches, grass, leaves and shadows, dark and light swirling together. Many of the people we passed had what seemed to be huge tumours on their necks. Their heads were bent slightly to the side, forced crooked by the growth which on some was the size of a large melon. Men and women alike had these swollen bullfrog throats. They looked grossly disfigured, burdened by this additional suffering in what was a hard living. A man on the roadside raised up something aloft, offering it to us. It was a small baby chimpanzee. The look on its face was infinitely sad.

We came to two more large bogholes, almost the height of the truck. The earth here was a deep red-brown, the colour of rust on shipwrecks. The bottom of the first hole was filled with rocks and logs, laid there as traction for wheels that spun freely in the smooth grip of the mud. Fortunately no other trucks were waiting, and we made it through both holes without stopping, using four-wheel drive.

Trucks weren't the only overloaded vehicles we came across. Two men were pushing bicycles down the road ahead of us. The first bike was bearing two huge sacks of peanuts, two goats held in bamboo cages, and ten chickens huddled together in long, closed wicker baskets. The other bike's burden comprised three sacks of flour, ten more chickens, a sack of peanuts and several other baskets and bags of unknown content. As we drove up, the rear bike pitched backward, its front wheel spinning in the air. Its owner wasn't strong enough to right it. Rob jumped out to lend him a hand.

Another truck blocked the road. It also had no starter motor and had stalled in a shallow pothole. We towed it out and continued, Bronwyn at the wheel. We rounded a bend. Coming fast towards us was a red Mazda truck.

"Pull across, Bron," said James.

"God, he's not slowing down!" I yelled.

"And I can't go any further across!" screamed Bronwyn.

We watched transfixed as the truck hurtled towards us. Our truck took up three quarters of the road. There was no way it could squeeze past.

"It's got no brakes," James said quietly, as the realisation struck.

The Mazda's engine screamed as it was slammed into a lower gear, but this hardly slowed it at all. At the last moment, not fifteen metres in front of us, the driver wrenched his steering wheel to the right. The truck ramped off the road and up the bank, crashing through the undergrowth, mowing down saplings and shrubs in its path before coming to a shuddering rest against a fallen log. The driver held up both hands in apology and smiled as we drove past, staring in disbelief. He obviously had no starter motor either for he had managed to keep the engine from stalling. We breathed deeply and drove on. I looked behind us out of the door. The Mazda carefully reversed onto the road and set off again on its reckless way.

Night fell. We drove on, still forty kilometres short of Buta. Our headlights picked up an old woman, deliriously drunk or mad. She screamed in terror as we approached and dived into the deep mud alongside the road, covering her head with a red cloth so as not to be seen.

Soon after, we decided to stop, exhausted by what had been a very long day. James hardly slept. He was using one of the A-frame tents which had seen seven months' use on their way down the continent and whose zips had long since perished, leaving the flaps hanging loosely open, invitation to a host of small night creatures. In the early hours of the morning he joined me and Rob in our tent, desperate with fatigue. He was covered in the small red bites of the insects that had kept him awake. Midnight had seen him wandering up and down the moonlit road, trying to escape the misery.

Bronwyn had slept badly too, and was also covered in itchy bites. We weren't sure if they were from mosquitoes. Or we might have bedbugs. We left late, James especially feeling subdued. Masimbuka left us at Buta where we dropped him off outside his house. He made a touching farewell speech, thanking us for accepting him into our family. From our side there was more than hint of relief to be back to four in the truck.

Derek stayed behind in Buta to stage an impromptu auction. He sold two pairs of gumboots for 100,000,000 zaires each, a 300% profit, and a large jerrycan for 55,000,000. Two men bid feverishly against each other for the gumboots to drive the price to such heights. After one of them capitulated, Derek produced the second pair which he offered at the same price.

Travelling further into the Congo Basin, we started coming to more and more bridges across the network of streams that drain the waters of the jungle into the Atlantic at Soyo 1,600 kilometres to the south east. The bridges consisted of large round logs laid across the two banks. Some had flat cross-planks but mostly these had been broken, or possibly stolen for other use. Felled decades ago, the logs were beginning to rot. The gaps between them were not uniform and we had to carefully choose a path before crossing.

At the first, James drove. Blind to the position of the wheels, he could only stare ahead, like a tightrope walker. I stood on the far side, indicating left or right. Bronwyn, beside me, was doing the same. James stopped the truck.

"You're signalling opposite bloody ways!" he exploded. "Jesus, Bronwyn, just leave it! Let Paul do it!"

The road became wetter too. We got stuck in a boghole just outside Buta and had to winch ourselves out. Our pace was slow, retarded by bridges, which we tried at first to strengthen using logs and our sand ladders, and an ever-worsening road surface. It was hard to believe the road would remain passable, given a few more rainy seasons of neglect.

The cover of cloud that had blocked what little of the sky we could see thickened and darkened. Heavy single drops turned suddenly into a continuous stream of water. We pulled over to have lunch and wait for the worst to pass, hoping it would end, hoping this wasn't the vanguard of the rainy season we'd been racing to beat.

Rain poured from the sky, drumming down onto the back of the truck where we all huddled. The deluge cut visibility down to twenty metres. After it abated, we set off again, into a landscape that had been transformed. Mist rose up slowly into the humid air. Water dripped from the leaves and branches above us, adding to the volume of water that churned along the edges of the road, thick and brown with the soil of its heart. Everywhere, long water-filled potholes scored the surface of the road. As we entered them the truck would list, beguiled by the uneven bed below the flat surface. Unable to gauge the depth of the holes, at times we would plunge unexpectedly, water splashing up to the warthog skull affixed to the front bumper as the wheels churned in the muddy darkness below. Like a frightened elephant fording a river, the truck lumbered through the holes, emerging heavily on the other side, water streaming from its flanks.

The smell of the rain stayed clean in the air. Fronds and leaves, bowed by its weight, slowly lifted themselves, shaking free its glinting drops. Insect sounds, drowned out, were brought back to life. Like blood beating through a body's veins, the rain was invigorating the jungle it flowed into.

We stopped to hack our way past fallen bamboo. I chopped through most of the last pole, leaving it to sever itself under its own weight and fall to the ground to join the others lying there, to be driven over by the truck. Turning from the work, I recoiled at the thought of climbing back into the truck, back into its lurching and buffeting noise, the contest of machine and road.

Barefoot, dressed only in a pair of shorts, I ran on ahead of the slow-moving truck, sprinting now, leaping the smaller potholes, splashing through the larger ones, ducking beneath the outstretched leaves. I fell into the mud and got up laughing. I had the panga still in my hand. The raw scents of mud and rain filled my head like a drug. The jungle loomed over me, threatening, protective. Its wildness resonated in me, shaking loose old screams. Unshielded now, I opened to its strength, its massive and impersonal capacity for inspiring life, and delivering death. I ran until exhausted, and climbed back into the truck.

The uncertainty of the pond-like holes and the softness of the road's rain-soaked surface slowed our pace to a crawl. Having left at ten in the morning, we drove until seven that night. In that time we covered eighty kilometres.

In what was by now a well-rehearsed ritual Rob and I erected his dome tent. Most nights we would sleep in it. It was the only one with gauze and I was beginning to feel concern about the number of mosquitoes visiting nightly. There was comfort too in this routine of preparing for sleep, in having some constancy in a lifestyle that was so unsettled.

In the dense reaches of the forest nocturnal creatures stir to life, awakening to the night. Crickets chirp incessantly. A bat flies by. They lie next to each other, talking softly. The others are asleep by now. Her cautious words conceal a tumble of emotion. Anger at his disdain, desire to impress on him something of herself, enjoyment of the attention of the present.

Need draws his hand up into the darkness, contravening a deeper knowing. He touches her. She starts slightly, then relaxes. Touch becomes caress. She is unable to resist. Hope outjumps fear in her heart and she submits to the lines staked out by his fingers. His hands move down. She lies suppliant. Clouds return to cover the moon. In the closing night they fill each other's need.

The Michelin map indicated that the roads would get far worse after Dulia. There the markings changed from red and white checks – *partially improved road* – to a jagged line parallel to a solid one – *recognised or marked tracks*. The deterioration was immediately noticeable. As we crawled our amphibian way through long, water-filled holes, the truck rocked constantly, buffeted by the uneven surface of the capricious road. Bamboo stems screeched along the its aluminium body as we broke past their clawing arms. Progress was slow. We came to more bridges. Breaths were held as we tiptoed across their wet and carious trunks. Many of the bridges had logs missing, smashed into the water below under the weight of some earlier cautious truck.

The relentless strain of the road surface was beginning to tell. A rear U-bolt sheared and we had to spend an hour replacing it with one that James had had the foresight to have machined in Zimbabwe. As we were tightening the nuts a hunter appeared. He was armed with a crossbow. His quiver held poison-tipped darts. The design was simple but deadly effective. He demonstrated it to us, loosing a dart into the jungle. It soared hundreds of metres into the air, arcing slowly to disappear into the interwoven treetops.

More worrying than the suspension was the weakening of our brakes. To obtain any pressure they had to be pumped vigorously several times. This lack of control as we approached holes or dips worsened the jolting the truck received as we plunged into them faster than we should have. James and I tried to reset them, but to no avail. The problem seemed to have appeared after entering the deep puddles of the day before, and this left us puzzled.

Just past Likati we encountered a wide river. The road bridge had collapsed years before, as had the railway network. Since then, road vehicles had taken to crossing over the 1927 railway bridge. Logs had been laid between the wooden sleepers, but it was still a tortuous, suspension-threatening crossing. Graffiti testified to this. Overland tour groups had painted on the bridge's metal framework their times for crossing: "Guerba 2/2/91 7hrs 43min"; "Afr Overland 3/4/92 1hr 22 minutes."

Derek wheeled his bike across, balancing it on the thin ridge of the railway track. As the rest of us walked on ahead, James drove the truck onto the bridge. The truck bucked and plunged like a stabbed bull as the wheels fell into the holes between the sleepers or slipped on the loose logs placed there for support. The suspension squeaked in protest for the fifteen minutes it took James to drive across. To relieve the stress of it all we spent an hour leaping off the bridge and swimming in the dark waters of the river below. The crew of the truck ahead of us was still flattening a boghole after the bridge and would continue to do so for two hours, so we decided to stop for the day, setting up camp in a disused quarry. We had covered another eighty kilometres in the day.

★

As the sun rose, I hurried to open the tent and ran into the jungle to ablute, as had been happening for two weeks now. After my morning panic I would be fine for the rest of the day. Although bad dreams weren't disturbing my nights, I thought it might be the days' stress unsettling my insides as I slept.

We crossed the boghole easily, but it was only the first of many, waiting in the road like patient sea anemones ready to close over whatever entered their lairs. Before one particularly deep hole, which covered the road like a lake, there was a detour which headed into the jungle, joining up with the disused railway line running parallel to the road. We decided to follow it, and regretted this as the truck jolted painfully over the metal sleepers. Discarded tyres, their inner rim ripped open by the sleepers' sharp edges, littered the long grass. After a bone-shaking hundred metres we bounced back over the steel track and rejoined the road.

Sandflies had begun to plague us. We didn't notice them bite, but the marks they left itched worse than chicken pox and remained for two days. Bronwyn's legs were covered in festering sores her frustrated nails had ripped open. She started a course of antibiotics to ward off infection. Despite the clammy and oppressive heat of the days, I had begun to wear tracksuit pants, preferring to swelter than suffer more of these bites.

In many places the road hardly existed at all. There were only metre-deep ridges and ruts ripped out of the ground by the violence of the rains. As we mounted the ridges and dropped into the ruts, the truck tilted dramatically, like a ship striking a reef. Inside the cab we were thrown around by these sudden and vicious shifts from the horizontal, like so many puppets jerked on strings by a heavy-handed puppeteer. Our lack of brakes exacerbated the perils of the road, leaving us to career into its cuts and tears, heightening the stress on the truck and our nerves.

The jungle is closing in. It has become oppressive. The cab is filled with the stench of mud. Ground into the carpets, it is rotting and the smell is always in my nose, slightly sweet, cloying, like blood. The strain on the truck transfers through to me. I wince with each jolt, and inside it is I who scream as the tortured chassis is twisted in the forceful hands of the road. Continually, our broken brakes drift us towards terror. I grip the seat and press down my foot as the truck crashes down into holes and then out, juddering. My legs are covered in welts. The noise of their itching is incessant in my head, high-pitched, occluding my thought. Anxiety has smothered my awe.

We reached the Uele River at lunchtime. After so many days spent under a canopy of green, broken only by the thin line above the road in front us, it was a relief to be under a wide expanse of sky again. The river stretched half a kilometre wide, flowing strongly. Its waters, smooth and heavy, like molten titanium, reflected in the sun. Men paddled pirogues across, angling against the current.

The ferryman was not to be found. Three other vehicles, two trucks and a Land-Rover, had spent the morning waiting for him. Eventually he did arrive and a bitter argument ensued. He was demanding twenty litres of diesel for the crossing. The normal price was fifteen. The other three drivers shouted angrily but he remained unmoved. There was no other way to cross, and no other crossing point for 200 kilometres. The ferryman stood on the ferry, confident of his suzerain power on the river. The only weapon the drivers had in this unequal contest was patience. They would wait for the ferryman to relent. They expected us to do the same.

"Let's give him the twenty litres," I suggested. "It's not worth waiting here for a day for just five litres of diesel."

"Ja," agreed James. "It's a scabby thing to do, but what the hell."

We approached the ferryman. He agreed to let us cross first for twenty litres. We took down a jerrycan of diesel which he poured into the huge tanks of the ferry. James started the truck and began to move down to the river. The driver of the Land-Rover, who was first in the queue, jumped into his vehicle, planning to drive down the road leading to the ferry and prevent us from getting on. Bronwyn and Derek ran into the road in front of him, barring his way. While he hooted and cursed us, James drove through the long grass at the roadside and onto the ferry.

Once across, we turned off the main road through Bondo, driving through the streets of its eastern suburbs to avoid the insurance salesman we had been warned about. A huge red-brick church sat empty alongside the road, its windowless eyes staring blankly towards the forest. In its graveyard stood the ornate headstones of buried Christian settlers.

We met up with Derek eighteen kilometres beyond the town. It was 5.30 and we decided to press on for another hour or two. Derek would go ahead to find a campsite. As daylight ebbed, we came more frequently upon the narrow bridges. At the first we decided to refill some of our water jerrycans. James said he would lower Bronwyn down to the stream. He crouched, right arm extended as she swung over the edge, each gripping the other's wrist. James was pulled off balance onto his chest, jarring his shoulder and ripping a flap of skin from it. Bronwyn let go and fell the remaining two feet into the water. A bit shaken, she filled the jerrycans. We pulled them and her up with a rope and proceeded.

Groves of bamboo hung across the road and had to be hacked down. A sliver of bamboo sliced deeply into James's finger, dripping blood heavily onto the dirt road. We tried to drive underneath a second grove but were held back, two thick bamboo poles catching the vertical blue poles on top of the roof. Rob and I climbed up to free them. Rob stood behind the chairs on the roof and heaved at the first pole. Like a piece of rock in the pod of a siege catapult, he was launched violently backwards. He flew two metres through the air, landing sprawled on the roof of the box of the truck, his calf muscle torn and back wrenched from where he had smashed against the box's edge.

A third grove took an hour to chop through. There was no sign of Derek. The mood in the cab grew heavy. Tired and sore, we all wanted to stop. We cursed Derek as we drove on into the night.

It started to rain. Crossing wet bridges in darkness wracked our nerves. Dazzled by the headlights, James could hardly see to direct me. I inched forward, heart in my mouth, pumping urgently at the brake as James raised his palm. Every few kilometres there was a bridge.

Frustration turned to anger, directed at Derek. We stopped to look for his tracks. "Surely he couldn't have gone this far?" I asked. "Is he completely mad? He must have realised the bridges and bamboo would slow us down."

Eventually we decided to forsake him and to stop for the night. We were looking for a campsite when we saw his bike standing outside a village. The people of the village were friendly and wanted to chat but, having driven the whole of this nightmare evening, I was exhausted and went to bed. In four hours we had covered thirty-two kilometres.

Chapter Fifteen

Killed by its own weight, a tree had crashed across the road, its roots ripping free of the rain-softened earth. Twin water-filled trenches gouged by the wheels of trucks ran under the thick foliage of the fallen tree's leaves and the plants it had brought down with it. Pinioned at one end by its remaining roots, and at the other by a huge anthill which sat between us and it, the tree looked immovable.

"How the hell are we going to shift it?" I asked. "The axe is bust, and there's no way we can winch it backwards with that anthill in the way. Unless we dig it away, which will take forever."

"Don't worry, Paulus, we'll make a plan," Derek reassured me. "All we need to do is find a suitable tree on the far side, loop the winch cable around it and it'll act as a pulley. We'll pull the tree away from us."

"Exactly," agreed James. "We need to find one as close to the road as possible, to use as a fulcrum, so as to obtain the greatest turning force."

While James released fifty metres of cable, Derek and Rob tramped into the forest where they looped it around a sturdy ironwood. The end was tied around the fallen tree. James engaged the winch and we watched happily as the tree was jerked to the side of the road.

Two miles on another river blocked the road, a swathe of molten blue cutting through the green of the jungle. Again we felt the exhilaration of space, revelling in the feeling of sunlight unfiltered by high leaves, in beholding horizons that did not end abruptly ten yards off in a wall of green. Protracted bargaining by Rob bought us a crossing for 40,000,000 zaires. While this was going on, Derek organised a cheap crossing for him and his motorbike on a wooden pirogue. He had to sit astride his bike to balance it, a difficult task, rocked as the tiny craft was by the current and the thrusts of its pilot's paddle.

The bridges continued to worsen. None had the crossplanks on top that had once offered a smooth and moderately safe ride. On all now the huge logs which acted as spars for the bridge were exposed, and it was over their round, smooth, rotting lengths that we had to drive.

One bridge had collapsed completely. The snapped halves of the logs hung into the water below. Trucks before us had cut an alternative route through the forest and across the stream itself. I wondered if this was the site of the story we had heard about a sixteen ton overland truck that crashed through a bridge and had to be taken apart and reassembled by its passengers on the far side over five days.

As we climbed into the hilly regions of the north, the road deteriorated still more. Erosion was aggravated by the gradient, and the insistent cold weight of the rain carved the road into metre deep ruts that snaked their way downwards, contorted, rough with stones. Mud flowed red along these wounds cut out of the ground by the unending tattoo dripping from the sky.

Our brakes had become spongier. Rob offered to drive, despite the terrible headache he'd woken up with that morning. The rain continued to fall. The road was treacherous, slick under its coating of rain. A steep hill sloped down below us. As we started down it the truck began to slither out of control. Panicked, Rob pressed both feet firmly down on clutch and brake. The truck rolled faster, gaining momentum. Rob's hands clenched the steering wheel, pulling backwards as his feet bore down on the two pedals. Twisting slightly sideways as it gathered speed, the truck careered downward, unchecked by either brakes or engine.

"Release the clutch! Release the clutch!" screamed James. Rob, steering grimly, his eyes widening in terror, obeyed. The truck slowed and then came to a stop as he pumped the brake and hauled up on the handbrake.

"Someone else can drive," he muttered. "I can't handle this."

James drove on, his foot pumping frantically to build up pressure in the brakes. Deep grooves caught at the wheels and bore us towards the road's edge, or ripped the wheels skew, causing the steering wheel to spin wildly under his hands. Permanently in four-wheel drive, we slid and bounced our way towards the mission station at the town of Monga where we hoped to spend the night. The villages we passed were poor, consisting only of a few small huts with grass roofs. There was no cultivation or stock animals. The inhabitants sat listlessly near the huts, gazing without expression as we drove by.

Near one such village the road disappeared. Instead of two tracks separated by a ridge of grass or mud, there was only a single pathway which we straddled. Even the road seemed to be subjugated under the relentless convergence of the jungle.

The process of evolution is shaped by the adaptation of species to suit a changing environment. Theory has it that humans have ended the course of this process because of our ability to shape our environment to suit us. This did not seem so obvious here. The fragility of human life was patent, even from within the security of the truck, our window onto this starker world.

★

Monga was a small town, built around the mission station and medical clinic. We arrived in the afternoon, weary and shaken. Rob had begun to shiver uncontrollably. He was sweating slightly and complained of a splitting headache. The missionaries, a Norwegian couple called Alf and Simonette, lived there with their son Jan and his tutor Monica. They said we could stay in the guest house. With electricity supplied by a small hydroelectric generator, hot showers and proper beds, it was a palace to us after four weeks in the open.

Derek drove Rob down to the hospital, a small clinic run by the mission station. In his delirium, the hospital Rob envisaged had cool white rooms with starched sheets on firm beds. He clutched on behind Derek, holding on with his last to make it to this sanctuary. The nurse seemed irritated as they pushed to the front of the queue of people waiting.

"I think I'm dying," said Rob faintly.

"What are your symptoms?" she asked brusquely. He told her.

"You've just got malaria. Do you have any drugs for it?"

"We've got Fansidar."

"Take three, go to bed and you should get over it soon enough."

Rob slumped to the concrete floor in a wretched heap, enervated by this unsympathetic response. Derek coaxed him to his feet and up to the mission station where he put him to bed.

Bronwyn and I, meanwhile, had gone off to town to find a chicken for dinner. There weren't any chickens available but the villagers said we could choose a duck, pointing to a flock waddling nearby. Bronwyn picked one out and was then wracked with the guilt of an executioner as it was caught and had its neck wrung in front of us. Derek plucked it and turned it into a tough but tasty duck à l'orange which we ate that night.

Passing through this alien jungle had raised several unanswered questions in my mind. I was pleased to find in Alf and Simonette people who could cast some light on the mysteries of this place their home.

"What are those growths on people's necks?" I asked Alf.

"They're goitres, swollen thyroid glands. It's a disease caused by iodine deficiency. It's tragic, really. We need so little iodine to prevent it, but these people get none, cut off as they are. You get iodine from things like sea fish. That's how most of us get what we need." This explained the cargoes of so many of the trucks we had passed.

"Interestingly enough," he continued, "the pygmies don't get it at all. No one is quite sure why."

"It's strange," Simonette broke in, "because they eat much the same stuff as the others. There's a barter economy here. The pygmies swap protein in exchange for carbohydrates."

"I suppose people's health has got worse as the roads have deteriorated and fewer trucks have got through."

"Yes and no," Alf replied. "There's a hidden blessing in these bad roads as well. They slow down the spread of AIDS. These long-distance truck drivers are the main cause of it spreading so quickly."

At supper that night Monica confirmed our impression that the people of the region seemed to lack energy, to have withdrawn into a lethargy.

"Even the children don't play," she said. "When Jan first got here he tried to get the other kids to play with his cars and things, but they just wanted to watch. Even now, two years later, only a few will play with him. The rest just sit and watch from a distance."

The subdued nature of the people here in the northern reaches of Zaire was in marked contrast to the outgoing, industrious atmosphere we'd found further south and in the east. The jungle is an unforgiving place. It was as though their harsh struggle with it had sucked their vitality out of them. It allowed them to exist, but not to live.

*

Rob lay on his sickbed sweating and shivering, his head hot to the touch. I cannot say I gave him much sympathy. I was preoccupied with my own concerns, with the need to get out from the jungle's constricting grasp. To find earth that was dry, views that were distant, and an end to the ceaseless jolting and jarring of our buffeted truck.

James and I spent the next morning bleeding and setting the brakes again. A light rain fell on us as we worked. After four hours the brakes were no better at all. We decided to stop for the time being, and returned to the house where we began to update our diaries. James noticed that it was a Tuesday.

"Hang on. We'll be cutting things too fine if we stay here another day. We've only got five days to get through the CAR," he said, referring to the five-day visas we had bought in Nairobi, "and we still have to get our Cameroon visas in Bangui, which means we have to get there by Friday morning at the latest. If we're going to make it we'll have to leave now and try to get to the border by tonight." The forward impetus was strong in us all now, the desire to get through Zaire, to find ourselves out of the jungle. No one objected.

"What about Rob?" asked Bronwyn.

"We'll ask him if he feels well enough to carry on," replied James.

Malaria has two distinct phases. In the first you become scared that you might die. In the second, you're scared that you might not die. Rob was in the grip of the latter and said weakly that he didn't care what happened. We packed quickly. Rob walked slowly to the truck, pale and shivering, supported by Bronwyn. He slumped in the front seat, his eyes closed, a pillow clutched in one hand. We climbed in after him and waved goodbye to the missionaries, and to Derek who had decided to stay on an extra night. He would catch us up the next day.

It became the worst of days. Another huge tree barred our way and had to be winched aside. The rain, which continued to fall, made the surface of the road slippery like the slime that coats fish. Without brakes, we slid helplessly, a loose toboggan on a ski slope. Several times, being dragged inexorably off the road, we had to dig deep channels to guide the wheels away from the road's edge.

If a wheel got caught in one of the deep ruts caused by sluicing rainwater, the truck followed it to the bottom of the hill, oblivious to the driver heaving at the wheel. Our undirected momentum threw us repeatedly off the frictionless road and into the ditch at its side, forcing us again and again to resort to the winch.

Halfway down a steep hill James lost control of the truck and it slid heavily into a ditch, crushing grass and creeper below it. Its box and cab canted steeply as the suspension tightened under its suddenly uneven weight. We clambered out hastily.

"Quick, Robbie!" cried Bronwyn. "Get out! It's going to topple over!"

The truck lay at an improbable angle, thirty-five degrees at least. The top of the yellow box stuck out a metre and a half beyond its submerged right wheels. Why it did not go over was beyond me. In my mind it fell, like a wall in an earthquake, gaining speed and crashing heavily, violently onto the ground. I could see it go over, the box ripped off the chassis, the engine torn from its mountings, the springs snapping like twigs. I wanted to close my eyes, not to look.

So precariously perched, it could collapse in at any moment, like a golf ball on the lip of the hole.

"Come on, Rob! Quickly!" I urged. "Before it falls!"

"Leave me," he moaned, his eyes shut tight, holding onto the pillow beneath his head. "I don't care."

"You must, Robbie!" exhorted Bronwyn. "Come on!"

He lay there, inert, withdrawn, curled in upon himself by the enervating strength of the malaria.

"We're going to have to winch it out," said James, determinedly. "I'll climb in and engage the winch. You pull the cable free. Tie it around that tree there."

"Shit, James. Be careful," I warned. The driver's seat lay at the bottom of the downward slope. It seemed that even James's light weight would be enough to shift the centre of gravity beyond the vertical and send the truck crashing over. He climbed in through the passenger door, gingerly lowering himself behind the wheel. Nervously we drew out the cable and made it fast. James revved the motor, taking up the slack. The smell of diesel smoke mixed with wet vegetation as the driving engine slowly reeled in the winch, taking up the slack. The truck jerked slowly upright as it clawed its way back onto the road. The right-hand stairwell was crushed in, but we seemed to have got off lightly. Bronwyn and I climbed back in, out of the drizzle.

Two hundred metres on was a bridge. Of the four logs that remained, it looked like no two were the correct distance apart to accommodate our wheels. The logs were soaked and their edges splintered under the weight of previous trucks. We took out the thin bamboo pole we kept in the cab, which we'd cut into an exact measure of the width between the wheels. Moving onto the bridge, and putting it down, we saw there was one possible route.

"God, if we go on these two only half the right wheel will be supported!" I exclaimed, looking down at the water three metres below the smooth wood of the log.

"We have to do it," shrugged James. "We've got no alternative. You direct me."

He got in behind the wheel, Rob huddled next to him. The truck moved haltingly onto the bridge. The rightmost log curved inward like a bow. As James neared the middle of the bridge, more and more of the wheel hung over the water below. The area of the tyre on the log compressed under the increasing force. I concentrated furiously, signalling the centimetres that could bring the truck across or send it, with James and Rob, plunging over the edge. At the centre of the bow no more than a quarter of the wheel rested on wood. The tyre bulged over the edge, squeezed down by the weight of the truck. Like a man hanging onto a cliff edge by his fingertips the truck lay suspended over the drop. Unblinking, with the excluding focus of adrenaline, I beckoned James forward. The truck rolled past halfway, regaining solidity, easing the strident jangling of my nerves.

We decided to stop. The border was still forty kilometres away, impossibly far. With the rain worsening, we pulled over at a village and obtained permission to sleep in their church. As the evening wore on, James too had begun to feel sick, with the malarial symptoms of a headache and chills. He took three Fansidar pills and went to bed. Rob was already asleep. Bronwyn and I decided to start taking Lariam again lest we also contract malaria. The plan to reach Bangui by Friday was shelved. We would extend the visas if we had to.

I chatted to two Liberians who were camped nearby. They were walking to Zimbabwe or South Africa. I told them we had come from there, but not on foot, and admired their bravery. Later on, as I sat writing in my diary, one of them came up to me and handed me an envelope. Inside, written on paper torn from an accounting exercise book, was a note:

> *22-9-93*
> *in-Vilage*
> *R/Z*

> *Tourists American*
> *from S/Africa*
> *in-Vilage*

> *Dear, Tourists.*

> *I'm very sorry of me embaresing, cause our situation is very devicult. we are kindly asking you to please help us, for we are on long journey no lot of food neither money, and there is no car to travel in; so we asken if you can help us with any amount of money or food for our charity.*

> *Sincerally*
> *Georges Kamara*
> *Liberian*

Touched by this letter, and the dignity of their asking, I gave them a large bag of rice, a few packets of dried vegetables and some of the remaining zaire notes we had. We left the next morning at ten thirty, with James and Rob both gravely ill. Derek soon caught up with us. He too was feeling the first symptoms of malaria.

The roads, impossibly, became still worse. The lack of brakes made me cautious, unwilling to risk a recurrence of yesterday's near calamity. I drove at walking pace, in first gear, pumping the brakes long before an obstacle neared. All along its length the road was ripped and broken, its blood leaking from these wounds. The deep scars caught at the wheels, luring us off the road. Descents were worst. I crawled down the hills like a blind man in a new place, carefully feeling the surface below, edging forward slowly, nervously.

"Can't you go a bit faster?" asked James, frustrated.

"No, I don't want to risk an accident," I replied, continuing the ponderous pace. A short while later James leaned forward.

"Right, stop here! I want to drive."

"But you're sick, James!" I protested.

"I don't care. You're driving too bloody slowly! I'm becoming frustrated," he replied, climbing in behind the wheel. James's lack of faith in me cut deep. I felt the never-doubted trunk of his support axed away from under me, leaving me falling into loneliness, vulnerable.

I sat in the back, silent, watching him manoeuvre the truck so much more adeptly and confidently, summoning his will against the clouding bands of his illness. Resolute, angered, he fought the truck and the road, now pumping at the brakes with his foot, or pulling viciously on the lever of the handbrake, now wrestling with the wildly spinning steering wheel, expertly using the truck's speed, guiding it along instantly chosen lines as it plunged and bucked along the back of that tortured road.

James stopped only when the rear tyre punctured, the worst of the passage behind us. Air from the hole blew into my face as I stood in the doorway, strong gusts beating a slowing rhythm as we came to a halt. James clambered down, exhausted by his struggle. The tyre was worn out. Huge chunks of rubber had been ripped from it, and the nylon worn through, exposing the rubber of the tube. Bronwyn and I replaced the tyre, putting on one of the new ones we'd been saving for Europe. We left the ravaged tyre to rot in the overgrown ditch lining the road. I drove on to the border at Ndu.

There we found Derek, freshly showered and eating doughnuts cooked for him by a charming woman dressed in a coloured robe and headscarf. We spent our last zaires around her fire and pot and drove past the customs boom, planning to camp on the banks of the Mbomou River that marks the border between Zaire and the CAR.

"You cannot camp by the river," we were told by a sullen-faced official, a machine-gun slung over his shoulder. "You have to camp here."

"In that case we'll go back down the road. There was a good spot a couple of kilometres back," I replied.

"No, you have passed the control boom. You must camp here."

Arguments and antipathy filled my mind, to be actively suppressed in the face of his uncompromising expression. There was no point in doing anything that might jeopardise our crossing the following morning. The next border post on the river was 150 kilometres west. To get there would mean retracing our path along the road we'd been on. It was better to comply, to accept his power over us. We pitched our tents there, outside the small, crumbling room labelled "Immigration." The half-dozen or so officials who clustered around a fire twenty metres from us were hostile, rebuffing any attempts at conversation and staring stonily towards us as we unpacked. We went to bed early.

As the stars brightened, a deep and steady thudding of drums rose up from the thick air of the jungle into the night. A different beat answered. Back and forth, all through the night, the drumming sounded, primal and resonant, now urgent, now yearning. I lay in my tent, held by it, hearing its echoes in my head. It was ominous in its beauty. Like a heart pounding in excitement or in terror, the drums pulled at my hopes and pushed at my fears.

★

I woke up with a headache, feeling dizzy and weak. Though still tired, James, Rob and Derek were over the worst of their malaria. After the hostility of last night, we were surprised to find ourselves welcomed smiling into the immigration building by the chief immigration officer. The reason soon became apparent. He had seen Derek using our volt meter to test his bike's circuits. The 12V battery the chief used to power his two-way radio was charged by two 6V solar panels, both of which were broken. Our getting through immigration was dependent on fixing them.

"Shit," I said, looking at the two battered panels, "I've got no idea at all about this kind of thing. How about you, Robbie?"

"Even less. Let's take them to James."

James and Derek studied the panels and then set about prising loose their plastic covering, and probing various intersecting copper lines with the two rods of the volt meter. They then rolled up some tin foil, taped it down between two points, and I watched amazed as the red needle rose slowly to the 12V mark.

"I doubt it'll last long at all," laughed Derek, "but I'm sure it'll only pack in once we're over the border."

It was 23rd September. While we were returning his repaired panels to the satisfied chief officer, Rob altered the date stamp lying on the table in the office. All our passports indicated we had left Zaire on the 28th.

"If I can pull a similar stunt on the other side of the river," Rob explained, "we'll have an extra five days to get across the CAR!" A minor official tried half-heartedly to make us pay taxes of $30 for the truck, $10 for the motorbike, and 60,000,000 zaires for each camera. We laughed at him, saying he was mad to think we'd pay such fees on leaving the country.

I was sitting in the truck with Bronwyn, waiting for the other three to return from the customs building a hundred metres away, when I saw them sprinting up the path towards us.

"Quick, start the truck! Let's go! Let's go!" shouted James, our carnet clutched beneath his arm.

"Christ, what's happened?" I asked as he and Rob clambered in.

"We've just had a massive fight with the roads official!" replied James, his eyes alight with excitement. "He tried to get the $65 road tax from us, but we said we'd already paid it at Mambasa."

"He asked for the receipt," Rob continued, "and we said we hadn't been given one. So he got stubborn, saying we had to pay. We could see it was all going nowhere fast, so we made a quick plan in Afrikaans. Derek grabbed his carnet, and James ours, but as we turned to run out this other guy stood in the doorway. Derek just bear-hugged him and hurled him aside, giving me and James the chance to get out. Derek then jumped out the window."

"Oh, Jesus!" I moaned. "What the fuck's going to happen now?"

"Nothing, I tell you. Let's just get going."

Our flight was brief. 300 metres from the customs building lay the Mbomou River. Almost 200 metres wide, its swift-flowing waters barred our way. While we were haggling with the ferryman, the roads official came running down the road, furious. Pointing at us he screamed that we mustn't be allowed to cross as we hadn't paid our tax. He appeared reluctant to approach us directly. After half an hour, during which he glowered at us from a distance, he went back up the road. We approached the ferryman again. His fee had suddenly risen from the fifteen litres of diesel that was standard.

"*Vingt litres*," he said belligerently, "*et dix dollars.*" Twenty litres. And ten dollars.

"What?" cried Derek. "There's no way we're gonna pay that."

Derek and Rob haggled with the ferryman but he remained obdurate, threatening to return to his home. In the end we paid. Going back now was out of the question and the only way forward was on Charon's ferry. Drunk, and revelling in the power he had over us, he folded the money into his shirt pocket. He then demanded cigarettes, which we gave him, and then some pens. Derek was fuming. The ferryman spotted a jersey on one of the seats and wanted it too. Derek grabbed it before he could.

"On the other side! I give you this on the other side!" he shouted, pointing angrily. At last the man seemed satisfied, and we drove the truck and Derek's bike onto the ferry and set off for the far bank. Derek sat in a cold rage. With forty metres to go, Charon approached him for his jersey. Derek held it up to him, and as he came to grab it, shoved him heavily in the chest. Charon's arms flailed wildly as he sought balance, knocking two little boys into the water. He followed in, disappearing over the edge as we drifted in towards the shore. With his left hand Derek had grabbed the ferryman's pocket, ripping it in an attempt to retrieve our ten dollars.

"Right, let's get out of here!" shouted Derek. We leapt into the truck, James behind the wheel. As the ferry touched the soft mud of the bank, he drove the truck forward, forcing the raised ramp down under its weight. Derek rode off, water spraying as his back wheel slid out behind him, spinning in the slick mud. We followed, plunging into the shallow water, our momentum forcing the ferry backwards behind us. The truck bogged down immediately, its wheels spinning helplessly. Water flooded in at the stairwells in front. The rear wheels were completely submerged. An excited crowd had gathered. They watched enthralled as we hurried uphill with the winch cable and tied it around a palm tree. Some of them helped us and were screamed at by Charon who emerged dripping and muddied from the water.

Free of the mud, we reeled the cable back in. The animated babbling of the crowd was silenced by three shrill blasts of a whistle blown by an official who had emerged from amongst them. He stood before us, immaculate in a starched white uniform and hat, his hand raised, palm towards us.

"*Passeports! Passeports!*" he demanded.

"We'll just park on the side of the road," said James, miming this intention, while saying something quite different to Derek in Afrikaans.

James drove the truck to the side, and then accelerated suddenly, heading down the road as the crowd opened up before us. Derek kicked his bike into life and powered after us. The angry blasts of the whistle faded slowly as the truck carried us into the Central African Republic.

Chapter Sixteen

"We've got to go back," I said.

"Forget it," replied James, "there'll be all sorts of shit waiting for us back there."

"But it'll be nothing compared to what we might get later on if we don't. They could easily radio ahead to Bangui, and it's not like we're inconspicuous in this truck."

"Those guys will nail us if we go back," said Rob. "This country's as bad as Zaire. Remember, this is the place where two weeks ago they released every prisoner from the jails, including the ex-president Bokassa, who was in there for cannibalism. He ate fifteen schoolgirls, for God's sake! We've just got to try and get through here as quickly as we can."

"And by now they've probably found out what happened on the Zairean side," James continued, "so they'll have us where they want us."

"We've got to go back! You can't just enter a country, go flying through the border like a bat out of hell, and expect nothing to come of it. It's a serious bloody offence, evading immigration. We'd better go and face the music here."

Somehow I convinced them we should turn back. We followed signs to the immigration offices, which were about a kilometre from the river. We arrived at the same time as Charon. Still dripping wet, and consumed by fury, he climbed off the bicycle he had taken from one of the locals and stormed across to the officials sitting outside, swearing abuse and pointing wildly towards us and the river.

The two men listened to him and then came across to us. They spoke no English and after realising that I could understand French, directed their inquiries toward me. My head throbbed and I felt tired. I wondered what the hell we were doing in such a position, thinking how unnecessary it all was. There was frustration too that I should now be the one to try to remedy matters, when the preceding events had been motivated by others.

The men asked me to come inside, with Charon, so that they could hear both sides of the conflict. We entered the office, a small and sparsely-furnished prefabricated room. The two officials sat across the table, judges in this tribunal. Charon and I sat next to each other on wooden chairs facing them.

"What happened?" one of them asked Charon. He began replying, heatedly, in his native language.

"Stop, stop," he was told. "We must all speak in French. That way no one has an advantage, and any lies can be countered. So what happened?"

Charon's hatred poured out. He told them how we had pushed him into the river, how we'd cheated him by not paying the agreed price. He said he'd nearly drowned, he'd almost been murdered, and he wanted what was rightfully his. He said we were evil.

They turned to me. "And what is your side of the story?"

"Yes, we did throw him into the river," I began, in my broken French. "We're very sorry. My friend became angry because this man asked for twenty litres of diesel and then ten dollars and then pens and then cigarettes and a jersey. More and more things. We had no choice but to give them. My friend just lost his temper."

The officials looked at each other. "Is it true that you asked this price, more than fifteen litres?" one asked Charon. He stared down, and nodded almost imperceptibly. I began to hope things might not be so bad. It seemed that they knew nothing of our tax evasion in Zaire and for some reason Charon didn't mention it at all.

"We are sorry for what we did," I reiterated. "We know what we did was wrong."

"Please call in the person who pushed this man into the river. He must be the one to apologise."

I fetched Derek. I told him he must apologise to the ferryman. He looked horrified. "*Moet ek?*" he asked. "Do I have to?"

"*Ja, doen dit net,*" I replied forcefully. "Yes, just do it."

"I'm sorry I pushed you into the water," said Derek, through clenched teeth. This satisfied the officials and they said he could go. They conferred and turned towards me again. "Good, good. We have now heard both sides of the case. Although there was provocation, it was wrong to settle things in your own way, especially using force. You should take matters like this to the appropriate authority. We have heard you apologise for what happened but we have decided you must pay a small fine as well, a tangible symbol to show that you are sorry."

'Here we go,' I thought. 'It's a kangaroo court after all. This is where they line their pockets. It's just a question of how much we'll be stung for.'

"As admission of your wrongdoing in this case, and as a symbol of your regret for your actions, you must give the ferryman, who became muddied as a result of what you did, a cake of soap."

I had been in the court of Solomon. When Charon refused to accept the soap, furious, they insisted we should not keep it and gave it instead to a grateful woman who was passing by.

*

They stamped our passports and we left. By a stroke of luck their stamp was beginning to perish and the 'S' and 'e' of September had to be traced over in blue ink. Rob would be able to similarly change the 23 of the date in all our passports to 28, giving us the five extra days to cross the country.

*

In the town of Bangassou itself we saw signs pointing to the American Mission Station, and decided to follow them, hoping to find somewhere where we could relax for a couple of days. I was feeling grim and the others were still weak from the malaria.

The missionaries were very hospitable, and said we could camp in the gardens of the station. We set up our tents on the lawns, in the shade of palm trees, hammering the pegs through the thick tropical grass. An elderly woman called Edie brought us a gift of banana cake. Talking to her, we were shocked to discover how expensive even basic items like eggs were. The CAR is still essentially a French colony. Since independence in 1960 its economy has remained dependent on France. Its dictators' self-aggrandising whims have been pandered to with donations from the French government. As a consequence of this the Central African franc (CFA) was yoked to the French franc at a fixed rate of 50:1. We were paying European prices in one of the poorest countries in Africa.

A young missionary couple, the Dannenbergs, invited us into their home for our first proper showers in weeks, and asked us to stay for supper. While John cooked Tomali, a Mexican pie, using imported ingredients stored in huge tins, Paula set the table.

"Should we use big plates or little ones, dear?" she asked in a small voice.

"Mmmm," he pondered. "The little ones will be fine I think."

And later, "Should we eat with forks or spoons, dear?"

"Forks, I think, Paula."

We sat around the table, under signs saying "Home is where the heart is" and "Marriage is the blessed union of two hearts, two souls." John talked about the country and Paula smiled. I escaped to bed as soon as I could.

I was sharing a tent with Rob, as had become a habit. We got into a debate about Christianity. Rob defended his faith as I launched into a tirade against unquestioningly accepting anyone else's beliefs as your own, blasting blind faith, and the self-righteousness that often stalks in its shadow. The altercation ended unresolved, with bad feeling. That night I dreamt I was a bully in a playground, making him cry.

The next day I still felt as though I had a bad dose of flu and gave what help I could as James and Derek disassembled the brake servos and slave and master cylinders and put them back together again. Despite their efforts the brakes remained flat. We spent the rest of the day washing our dirt-ingrained clothes and beating the carpets of the truck's floor, shaking loose the mud that had been ground into their pile.

As thanks for their hospitality, Rob offered to cook that night for the Dannenbergs. He set about preparing a pasta dish. An excellent cook usually, he managed to burn one of the two pots of pasta, but got around this problem by dishing up from the other pot first, and leaving the blackened spaghetti to James and Derek, who sat at the end of the table. After dinner I went to bed while the others stayed to watch a video. They chose *101 Dalmatians* ahead of *Mary Poppins* and *Bambi*.

I awoke the next morning with a vice crushing my eyes and a jackhammer in my head. My pillow and the duvet cover I slept in were sodden. My skin felt clammy and cold, like a dead chicken's.

"I think I've got malaria," I told James. "I'm going to take some Fansidar."

I sat quietly as we headed for Kembe Falls, 130 kilometres away. My discomfort was eased slightly by the joy of being on firm roads once more. The high cost of fuel had forced Derek, ever money-conscious, to put his bike in the back of the truck, so there were five of us in the cab as we moved west. This also cut our costs as he would pay for one fifth of the diesel we bought. The price in the CAR was the equivalent of $1.35 per litre, and of the cheap diesel bought in Kenya and Uganda only a few litres still sloshed around the bottom of the tanks.

We camped next to a flat rock which sloped down to the cascading waters of the falls. The evening air was thick, almost solid with the heat of the day. Illness prevented me from fully appreciating the beauty of the place. After eating the meal Rob and Bronwyn had cooked, I got up.

"I'm still feeling crap," I announced to the others. "I'm going to hit the sack."

"You're not going to shower first?" asked Derek, who was heating water in a large pot over the fire.

"No, I just don't feel up to it."

"I just couldn't do that," he said, "go to bed without showering. I've managed to get a shower every night of the trip so far."

"That's pretty keen," commented Bronwyn. "Not like most men I know. Have you always been like this?"

"Mainly since I came out of the army. When I got back from the border, if my Mom couldn't find me she'd always try the bathroom first. I'd easily spend two or three hours in the bath, getting clean."

The night is dark, covered in cloud. The other tents lie still in their sleep. As his hands move over her, confusion churns her mind. His touch feels gentle, his voice sounds kind. When he is like this, how can she believe the words that she read in his diary? When he is like this, how can he despise her? He is sharing his so beautiful body, so how can it be true? As she clings to him the comfort she takes is rent by the piercing echoes of those words. Impelled by a deeper need, she shuts them from her mind and seeks solace from their very source. She drinks poison because he says it is wine.

I was feeling better, although my liver felt as though I'd been on a two-week drinking binge, a result I assumed of the Fansidar I'd taken. We took two days to reach Bangui, travelling on roads that, although built in the same way as those in Zaire, were kept in good shape by the simple expedient of rain barriers, *Barrières de Pluie*, which prevented vehicles from continuing along the road until several hours after rain had ceased to fall. I had seen similar booms in Zaire, open and rusted, long since ignored as the heavy trucks gouged their anarchic way forward.

At the first barrier we were stopped for three and a half hours. Derek, annoyed by the badgering of small children, started pre-empting them. "*Donnez moi cadeau. Donnez moi cadeau,*" he would say. "Give me a present," at which they either laughed or ran off. But generally we found the atmosphere unfriendly. For the first time since leaving Cape Town, we met with antagonism from people not in authority. As we passed through one village, a group of children threw stones at the truck, screaming angrily at us.

I met a man at the barrier called Charles Hamilton Watson, a Sierra Leonean hitch-hiking the other way. He was headed for South Africa, Namibia or Botswana, anywhere where he could find work on a diamond mine.

"What's it like in Sierra Leone?" I asked.

"It's a weird place. I come from Freetown, the capital. There's a constant tension between the old ways and the new. My father's got forty-two children, twelve by my mother. You can't expect to educate that many kids. So on the one hand you've got people like that, who find it enough just to get their daily bread, and then there are those wanting to get into the Western way of doing things."

"And did you get any formal education?"

"None at all. I've been working since I was fourteen, mainly on diamond mines. The problem is even if you want a simple and traditional way of life you can't have it. The politicians and the military get in the way, always fighting for power, leaving the people to suffer. We had a coup just last year. The new president is twenty-seven and the vice-president nineteen. What kind of a country has a nineteen year old in charge of it?"

"Is that why you left?"

"I'd had enough. I decided to leave one day and got out the next. I didn't even have time to organise a passport."

"So how on earth do you cross the borders?"

"I just tell them I'm an African and should be allowed to go anywhere in Africa. It's been fine up to now."

"Sierra Leone was set up by the British, wasn't it, like Liberia was by the Americans?"

"Yes, and I tell you, although everyone complains about how bad colonisation was, far worse was how quickly the colonisers got out, leaving nothing behind, educating no one to take over. That's what we're paying for now."

We continued to chat as the rain fell softly. Despite having had no formal education, he was obviously highly intelligent, and spoke four languages. Eventually the boom was lifted. As we prepared to set off I asked him one last question. "Are there any pygmies further west?"

"No, there's been too much interbreeding. You only get giant pygmies there."

*

Our wheels rolled over tar for the first time in almost a month 200 kilometres before Bangui. The 350 kilometre stretch leading to the capital from either side is the only tar in all the country's trunk roads. The eastern and western arteries meet at a point ten kilometres before the town, where a permanent immigration post and roadblock is positioned.

"Where's your visa?" I was asked.

"I was told in Nairobi that Greeks don't need visas."

"That's not true. They do. In fact countries of the EEC pay double the normal price. Your visa will cost $40. You can fetch your passport at the administration offices tomorrow."

I watched as the others had their $5 five-day visas stamped. I felt hugely frustrated, hating the officials in Nairobi who had misinformed me. I worried too that my passport had been taken from me.

We camped at the Tourist Welcome Centre where we bought Cokes, breaking the diet of water and tea we'd had since leaving Kampala six weeks before. There were no other campers apart from us. An armed guard stood at the entrance, lounging next to the high barbed wire fence that surrounded the grounds. The atmosphere was quiet, weary.

While we were within it, Zaire had been all-consuming. Faced with the immensity of the journey that still lay ahead, we had had to break it down into smaller sections, focusing on one at a time, to make it less daunting. Our vision in Zaire had been limited to reaching its border intact, our daily activity to the practicalities of forging a way forward. It was only now, outside of it, that we could look ahead again, and look back and realise how much of our energy and will had been drained by its mud and rivers and trees.

We felt stronger for the contest too, competent now, capable. London was a realisable goal. Each obstacle between us and it was surmountable, we knew that. But the thought of having to summon the energy to tackle these obstacles left us deflated. Zaire had gripped our minds, externalising our fears in the intensity of its hold on us. It made our concerns immediate. Now that we were out of its grasp loneliness returned, filtering into the isolation.

"Only 7,238 kilometres left of Africa," remarked James, looking up from the logbook. "We've come 14,700 from Jo'burg, 17,000 from Cape Town. If all goes well we'll get to England in early December."

"That gives us just over two months," I commented. "Plus we've got to get across Europe. That's another few thousand kilometres. We would have to push bloody hard to make it. I reckon we should take it a bit easier and aim for January."

"I definitely want to be back before Christmas so I can spend it at Amsterdamhoek with my family. It'll probably also be my last opportunity to spend quality time with my brothers before I start working. I want to take them hiking in the Drakensberg."

"And I heard from Bridge today that Chris Lovemore's marriage is set for mid-December," added Rob. "I really want to be back for that."

The next morning, while Derek took me to fetch my passport, the others went to check for mail at the post office. I was told it would only be ready tomorrow and returned even more frustrated. When we got back, James and Bronwyn came up to me, their bodies betraying a suppressed excitement, or perhaps an anxiety.

"Guess what?" James asked, attempting to hold a deadpan expression. I wondered what news the post could have brought. Bronwyn's face told me the news wasn't bad. Then I knew. "Sandy's coming back!"

"That's right!" cried Bronwyn. "God, how did you know? There was a telegram waiting for us at the post office. She's arriving here tomorrow, coming via Gabon. I'm so excited!"

"God, she's brave!" James exclaimed. "There was no guarantee we'd get here at all. Or we could have left before she arrived. Or we could even have decided to go through Sudan instead. She'd have been stuck here forever. And Bangui is no place to hang around on your own."

He was right, it was a tip. The resplendent houses of the privileged few, and the two luxury hotels catering to French tourists, were surrounded by the squalor of litter-strewn streets whose dust mixed with sewage in stagnant pools by the roadside. Unpainted houses, packed together, sprouted off the streets and alleys, their tin roofs held down by rocks. Deep trenches in the earth ran parallel to the walls, beneath the roofs' downward slope, dug there by the force of the torrential rains.

The thought of Sandy's return lifted our spirits. I hoped the feeling of jadedness pervading us would pass. The risk Sandy was running by rejoining the trip was more than just the logistical difficulties of finding us in the jungle. Whereas her journey was just beginning, our attention was increasingly being focused on its end.

But for now we were elated, and set about planning our route and schedule, and repairing the truck. We had been warned about a roadblock twenty kilometres out of town where heavy fines would be levied for even minor offences such as a hooter not working. Derek had noticed that our brake lights weren't lighting as we braked. James tried to fix them but found that the pressure switch was broken; he couldn't repair the connection without obtaining a spare. Instead he rigged up the lights to a switch in the cab which could be flicked on and off. Again we tried to tighten the brakes but failed.

The time was used to undo some of the other damages incurred in Zaire. Our table had fallen out somewhere on our last day there, shaken loose from its mooring by the endless jolting of the broken road. Derek and James set about making a new one, using wood bought with the proceeds of a spare cassette player Derek had sold for us.

The next day, after taking me to fetch my passport, Derek drove me to the airport to meet Sandy. She walked across the tarmac wearing a wide straw hat and a very relieved smile at seeing us waiting. We embraced happily, laughing at the daring and chance that brought us together again in such an alien place. While I stayed with half her luggage, Derek drove her back to the camp. When I returned a short while after, it was to a scene of celebration. Bronwyn was talking animatedly about Zaire, her hands chopping and spreading as she spoke, expletives emphasising the wildness of it all. Sandy too had had a difficult time getting to Bangui, and told us of a harrowing night spent at Libreville airport as she waited for her connecting flight. Like before, she came bearing gifts and I was overjoyed to receive almost a dozen birthday cards and letters and a box of biscuits and sweets sent by my family.

"It's so wonderful to be here!" Sandy exclaimed. "It's been such a dark time, but now with Maman's amazing recovery, and being back here, I'm excited again by what lies ahead. I've been reading up all about West Africa. I can't wait to get there."

"You do know we won't be seeing all that much of West Africa, don't you?" asked Rob. "Just Nigeria, really. And Niger. After that we'll be in the desert."

"But I thought the plan was to go around the bulge, via the Ivory Coast, Senegal, Mauritania, and up into Morocco. That's what we discussed in Kenya."

"That was before we knew the Hoggar Route was open again," said James. "From the very first we always said we'd go through Algeria if possible."

Sandy's disappointment was tangible. "But don't worry," James assured her. "Algeria will be well worth it, and we still get to go through Morocco."

"And when do you expect us to arrive in London?"

"Early December, I hope."

"Not January?"

"No. December was always the plan. We only kept January open in case we encountered problems."

"Well, it does seem like I've rejoined a trip that's quite different to what I expected. But it's still wonderful to be here."

★

All eager to leave Bangui behind and continue our adventure, we set off early the next day, leaving Derek to check for any post that might have come in with Sandy's plane and to fetch her passport and mine from the Cameroon embassy. We avoided any hassles at the ten kilometre checkpoint by saying we were going on a day trip to the Boali Falls while waiting for our Cameroon visas. Lying like this was second nature to us now.

A few kilometres out we met an Encounter Overland truck, the first overlanders we'd seen since our second day in Zaire. We told them horror stories about Zaire and received useful advice about routes through Cameroon and Nigeria in return.

"You're bloody lucky Algeria's open again, mate," the driver told me. "Getting west to Senegal is almost impossible, now that it's started raining. We had to ship all the way round to Ghana just to get going. Cost us a bloody fortune. And watch out for that shark ten kays up the road.

He'll jump on you for anything. Took us for $50 for a cracked windscreen."

As always, it was exciting meeting others sharing our journey and as we continued we felt optimistic about the road ahead, happy to be all together again as we aimed our truck west towards the sea and from there to the other wilderness of the Sahara.

Chapter Seventeen

The roadblock consisted of a small hut next to the road. A uniformed man waved us to a halt. He walked up to us. "Papers," he said gruffly. I passed him the photocopies of our passports, carnet and drivers licences. He moved to the front of the truck.

"Indicators. Lights. Hooter." James turned them on. He moved around to the back. "Brakes." I surreptitiously flicked the switch. He remained there a while before walking back, shaking his head sadly.

"I'm afraid you are going to have to pay a fine," he said, in a sorry tone. "Your rear lights are too close together."

"What?"

"Yes, they do not conform to the standards," he said, pointing to a paragraph underlined in red in a French manual of road regulations. "The fine for this is $100." I couldn't properly understand the convoluted French written in the manual, which was at least a thousand pages thick, but it made no difference. There was no way we were going to pay this extortion money.

We waited for ten minutes, hoping to wear him down. The decline in overland traffic seemed to have increased his patience. He sat in his little shack, pretending to read through our papers. Across the road, three soldiers armed with machine-guns lounged beneath a tree. We could have just driven off, abandoning the papers, but it would have meant having to photocopy more. Out of principle, too, we wanted back our stolen goods. James became fed up.

"Right! I'm going to try grab the papers. Paul, drive the truck forward so those soldiers can't see what's going on. Be ready to make a dash for it if needs be."

I moved the truck forward and left it idling. James started talking to the official, waiting for an opportunity. The man sensed James's intent and, picking up the papers, turned to put them into his briefcase. James moved into the shack and held him from behind as he bent over, seizing the papers in both hands. As James tore them from him, the man straightened and turned, launched into a fury. James made for the door. The man lunged at him, grabbing his collar and ripping the buttons off his shirt. James swivelled violently to free himself, knocking the man's glasses flying, grappling his way towards the door. I revved the engine, hoping its noise would drown out the shouts. James came storming out of the hut, like a rugby player surging for the line, the official clinging onto his back like a leech.

"Go, go, go!" he yelled. I accelerated down the road. James grabbed onto the door frame as it passed and was wrenched out of the man's grasp. We drove off, leaving him sprawled in the dust behind us. Caught up in the excitement of anarchy, we drove past two subsequent roadblocks, slowing down and waving before driving off. Sandy watched our hardened behaviour wide-eyed, caught between horror and excitement.

We stopped for breakfast soon after. Derek caught us up, bearing the passports and mail he had collected. He removed his helmet to reveal a shaven head. With his thick beard below it made him look like a mercenary.

"What happened at the roadblock?" I asked him.

"Well I got there and they stopped me, so I asked 'Have you seen my friends in the big yellow truck?' I took off my helmet as I asked this. The guy took one look at me and pointed down the road. 'They went that way,' he said!"

*

Derek pushed his bike into the back again and we drove almost 400 kilometres before we were stopped at a *Barrière de Pluie*. We decided to camp there for the night. Other than the rear-view mirrors of the truck and those on Derek's bike, we had no mirrors with us. Being so far out of what we knew as society, we had become unselfconscious. It was this, and something of camaraderie too, that got James and me to shave our heads in the convict style Derek had adopted. With a Captain Haddock beard and nearly bald head I looked like a psychopath. My own mother failed to recognise me in the photographs we took that afternoon.

Rob resisted the pressure to conform. "I'll be seeing Bridge again in just over two months' time," he said, "and I don't think it'll have grown back properly by then."

The rain continued to fall lightly as we proceeded. We were stopped five times at rain barriers but had only short waits. It seemed that a careful bribe dilated the barrier officials' sense of time. At all five barriers the boom was lifted after a local driver engaged the official in earnest conversation out of sight. We drove through in the wake of these trucks, despite the pouring rain. We became sick of the endless roadblocks, with policemen waving at us to slow down. More often than not we just drove past, pretending we didn't understand.

In the evening we came to another rain barrier. The official there was dressed in a bright blue and yellow floral shirt. He asked for our papers and we asked for his. We then began abusing him, laughing as we told him he looked like he should be selling ice creams on the beach. The poor man looked hurt. He was just trying to do his job and we softened. The endless hassle we were receiving was making us lose our fellow feeling.

While rotating the wheels that evening, James noticed that another leaf spring had snapped. We'd fix it while resting in Cameroon. I was still not fully recovered from my illness. I tired rapidly come evening and was looking forward to relaxing on the beach for a few days, to a respite from our nomadic lifestyle. Apart from the three nights in Bangui, we had not camped in any one place for more than two days since leaving Nairobi. Like a plant that is continually uprooted and replanted, never being allowed to settle, I felt the flow of life in me being staunched.

Rob doctored our passports. We'd received another stamp as we entered Bangui on 27th. He crudely superimposed an 8 over the 7, using our printing kit, and altered the 23 of the entry stamp to 28 as well. Our fraud remained undetected, and we crossed into Cameroon on 2nd October, 1993, my twenty-fourth birthday. The sun blazed all day and we stopped to swim in the rivers we crossed, leaping in from the bridges. The roads were worse than in the CAR, and we followed a detour recommended by the driver of the Encounter Overland truck. It took us to a river.

The ferry was on the other side, loading up passengers, a group of women and two men, one pushing a bicycle. The women talked amongst themselves, their clothes, bright reds and yellows and oranges, standing out against the rainforest behind. The sounds of their language were unfamiliar. I wondered what other, hidden, differences their lives held, what rites of circumcision, so prevalent in this part of Africa, what religious beliefs.

As the ferry docked, its passengers stepped off and I drove the truck on. The method of propulsion for the ferry was ingenious. A thick hawser spanned the river, anchored at either end. The ferry was attached to it by a smaller cable. All power came from the river itself. While a series of underwater rudders angled the ferry forward, the inertia provided by the hawser kept it from moving downstream. As it glided across the river, the only sound came from the occasional creaking of the cable, and water breaking against the bow. James and Derek took off their clothes and dived in, to be towed across, hanging onto two ropes that trailed in the ferry's wake.

We camped that night in a soccer field. The moon was full and fireflies winked all around us as we set up our table outside. James arranged some flowers in a milk powder tin and placed them on the centre of the table while Rob cooked a special dinner for me, using the triangular tin of Colcom ham we'd hoarded since Zimbabwe. I was feeling much stronger, and shaved my beard off in celebration of this return to myself. Catalysed by Sandy's return, our enthusiasm was coming back.

The road improved after Abong-Mbang, a nondescript town due east of Yaoundé, which consisted of a few brightly painted shops along the main road, a couple of small churches and an airfield. We had moved back into the jungle again. It thrived on either side, dense and shadowed, giving Sandy an idea of what we'd passed through in Zaire. But it did not have the same intensity of character here. The road, with its potholed but unravaged surface and edges sloping evenly away on either side, held the jungle in check, taming it. We no longer felt the same sense of threat we had in the encroaching fastness of Zaire.

Again we stopped at all the large rivers we crossed, to escape the heat, leaping from their bridges into the water. We came to seven rain barriers which we passed after varied waits. At one we had to part with half a bottle of whiskey. A bridge that was being repaired had a weight restriction of three tons and we had a hard time convincing the official that this was all our seven ton truck weighed. We crossed easily, the bridge offering no peril compared to the tightrope crossings of Zaire.

Shortly afterwards Bronwyn noticed Derek's bike parked outside a bar in a village. We found him inside, with over fifty other people who were crammed into the small room, staring raptly at a flickering television set. Cameroon was playing Zimbabwe in a World Cup qualifying match, and leading 3–1. The mood was joyous and people shifted up smiling to make room for us to sit. A short documentary on Roger Milla followed, to cries of adulation. We left in high spirits, with the words of Papa Wemba's song to this people's hero echoing in our heads.

Yaoundé is an attractive city, set amid rolling hills. The traffic system, French-inspired with huge traffic circles, is diabolical. For some reason right of way is given to vehicles entering the circle, causing intense congestion. We camped at the Foyer International, run by the Presbyterian mission. The only other person camping there was a young white Zimbabwean called Dion, who said he was in political exile after being ousted for supporting Edward Tekere's opposition party. He stressed to us the political motivation behind his undirected life in the charity of the mission.

The next morning Derek took Sandy's passport to the Nigerian embassy for a visa, refusing to leave until it was granted. While waiting for him, we visited the post office. There were seven letters waiting for us at the *poste restante* counter. As we were told to pay CFA 200 – almost a dollar – per letter, we stole them.

Coming out of the post office, we noticed a Land Cruiser parked up the road. The sand ladders strapped to its side identified it as an overland vehicle, and we went across to chat to its occupants. The couple sitting inside were Dutch and had come south along the Hoggar Route two months ago.

"Algeria is okay," Michael told us, "but Niger is full of Tuareg bandits. We were driving from Agadez to Tanout when these two cars came up on either side of us, filled with men carrying machine-guns. They put a gun to my head and forced us out the car. Thank God I didn't panic or else I'd have been shot like that German woman two weeks before."

"So why didn't they take your vehicle?" I asked.

"They would have, but for some reason their chief intervened. They were using our car to ram-start one of theirs when he arrived. He's an educated man and after he spoke to us a bit ordered them to return the vehicle, and the equipment that had been stolen from it. I don't know why. We were very lucky."

"We'll be doing the Hoggar Route in a few weeks."

"I wouldn't go back there. But if you do go, go via Tahoua and not Zinder. If I were you I'd seriously consider a different route. Niger's out of control."

This news soured our excitement. As we drove towards Douala we debated our options.

"I reckon we go for it," said James. "We'll just be careful."

"There's not much care we can take," I pointed out. "If Land Cruisers come chasing after us we're not going to outrun them. What about heading west to Dakar?"

Rob sat quietly. He had become set on reaching London in the first week of December. This news about the Hoggar Route, the quickest way north, depressed him. "We must go north," he said, subdued. "It'll take too long going west. From what that guy said just outside Bangui the roads west have been washed away. If we don't go north, or if we decide it's too dangerous, I'll think about flying out to Spain."

"Don't hassle, Rob, we'll get through," encouraged James. "The worst that seems to happen if you don't panic is that they steal your vehicle. And what self-respecting bandit is going to want this old thing? Also, they crossed two months ago. Things could easily have changed by now."

"Well I don't mind which way we go," Bronwyn opined. "So long as I get to see the desert. How do you feel, Sandy?"

"The more I get to see of Africa the better. It's come as quite a shock that we'll be arriving in London so soon, you know, December instead of January. For me the travelling's far more valuable than the arriving. I'd hate us to blaze past fascinating places just so that we can arrive in London at some arbitrarily decided date."

Leaving Yaoundé, we headed west, passing through Douala, Cameroon's largest city, an industrialised, garbage-strewn place where we got caught in a dense traffic jam. The roads leading into the town were excellent, maintained with toll funds. Police roadblocks attempted to extract further tolls every ten kilometres or so. By now we were sick to death of stopping to humour avaricious officials, and just drove past, ignoring their waving arms.

We continued to Mile 6 Beach, near Limbe. Driving down a steep sand road we saw, shimmering below us, the blue waters of the Atlantic. We had now crossed the width of the continent twice, and were two thirds of the way up its length. The campsite was beautiful. We pitched our tents on lawns lying next to the beach. Ancient figs soared two hundred feet into the air above us. Palms rustled quietly in the breeze that blew down from Mount Cameroon towering behind us. Colobus monkeys swung and chattered in the trees, their long tails hanging stiffly below them. We decided to stay for four days, and enjoy a sorely needed rest.

Two couples arrived the following day. The had both come down through the desert, in wildly contrasting vehicles. Gregor and Nadine, two East Germans, were in a huge military truck they'd bought for $1,200 after the unification of Germany. They had travelled through Mauritania and Mali. The truck was equipped for chemical warfare, had a radiation-proof shell, a welding kit, and thick, bulletproof tyres that could be inflated by flicking a switch in the cab.

Dwarfed by this ochre leviathan was a battered old Citroen 2CV named Herbert, swathed in brightly-coloured ethnic designs. It had been driven down through Algeria by two Swiss, Uris and Sarah. Their little car had thin biscuit wheels, and a 600cc engine, smaller than Derek's bike's. I was amazed that it had made it through the desert. Uris explained that whenever they got stuck they could just lift it up and move it.

We spent our first day at Limbe swimming, writing letters, and playing the inevitable games of beach cricket. On the following day we began the repairs and maintenance on the truck. Leaves had snapped in both sets of springs in front, and all the oil and filters needed to be changed. Sandy was eager to break down the gender-stereotyping into which we had fallen, and offered to help James replace the broken leaves. I was only too happy to be relieved of this difficult and dirty task. Sandy put on one of the overalls, removed one of the shackle pins as James hammered it out, had her photo taken, and began to realise how unpleasant the life of a grease monkey is. So I ended up back under the truck as James's helper.

As ever, we seemed to break as much as we repaired. Tightening the nuts on top of the right tractor joint, James snapped one of the studs. To remove it, we had to dissect the entire wheel mechanism. It was while doing this that we noticed that the kingpin bearing was broken. A familiar despair welled up in me. I though we might have to get a replacement mailed in. Derek agreed reluctantly to return to Douala to search for a new bearing. He returned shortly, smiling broadly as he had been able to find one in Limbe, just down the road.

To our immense relief we at last managed to fix the brakes. There had been nothing fundamentally wrong. We just hadn't been setting the rear linings properly.

★

The ten of us were sitting around the campfire, joining in the chorus while Bronwyn played her guitar and sang, the Maori words befitting the atmosphere of this African beach. We chatted easily with the other travellers, exchanging anecdotes about our lives on the trip and before. They had all journeyed extensively in North Africa, and managed to allay our fears about driving along the Hoggar Route.

James and Sandy stood up and made for their tent. The others had already gone to sleep, leaving Bronwyn and me sitting next to the campfire.

"He's actually a tragic figure," she said, a trace of bitterness in her voice.

"In what way?"

"He's so aloof, so remote."

"James? I've always thought of him as a passionate person, more concerned than aloof."

"Only in a superficial way. Emotionally he won't allow anyone to get close to him. He's like a lone wolf, a Steppenwolf."

"He has got a powerful intellect, I know, and that can often hold people back from opening up emotionally. But I do think James is able to confront himself, to admit to failings, and open up in that way."

"I can't see it. He always wants to be in the right, in control. It's like my opinions don't count for anything. He just ignores me. Whatever I say is worthless."

"I suppose our different perspectives is largely because his relationships with women are so different to those with men. I've always said I would never go out with him if I were a woman. He needs to dominate women. In his relationships he can be viciously critical, putting his partners down – to elevate himself I suppose. It must stem from an inner insecurity. But he's aware of this, I know. And he's got so many other wonderful qualities that outweigh his being domineering at times."

"That's easy for you to say. You've never been directly affected. Just imagine how those women felt! I don't think you realise just how destructive that kind of criticism can be."

"I suppose it must be especially difficult for someone going out with someone like that. But in your case the thing is not to take it too personally, Bronwyn. He'll only affect you if you let him. Just ignore it. Don't let it bother you."

We went to sleep for the night. I felt better for the conversation, hopeful that it was the beginning of a closer friendship between us, to replace the cordial but distant mis-communication that marked our relationship. The intensity of Bronwyn's antipathy towards James surprised me. More like someone jilted than ignored. Only months later would I know.

*

Fighting the lethargy our stay there had induced, we prepared to leave Mile 6 Beach. We had all been jogging in the mornings, and felt fit and rested, ready for the next leg. We wished the other travellers luck, swapped addresses and set off north toward Nigeria. We were forced to stop soon after to examine a shake that had developed. It didn't take long to discover that we'd forgotten to tighten the wheel nuts on the left rear wheel. With a potential calamity averted, we continued, along roads cratered with potholes.

I'm sitting in the rear of the cab. Music is playing and the others are talking over it. Suddenly my heart loses its rhythm. It drums quickly, then seems to jerk and kick, like the heels of someone hanged. A minute goes by and still it spasms and flutters. Dread floods me, pumped by the staccato beating of my failing heart. My chest constricts under the python squeeze of fear. No one notices the violence inside me. I cannot speak. The suddenness and uncertainty lock me in. Slowly the rhythm regains its regularity. I breathe in deep, bracing for a recurrence. My heart keeps its metronome beat.

How do you convey the fright of such a thing? As a child I was once washed out to sea and struggled to swim, exhausted, to the shore. With firm land underfoot, my story seemed so alien, improbable, that I could only mention it in an offhand way. Like then, I now found it hard to express where I had just been. I interrupted the conversation, hesitantly.

"Uh, I've just had some kind of weird heart palpitation. It was fluttering inside my chest completely out of rhythm."

"How long did it last?" asked James.

"It's hard to say. About a minute and a half I think."

"And how do you feel now?"

"A bit shaky. And my chest feels tight. God, what do you think it could have been? It can't have been some kind of heart attack, could it?"

"No, no, I'm sure it wasn't. You might have strained it a bit though, with all that jogging after the flu you had."

We drove on. I looked fine, and felt okay too, so the experience was set aside as an oddity. I tried not to dwell on it, but that arrhythmic beat still echoed in my head, like a raven struggling in a cage, croaking my mortality.

Chapter Eighteen

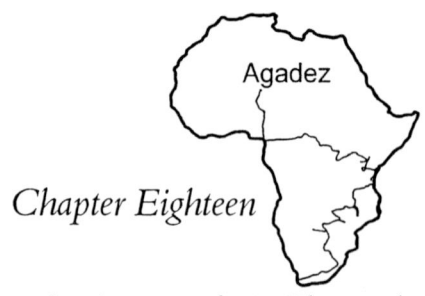

We camped that evening in a gravel pit. The croaking of hundreds of courting frogs filled the air. Mist hung thickly over the jungle-covered hills sloping up from the road. A river flowed past nearby, forty metres wide. Across it stretched a footbridge made entirely of lianas, the vines woven and knotted together into the shape of the hull of a boat. Seven thick skeins ran across the river. Perpendicular to these were looped hundreds of thinner strands, holding it together. Rob and Derek walked to the middle for a photograph. From below they looked like insects trapped in a giant spider's web.

I met an Italian man, an engineer who was living in prefab housing down the road. He said he was constructing a permanent road through the valley a few miles on. I could understand the need for a proper road as the surface had become more ravaged and was beginning to resemble the trenches of Zaire. But his description in no way prepared me for what we saw.

We rounded a corner. There before us, arcing its way through the folds of the valley, on massive concrete stilts five metres wide and thirty metres high, was a magnificent, two-lane concrete highway. Like a vision from a fantasy it floated above us, stretching onward for eight kilometres, rising and curving gracefully up towards the neck of the valley where it disappeared into the lowering mist. Below it crawled the old road, twisting and contorting its way uphill. For a hundred kilometres on either side of this aerial highway the road lay rutted and broken. It soared surreally above the jungle, enigmatic and sublime.

Because the flyover was not yet ready for heavy vehicles, we had to take the old road up, watching Derek as he cruised up effortlessly on his bike. We drove for another clanking, jarring hundred kilometres before stopping for the night beside a large river, thirty-five kilometres south of the Nigerian border.

Again come evening I was heavy with lethargy. My chest felt tight, like I was running uphill. The strangeness of my symptoms worried me, evoking sudden clenches of fear as I considered the worst. My heart might be weakened. I began to withdraw into a kind of nervous self-regard, preoccupied by this sudden and possibly terrible change in me. I sat quietly, my hand over my heart, seeking to find in its steady but occasionally hiccuping beat clues to dispel the dark uncertainty that was clouding in.

Floating down the river, in a busy stream of wooden boats rigged with outboard motors, were barrels upon barrels of fuel smuggled in from Nigeria. Men sat amidst their contraband, drifting slowly to the bank beneath the bridge where they would transfer it onto trucks. Shotguns lay menacingly in the bows.

James and Sandy went exploring together and returned to tell us of some natural pools in a stream leading down to the river. I took the soap from them and went to bathe in the lukewarm water. A little later, near to the pools, Derek found eight drums of smuggled petrol stashed away nearby. He siphoned five litres from each drum, filling his two twenty litre jerrycans, saying it was stolen anyway. The diesel that was there we left where it was.

Crickets call out to each other in the darkness outside the tent which they are sharing. The energy of Africa, of its jungle heart, courses in her, diffusing into her blood from the anarchic air she has breathed since her return. The world is more primal here, and she is stirred by the call that it makes. Echoing this, he touches her, an offer. She gives herself over to him, abandoning herself to attraction, to the liberation of the moment. Past and future cease, annulled by the reckless joy of what she has now.

They move together. After, he holds her, like a swimmer onto flotsam in a shipwrecked sea, seeking to fill the void where he is solitary. The sounds have carried, however. Another's ears have heard.

We had been told about a group of bikers who were crossing from Johannesburg to Hamburg. Organised by Tours for Africa, twenty-six of them had left South Africa five weeks after us, heading north through Zimbabwe and Zambia into Zaire. Equipped with powerful BMW bikes and three back-up trucks, they planned to cross Africa in six weeks. At Ekok, the last town in Cameroon before the Nigerian border we found, and were aided by, signs of their passing. They had gone through only two weeks before, more than a month behind schedule. A man came up to me, Rob and Derek.

"Where are you from?" he asked.

"South Africa," I replied.

"You want to change money? Naira for dollars?"

We were wary, thinking it might be a trap. He sensed our hesitancy. "You can trust me," he said. "Your friends did good business with me. Wait here, I'll show you." He brought back a note book. Dated fifteen days before was the entry "*Hierdie ou is vertroubaar. Ek het 'n goeie koors gekry.*" This guy is trustworthy. I got an excellent rate. We changed $500 at 40:1, double the official rate, as we later discovered.

"Where are the other two?" asked Rob as we returned to the truck.

"They've gone for a walk," replied Bronwyn.

"I think it's more than just walks they've been going on lately," insinuated Rob. Brownyn, staring at him, blanched, her lips pressed tense together.

"What makes you say that?" I asked.

"Just some nocturnal sounds I heard."

"Ah, I can't believe it. You must have been mistaken. If it is true, whatever reason could they have for keeping it hidden?"

★

The Nigerian border officials were the friendliest we met. One even brought us six Cokes as we sat waiting in the dripping heat. It was also the only border we'd come to where as South Africans we couldn't have bought our visas at the border if we'd arrived without. Nigeria immediately seemed solid and ordered after the disarray of Central Africa. There were even good tar roads ahead, spreading like a net across the country.

We soon realised that this appearance of order was only a thin skin stretched tight over an expanding chaos. The service stations of the country, the world's fifth largest oil producer, had hardly a drop of petrol or diesel to sell. The official price for diesel was 55 kobo – just over $0.01 – a litre, and it had all been bought by black marketeers. The stations that did have fuel were surrounded by mile-long queues of cars and trucks waiting patiently to be filled. Unwilling to join the queues, we bought diesel from a black market barrel on the side of the road, at the extortionate price of 1.5 naira per litre, about $0.05.

The cheap price of fuel meant that cars cost next to nothing to run. As a result the roads were filled with decrepit vehicles, mostly ancient Peugeots, that should long since have been consigned to the scrap heap. These cars would crawl along at thirty kilometres per hour. We watched as the infuriated drivers of faster cars took unbelievable risks to overtake them. Again and again cars were forced off the road to avoid a head-on collision as these drivers sped down the left-hand side, hooters blaring and lights flashing. We passed a bloody accident. A minibus had smashed into a mangled Peugeot. The minibus lay on its roof, its windows shattered. Two bodies lay under blankets next to the road. Drivers slowed to look, and then accelerated again to resume their deadly game of chicken.

We stopped at an outdoor roadside restaurant for supper where we had curry and rice, fried yam and Guinness for under $0.60. Local men began pestering Bronwyn and Sandy, but stopped when Rob and James said they were their husbands.

I gaze up at the walls of the tent. Translucent, they glow blue in the glare of the morning sun. The pillow beneath me is sodden. My skin is clammy and I can smell the now familiar odour of my illness, dank and cloying. My head throbs and I clamber out of my wet bedsheet, anxious to escape the sticky, plastic, used heat inside the tent and wash way the decaying smell that coats me. I tug down on the worn zips of the gauze tent door and crawl outside. Showering, I feel despair, the loneliness of illness. I want it to end now, to be well again.

"I need to see a doctor," I said in the cab as we set off again. "I need to know what's wrong with me."

"Okay, we'll find somewhere in Jos," replied James. "We'll get there in about two hours."

Entering Jos, a major town high up on the Jos Plateau in central Nigeria, we looked for signs indicating a hospital. I ended up at the Emdee Medical Centre, a quiet private clinic.

"Well, your lungs sound fine," said the doctor, listening through his stethoscope. "And your heart too." He tightened a cuff over my upper arm. "Hmmm. Blood pressure's fine too. Wait in reception for the blood tests to come back and we'll see what they have to say."

I waited for half an hour, wondering what could be inducing these strange sweats and the constant tightness in my chest. The doctor called me back into his office. "Well it's not malaria. And your white blood cell count is normal. There's no infection. Quite what is causing this tightness in your chest it's hard to tell. You're driving a big truck you say? It's possible you've strained some muscles in your chest while driving. I wouldn't worry about it too much."

I left the centre with my mind uneased. But despite the continued uncertainty about my illness, I was glad it was not malaria. The unconscious thought that I might have to take Fansidar, and suffer again the toxicity I had felt after the last time, had left me unwilling even to consider that I might have it.

As we drove north the jungle thinned rapidly. The countryside began to look remarkably similar to Zimbabwe's. Huge granite hills rose up out of flat expanses of veld, thick sheets of rock peeling off under the insidious force of water and plants. Baobabs stood squat and lonely. We camped in the bush, under the lee of a domed granite kopje. As had become customary, Derek had done all the food purchasing and he cooked a vegetable stew using an array of ingredients he'd bought at the ample roadside markets.

It is need that impels her back to him, despite what she has heard. She chooses not to think of that, to believe instead the message of his hands, clinging to the acceptance they offer. So far from love, she has made him into all she lacks. But it is harder now to quell the doubts that scream 'No' in her head, to ignore the gargoyle hands straining to flip her deep love into hate.

I awoke the next day cold and clammy after another night of sweating. I felt too weak to join the others as they scaled the kopje for the view it would offer across the expansive green and brown plains, and sat by myself, browning toast over the fire. After breakfast we set off for Yankari Game Reserve, which Rob had spotted on the map. We planned to spend a couple of days there relaxing at Wikki Warm Springs.

I sit in the back of the cab, gazing at nothing, feeling the weakness inside me. I do not have malaria. Could it be that I have contracted some rare tropical disease? The tightness in my chest, a dull ache centring over my heart, gives birth in me to the fear that my heart might have been riddled by some virus, the palpitations a mere portent of worse to come. For the first time in my life I confront my own mortality. I could be going to die. Fear and self pity swirl in me, and I mourn for what I might never do, for books unwritten and children unborn.

I do not speak of this to the others. For there is in me too the thought that my illness might just be my collapsing under the stress, a psychosomatic manifestation of the weakness I have felt where others have been tough. It might be that my condition is nervous. Where others exalted, I quailed, as we tussled with guards, or sped past roadblocks. The struggle through the jungle, and the endless jostling and bouncing, the pitching of camp only to strike it the next day, have left me exhausted. What if these symptoms are just my will buckling under these accumulated layers of stress?

On the seventy kilometre drive through the park to the main camp we saw only four guinea fowl. What other wildlife lived there remained hidden behind its long brown grasses. The camp was the perfect place to relax. Apart from my mystery ailment, Bronwyn and Rob were both suffering from diarrhoea and Sandy had sores on her legs that wouldn't heal. She too had been taking Lariam. After having covered the 1,300 kilometres from the Atlantic in six days we all felt in need of a break. We booked the six of us into a bungalow, at a cost of only $7.50 per night, and walked down to the spring.

The spring emerged from beneath a vertical sandstone cliff face into a pool whose floor was of pure white sand. The water was a brilliant turquoise blue, and at a constant temperature of 31.1 degrees. Groves of palms hung over us as we floated idly in the waist-deep water.

I felt capable of nothing more than walking slowly down the concrete paths to the pools, and spent most of the time lying in bed, stultified. The fan whirled slowly above me, gusting flies off their course. With its ties to my mind stretched thin by its own weakness, my body lay there, sweating, inert. My mind was crippled to other thoughts by the not knowing, as I wondered endlessly what it could be that had induced this dragging lethargy.

Rob kept us well fed, with meals of steak, chips, salad and spinach in cream sauce, and huge fry-up breakfasts. Two days later, as we prepared to leave Yankari, we all felt healthier, and lighter in spirit. We would have stayed longer, were it not for the growing momentum impelling us north. James, and Rob especially, had become determined to reach England in the first week of December and began to chivvy us forwards to ensure we met this goal.

"It's 152 days since we left Jo'burg," Rob was telling me as we packed the truck. "Just over three quarters of the trip done."

The ancient city of Kano, the largest city in northern Nigeria, rose up out of the dry scrub we had been driving through. The late afternoon heat filled the cab. An orange sun hung torpid over the horizon, shining weakly through the haze of dust blown south by the desert winds. It was a busy place. Small scooter taxis buzzed everywhere, ferrying people along the dusty streets past mosques and markets, and beneath the turrets and arches of the surrounding city wall, ten centuries old.

The markets were vast, sprawling villages of shops. Dirty water seeped slowly down the alleyways, which were filled with the babble of voices hawking their wares. From within mud rooms along the maze of streets merchants were selling carpets, jewellery, spices, metalwork, furniture and clothing. They approached us excitedly, pointing out their goods, urging us to buy. With dusk setting in, we decided to find somewhere to camp, and return to the markets the next day.

A sign led us to the Torono Guest House, a comfortable hotel. We asked the Lebanese couple who were running it if we could camp in their grounds. They accepted us as their first overland campers and said we could make use of the hotel's extensive facilities. Derek was feeling the symptoms of malaria again and took three Fansidar and went to bed early. He woke the next day feeling a bit weak but over the worst.

After Rob challenged the tennis coach there to a match, which he lost, much to his chagrin, Derek and Rob played a game of doubles against James and Sandy. This, and swimming in the pool, returned us to our pasts. For the first time in months it felt like we could have been back home. In the hours swimming or playing tennis we were able to slip the grasp of the exotic and relax in the arms of the familiar.

Preoccupied with the weakness I felt within me, I was unable to enjoy the place. The disappointment of each morning, as I awoke hoping to feel better, my chest loosened, my body invigorated, and found instead the same tightness, the same weariness, or even worse, sopping bedsheets and a clammy skin, nurtured in me a quiet misery. It required an effort to rise above the dragging weights of depression and doubt, to engage in conversations and chores.

More than anything, I wanted to know what was wrong. While the others went into Kano to organise our Niger visas, look for spare parts and do some curio shopping, I sought out a second medical diagnosis. A doctor at the main hospital, where I waited for three hours, said I had high blood pressure and gave me some pills. As it hadn't been high three days before, I went to a private clinic for another opinion. There I found a doctor I could trust. Patient and affable, he told me about his time spent training in England as he listened to my heart and performed an ECG.

"Your heart's fine now," he said. "You might have had a viral infection that affected it but it's okay now. That tightness in your chest is probably just an inflammation of the membrane between the ribs. It'll ease soon enough."

"And the strange palpitations I had? What could those have been?"

"These can happen under stress. But as the ECG shows, there's nothing at all wrong with your heart. It's beating quite rhythmically."

I felt hugely relieved. "Thank you, doctor," I said, buttoning my shirt. "That's wonderful news. How much do I owe you, by the way?"

"No, no, you needn't pay. You're a guest in my country. Send me a postcard from England when you get there."

I left with my mind assuaged by his confidence. I wasn't going to die. It must just be stress keeping me from recovering fully, but I would be okay again soon enough. In fact, by the time I rejoined the others I thought I was beginning to feel better already.

Bronwyn and Sandy were wearing light-coloured muslin vests and pants they'd had made for the desert ahead.

"So what do you think of our new clobber?" asked Bronwyn.

"Very fetching," replied Rob. "Although I can see a glimpse of an ankle. And as for those vests, you'll drive any hot-blooded Arab mad with lust."

"They're more to keep off the sun than the attentions of men," said Sandy. "I'll probably save them for the desert itself, and wear shorts in the towns. As a matter of principle. I completely disagree with having to sign obedience to the whims of an oppressive patriarchal culture."

"So you think you've got the right to act entirely as you like in a foreign culture?" James interrogated her.

"Yes. So long as I'm not actively harming anyone else. If an Islamic woman wishes to wear her veil in Cape Town I'm not going to stop her. I feel I'm entitled to act according to my culture, as she is to hers."

"That's all very noble," James returned, "but totally impractical. People in Algeria aren't going to be as open-minded as you. Moreover, they'll interpret your actions differently to you. Whereas you'll perceive yourself as merely wearing shorts, they'll see you as a slut, as we would a woman flashing her boobs in the street. It's terrible, I know, but what good will it do us enticing conflict?"

"The more women who do it," ventured Bronwyn, "the more people will become accustomed to it."

"I just want to get through as quickly as possible," said Rob, "so try not to burn too many bras and end up in jail or something. I won't be bailing you out. You should rather get one of these things, like me," he continued, pulling over his head a bright blue flowing kaftan and robe. "Only $20 in the end, after about two hours of haggling. But I'm so chuffed with it. I'm going to wear it all the time when I get back. It was a bit hard to spend that much after forking out for the Niger visas. Fifty bucks! I couldn't believe it. The book said they should have been only $5."

"We thought they were trying a con, so we phoned the embassy in Lagos," Derek continued, "but they said it has just been increased to $50."

"So we had to pay. Derek was keen to run the border but somehow I managed to convince him to cough up the money instead."

James had been unable to find the spare springs, grease and tyre pressure gauges we wanted for the desert crossing. We'd have to do without. Derek had been far luckier. He'd needed to replace his tyres, chain and sprocket, and had bought them all for an absurdly cheap price.

"The sprocket wasn't quite the right make," he told me. "I had to machine it to get it to fit. There were tons of bike spares at this shop, all left by those South African bikers. Evidently they arrived here three weeks ago and decided to fly out to Hamburg."

This news that this earlier group had abandoned their trip somehow gave me greater resolve to complete ours. With only the desert now lying between us and the Mediterranean, we had to cross. The measure of pride outweighed that of anxiety in the scales of my mind.

While at the Torono Guest House we had all made calls home. Bronwyn had left messages for her two closest friends to phone or fax her back. By the time we were ready to leave, none of them had replied.

"Don't worry, Bron," said Rob, trying to console her. "You know how bad phones are in Africa. They probably couldn't get through. Or maybe they're away and didn't get the messages."

But Bronwyn, who had staked so much hope on this contact with home, suffered heavily under the isolation she felt. As we drew away from Kano, aiming for Niger, she sat in the rear of the cab saying nothing.

After camping the night in a quarry just outside Funtua, 150 kilometres west of Kano, we drove north to the border at Illela. The Nigerian immigration officials told us we were the first South Africans they'd ever met.

★

Rob had to stand on a chair to extend the red line of our route up the map painted on the side of the truck. Whereas to the east it meandered and curved, it now shot upwards, straight, undeviating, like an arrow loosed at the roof of the continent outlined thickly above it. The force behind the bow had come increasingly from Rob. If we were to reach London by the deadlines he and James had imposed, we had less than six weeks to cross the Sahara, the Mediterranean and Europe. Sandy, her trip only three weeks old, was being swept along by the momentum of their will.

I looked at the thin red line set against the expanse of yellow. Yes, we were crossing Africa, but there remained broad swathes of space untouched, the many-thousand mile expanses on either side of the line that held the myriad forests and deserts, the people and cultures, passed unseen. The vastness of the continent dominated the path of our journey across it.

There were two major security reasons why the Tours for Africa bikers had flown out from Kano. The first lay in Niger where bandits, mostly Tuareg Bedouins, were reported to be hijacking travellers, taking their vehicles and possessions and leaving them stranded in the desert.

The second lay in Algeria. In December 1991 the government had cancelled the elections they saw they were losing to the Islamic fundamentalist party, the FIS. Since then the FIS had engaged in an active terrorist campaign, aimed at destabilising the country. Their targets were mainly foreigners with links to France, but had become more indiscriminate. The BBC World Service had begun more frequently to report on the killing of tourists visiting Algeria. French nuns had been murdered in a retreat, as had Italian sailors on a ship docked in the harbour and academics at the universities.

We discovered that convoys left Tahoua, the largest town near the southern border, for Agadez and Arlit, the two major towns to the north, fairly regularly, guiding traffic through the worst of bandit territory. We decided to be cautious and join the convoy at Tahoua. Driving north, the influence of Islam was immediately more apparent than it had been in Nigeria. The mud houses, square and flat-roofed, were like small fortresses, surrounded by low walls with squat towers at the corners. The walls kept the women within in purdah, out of sight from strangers. The few women we did see were heavily veiled.

The terrain began to change too, drying rapidly as we entered the parched regions of the Sahel, the thousand mile expanse of semi-desert on the southern border of the Sahara. The road groped its way across plains of hard, red sand broken by stony outcroppings. Camels loped over the baked mud of the wadis, carrying huge burdens, their gangly legs, platelike feet and prehensile lips making them an ungainly sight. Men sat astride the camels, their faces masked by turbans. Long curved swords lay sheathed in leather scabbards on their belts.

The atmosphere on board had dried as well. There was still laughter between us, but less than before, and the laughter there was was harsher now, rough like gravel. Within the camaraderie that continued to knit us together as a group was a growing dissension. The pace of the trip, the heat of the days and the close proximity of our own company made the mood more cutting, tetchier. Remarks passed had a coat of acid. Criticisms voiced were sharper, more personal. The illness and loneliness, the stress and discomfort which afflicted us all was making us more defensive, self-protective. The group remained paramount, in an unspoken acceptance. But as individuals within it we were drawing our arms in around ourselves, weakening the nexus.

Factions hadn't formed, but there were loose alliances, created out of our different needs as we travelled and contrasting approaches to how we could best forge our way forward. Whereas the desire for pace had been voiced most strongly by Rob, James and Derek, it was against Rob and Derek that James stood, usually with my support, on issues such as how we should deal with the people we met and in the discussions on religion and morality that started in the cab and spilled over into our camps. Between the three men there was something of a power struggle developing. Whereas in the first half of the trip James had been the tacit, though democratic leader, now Derek and Rob were strongly asserting their wills.

In all this Sandy tended to see things from James's perspective, except on the matter of arriving in London so soon. Bronwyn vacillated, drawn both towards the energy and charisma given out by James on the one hand, and the support offered by Rob and consideration by Derek on the other.

I was becoming frustrated with my relationship with Bronwyn. I felt she did not recognise me, had no idea who I was. As much as she seemed to crave James's attention and venerate his strengths, she criticised him as being intolerant and closed, aloof. She would react strongly to his ignoring her or putting her down, and in her subsequent rejection of him she drew back from me, as James's friend, as well. Unable to read me, and because I supported him, she saw me as James.

Her misapprehension of who I was was encapsulated for me by a statement she'd made a few weeks before. "Of all of you," she'd said as we sat in the cab, driving through Cameroon, "I'm most scared of Paul. You're the one most likely to commit violence, I reckon."

Bronwyn's words had hurt me. And they aggravated the cuts of self-doubt that had been made in me on the trip already. I began to wonder whether, with enough provocation, I might readily explode into violence. Perhaps there was a hidden part of me, feeding on the anger I knew I too often wouldn't express. Perhaps the calm I felt, the lack of aggression, was only pretence. Being so long with these other people, who were in some ways so different to me, so much tougher, made me doubt myself. Whereas in the past I had been used to holding arenas in which I could excel in safety, I now found myself caught up in something for which I lacked competence. The confidence I used to have in myself was ebbing away.

*

We reached Tahoua early on Friday and discovered that the next convoy would be departing on Sunday morning.

"Let's go on ahead without it," suggested Rob.

"I reckon we'll be okay," Derek agreed.

"No ways," I said. "It's only two days. Let's find somewhere nice to camp and spend the two days relaxing."

James, who had begun to feel ill with flu-like symptoms, was adamant. "I'm just not prepared to go on now. I need a rest. I'm feeling completely buggered. There's just no bloody need to kill ourselves getting there."

"I would like to spend a few days here as well," said Sandy, anxious to slow down in any way the hurricane wind blowing her north. We were told the first stretch, to Abalak, wasn't dangerous, and so drove towards the town, looking for a suitable campsite from where we could easily drive to meet the convoy.

A shallow lake shimmered under the white heat of the sun. We drove off the road towards it, bogging down repeatedly in the soft sand that lay thickly between the dry scrub and thorntrees. Eventually, after winching ourselves out a few times, we put in the four-wheel drive prop shaft and churned our way slowly forward.

The two days at the lake were spent swimming, writing and reading. The lake was shallow, a few metres deep at its centre, its water lukewarm from the relentless sun. We walked thankfully into its offer of relief from the day's heat, our feet sinking into the soft mud of its bed. James's illness worsened and he spent most of the time lying in the shade of the truck's tarpaulin, eyes closed, wondering how he would make it across the desert if this weakness continued. My own feeling of weariness remained, exacerbated by the oppressive heat. Derek overhauled his bike, taking it to pieces and putting them back together again. He even oiled his chain, leaving it to boil in a pot of bubbling grease. This done, he became frustrated at the inactivity, the lack of something to do.

Bronwyn's spirits were lifted by the appearance of a black stallion that wandered near to our camp. She walked up to it slowly, calming it with her voice. The horse allowed her to handle it, stroke its cheeks and muzzle. Assured of its trust, Bronwyn jumped onto its back, lying across it before straddling it. Barefoot, dressed only in a kikoi, she goaded the horse into a canter, gripping its mane in her hands and its unsaddled flanks with her knees. Confident now, she urged the horse forward, galloping between the thorntrees that littered the sand, whooping and hollering with joy. After she dismounted, to give Derek a turn, her mood was transformed. "That's a fine, feisty, spunky stallion!" she exclaimed, her eyes dancing with the thrill of her ride.

We drove to Abalak early on Sunday morning. The convoy arrived a while later but we were forced to wait a further two hours before it departed. We spent the time chatting to the locals, giving pens to children and asking them to draw pictures for us, and eating the dry goat's milk cheese we bought from vendors. The convoy consisted of two open Land Cruisers, filled with soldiers and on which were mounted 20mm cannons. Both Land Cruisers sat at the front of the convoy, ahead of the forty other assorted cars and trucks they would be escorting.

Eventually the signal was given to proceed. Forty-two engines all fired and the vehicles began moving forward. We were on our way, in safety, to Agadez. Within minutes we were overtaken by the vehicles behind us. While we chugged along at fifty kilometres per hour, we watched as the rest of the convoy drew away and disappeared over the horizon at ninety.

Chapter Nineteen

We reached Agadez unscathed, several hours after the convoy. As soon as we stopped the truck we were besieged by a crowd of people, selling swords and jewellery and offering to take us to cheap hotels or guide us around the town. A turbanned man with a pockmarked face introduced himself. "My name is Sidi Mohammed. You are going into the desert, yes?"

"Yes," I replied. "To Assamakka and from there to Tamanrasset."

"I take you," he said. "I know the desert. I will be driving my truck to Algeria in two days."

The thought of having a guide across the Sahara appealed to me. My visions of it were of trackless expanses of sand, an empty sea with all direction melted under the blazing heat of the overhead sun. My foreboding made me want to trust him, to follow someone who knew this alien world.

"Maybe," said Derek. "We'll see." And to us, "I don't trust any of these guys. They're only trying to get something out of us."

James was still feeling sick, so we decided to follow one of the more trustworthy-looking men, one of four Mohammeds who had approached us, to a hotel. As he led us to the Hotel Agreboun, he cautioned us against Sidi Mohammed.

"He doesn't even have a truck," he warned. "He's a bad man. Don't believe anything he says. There are many bad men in this town."

The hotel was situated behind a three-metre-high mud wall. We drove the truck through its large double gates into a spacious courtyard. Planted in the sand on either side of the driveway were a dozen small citrus trees. An old man was watering them with a bucket, carefully pouring water into the hollows that had been formed around them. After protracted haggling, Rob secured two double rooms for us at $3 each per night.

The rooms were austere but clean. Their thick mud walls held the day's heat at bay. I was pleased we weren't camping, stifling in the baked heat of our exposed tents. James lay down on one of the cane beds.

"I'm going to try to sleep," he said. "I'll see you later."

The rest of us went off to explore Agadez. We walked along its sandy, narrow streets, a group of children and traders following in our wake. Occasional trees stood out against the houses behind them, their greens brightened by the orange-browns of the walls. The buildings were all square and flat-roofed, built of hardened mud.

There was a timeless feel to Agadez. Its slow languor and unmechanised economy evoked a feeling of a centuries-old continuity, as slow-changing as the slopes of a mountain. Only the telephone lines and the occasional vehicle drew it into the present from the Biblical days its atmosphere conjured.

Mohammed caught up with us near the camel market. He invited us to look at jewellery at his cousin Hassan's shop, and turbans at the shop of a friend, another Mohammed. Afterwards he invited Sandy and me for tea. We entered the grounds of his family's house through a plain wooden door, passing through a small courtyard into one of the inner rooms. He gestured that we should sit on cushions arranged next to an intricately patterned rug.

The tea-pouring ritual was elaborate. Two small tea pots were brought in by his sister, Alima. She was a beautiful woman, very demure and displaying the coy submissiveness which had characterised so many of the African women we'd met. She cast her eyes down as she lowered the tray to the floor and retired in silence.

Mohammed spent several minutes pouring the tea between the two pots, holding one high above the other, a thin brown stream arcing down from its spout. Once brewed, he poured the tea into tiny cups. It was strong and sweet. He was a gracious host and we felt there was no ulterior motive lurking behind his hospitality. Although when he did enquire about Sandy's marital status, we again said we were married.

"It has been a difficult time here in Agadez," Mohammed was saying. "As you know the road through to Algeria has been closed because of all the bandits. So there have been no tourists here for a year now. We need tourists in Agadez. That is why I want you to have a good time here. So you will tell your friends to come as well."

★

The next morning Rob and Derek returned from the Algerian consulate.

"We could be here a while," said Rob, grimly. "South Africans have to have their visa applications approved in Algiers."

Derek threw up his hands. "It's ridiculous! Greeks and New Zealanders can get visas immediately. And whereas they pay $30, the South African visas are free."

"One of the reasons why it might take so long is that the weekend here is on Saturday and Sunday, but in Algeria it's over Thursday and Friday, so there are only three days of the week when the consulate here can communicate with Algiers."

"Well, that's what we think the guy said, anyway," Derek continued. "He kind of understands English but will speak only French to us."

"I'll go with you next time then, to sort things out," I suggested.

"No, it's better that you don't," Derek replied quickly. "Speaking French to him won't help things, and you've got to be tough with these guys to get them going. We'll go back tomorrow and put some pressure on him. Hopefully we can get them by Wednesday."

We continued our exploration of the town. It was obvious that tourism was the major source of income in Agadez. Jewellery and souvenir shops abounded. There was even a place called The Ski Shop where you could buy vehicle parts or hire out well-worn poles and skis for dune-skiing. What was also obvious was the effect the closure of the Hoggar Route for more than a year had had on the industry. There was desperation in the voices of the people selling their goods. Wherever we went we were followed by a retinue of people importuning us to buy their swords and trinkets.

The smaller children would grasp our hands as we walked, running along next to us, asking for *cadeaux* and laughing at whatever we said to them, with an innocent pleasure in the present, a *naïveté* about the probable hardness of their lives ahead of them.

The markets were filled with fresh produce, grown with the water pumped from the city's wells. The tables of the stalls were covered in deeply coloured oranges and peaches, and an endless selection of large brown dates. We ate fresh fruit daily, and yoghurts that were sold in plastic bags, a treat after months without. Most evenings we had sundowners on the garden roof of the Hotel de L'Aïr, looking out over the flat, baked roofs of the town's buildings, and across towards the main mosque which rose up five stories high, shaped like an elongated pyramid and spiked with poles sticking out from its walls on all sides like a sparsely-quilled porcupine.

It felt strange to sit there, in the comfort of a good hotel, drinking beer and being waited on. It was a reminder of a world long since left behind, almost irretrievably long ago, it seemed to me, here on the southern shores of the Sahara desert. Being there felt almost disruptive, a too-sudden dislocation from the simplicity I had become used to, the life of tin mugs, cooking fires and tents.

★

I was lying on the bed in one of our two rooms reading when Bronwyn came in. "James isn't getting any better," she told me. "In fact he's quite a lot worse today."

"What do you think it is? Malaria?" I asked.

"I don't think so. He took Fansidar a couple of days ago, which should have knocked it. But the symptoms do point to it. He's got an almighty headache, so it might also be sunstroke. It's hard to say."

I went in to see him. He was lying on his back wrapped only in a kikoi, his eyes closed. He was awake, though, his mind racing as he fought to understand his illness, to overcome it.

"I don't know what it is," he said, his voice hoarse with frustration. "I've got the most unbelievable headache. And every now and then I get these chills, and feel so cold I have to crawl into my sleeping bag. Then it passes and I start sweating like a dog, like now. I just wonder if it's some vicious strain of flu."

I dampened a towel and placed it over his forehead. His face was pale, blood drained from it by the illness. A sheen of sweat coated his chest. Rob and Derek came into the room.

"Some bastard's stolen our table!" said Derek angrily. "They've taken it off the roof of the truck. Hell, I'm pissed off! James and I spent ages making the damn thing in Bangui."

"And they've bust our warthog skull as well," added Rob. "They crushed it as they climbed down."

I went outside with them. The straps used to hold the table down lay empty. Bits of bone were scattered on the ground, the remains of the warthog skull we'd picked up as a talisman in the Masai Mara. I felt angrier about losing it than the table.

"To get it out they must have taken it through the gates," said Derek, pointing towards the large double gate we'd driven through two days before. "The people here must have known. I reckon we should get them to pay for it."

"You don't think it could have fallen off the roof on the way here?" I asked. "If one of the straps came loose the wind could easily have flipped it off."

"I'm sure we would have noticed," replied Rob. "And anyway, someone's definitely been up there if the warthog got crushed."

"Well, there's nothing we can do about it. We'll have to make do without it," I said, little realising that we'd have our table back again in a few days' time.

The next two days followed a similar pattern of shopping in the morning for a lunch of bread and tomatoes and fruit, Rob and Derek pressurising the Algerian consul to speed up the process of us getting visas, and sightseeing in the markets. I had begun to feel weak again and spent most of my time in one of the rooms, reading or staring listlessly at the wall outside which glared brightly under the reflected rays of the sun. Flies buzzed steadily in the sullen heat of the rooms.

Again it was good to split up, to be apart for a while, and we spent our time mostly in ones and twos, coming together for lunch or supper. For the most part supper was eaten in the local open restaurants, where we bought cheap salads and curries or stews. The truck was left alone, apart from one morning's work when Rob and I rotated the tyres to compensate for the uneven wear they had received.

I came to recognise the varied and distinctive looks of the people of Agadez. For millennia the different tribes had vied for power in the region, for control over the trade routes north. The Tuareg, historically the dominant group, stood tall and enigmatic in their sky-blue robes, heads covered in black turbans, upholding proudly their centuries-old nomadic ways. The majority of traders and restaurateurs were Hausas, dressed in kaftans and the white hats of their Islamic faith. The Fulani had angular, exotic looks. Tall and dark-skinned, with long, delicate hands, they wore their hair pulled back tightly from their scalps, parted in the centre and hanging about their ears in large braids.

Mohammed had warned us that all tourists were obliged to register their arrival at the police station. *Africa on a Shoestring* warned we might have to pay for the privilege. I went down to the station with Rob.

"Give me the passports," the officer there said in French, gesturing towards them. Rob shook his head. Leaning over the desk, he opened the first passport and pointed towards an empty page, holding the passport down with the other hand. "Here," he said. "You must stamp here."

"You must pay CFA 150 for each passport."

"No!" I said, angry with this incessant extortion. "What for? We have already paid CFA 3,000 for our visas for Niger. We are not going to pay any more."

The man gave in surprisingly easily, and stamped the passports, Rob holding firmly onto each one as he did so. A prisoner stared abjectly at us from behind the bars of the jail's single cell, looking without hope as we walked out into the heat.

★

A Chilean was staying at the Hotel de l'Aïr, and we became friendly with him. In his early thirties, Beltran was a fascinating man. A qualified doctor, he had a commercial pilot's licence, had made a few films, and had taken leave from his current job as a computer programmer to come to the Sahara to get inspiration for a novel he was writing. He could communicate fluently with us, English being one of the four languages he spoke. He had been in Agadez for almost three weeks, having arrived there by bus from Niamey where he had flown to from Santiago. Beltran was hoping to find a lift across the Sahara and was fast becoming despondent when we met him. The only lifts he had been offered had been from men who looked like pirates. Torn between his desire to see the desert and his anxiety over his safety, he sat stuck in Agadez.

"Let's offer him a lift," suggested Rob. "It'll be a bit of a squash, but that's not too serious."

"Oh, we've got to," I agreed. "It'll be brilliant to have him along. I've really enjoyed his company so far."

"I'm not so sure," said Bronwyn. "Six in the cab's a bit much. And the desert's going to be one of the hardest sections. Remember Masimbuka."

"I'm not so keen either," said Sandy. "I think he's quite chauvinistic. He just disregards me because I'm a woman.

It's like the hard time he's getting here is threatening him, so he takes it out on me and Bronwyn by bossing us around."

"We can't just leave him here," I objected. "He said he can't stay for much longer, and there's no other way for him to cross. Unless he goes with Sidi Mohammed in his non-existent truck!"

"I agree," said James. "It's the only decent thing to do."

"That's it then," said Rob, "a democratic majority. And we'll be able to get him to pay for the ride, so it'll make it cheaper for us."

Beltran readily accepted our offer. We would leave as soon as we received our visas. He would pay us $25 a day to travel with us.

"I'll give you some extra money as well, a contribution towards any bribes we might have to pay," he offered. "Sometimes it's better just to pay."

"Don't worry about that," Rob told him. "We don't intend paying anything more than we have to."

★

We had been in Agadez for a week now, with no positive news about the visas. Rob and Derek returned from the consulate each day with contradictory messages from the consul, that he'd received no reply, that we probably wouldn't get the visas, that we should think of going via Mali. Our frustration grew at being held back like this from where we needed to go, like a dog at the end of a chain. We had our minds set on going north. Our fatigue refused to entertain any thoughts of retracing our steps or finding another route via the west.

Only Sandy was still happy to be there. She roamed its exotic streets, taking photographs of its people and markets, with a love for the foreignness of it we had long since lost.

Rob renegotiated our hotel price, forcing the proprietor to accept half the previous amount, threatening that we'd move out if he didn't.

James's temperature had continued to soar. I took the thermometer from his mouth and looked at it. 40.3 degrees, it read. I put my hand on his chest. It was scaldingly hot. "Shit, James, you're burning up! Hang in there. Rob's gone to get a doctor. He's part of an American palaeontological team that's just arrived in town."

The doctor came into the room, a large, cheery man called Greg. "It's almost certainly malaria," he diagnosed after a few tests. "Have you got any Lariam left? It can be used as a curative as well as a prophylactic drug. I'm not sure what the prescribed dose is, but it should tell you on the leaflet inside the pack."

Bronwyn fetched a box from the truck and unfolded the leaflet inside.

"Jesus, it says here you've got to take six pills in a fourteen hour period. Three, then two seven hours later, then one. Shit, that's six weeks' worth in less than a day. Kill or cure!" James stoically took the first dose, and fell back, relieved to be acting against the illness, but wearied by the battle.

I awoke from an afternoon sleep later that day feeling wretched. My head ached and my stomach was badly upset. I feared I too might have malaria, but Beltran said that I probably had gastroenteritis, contracted most likely from the salads we'd been eating, and that it would pass soon enough. Bronwyn had also been ill with headaches and diarrhoea, but these passed after a couple of days.

The Lariam worked, and James's malarial symptoms passed, although he still felt weak, toxic from the overdose of the powerful drug. He was up to camel riding, however, and joined the others and Beltran as they went on a day's ride while I remained behind.

I put down The Sheltering Sky, its text just a jumble of words to my distracted mind. Self-pity at being sick mixes and augments my growing sense of inadequacy. My heart is clogged by the depression of this constant illness. It exaggerates my passivity, excluding me even more. I have no role on board. The skills I do have, speaking French, getting on with strangers, are continually pushed aside as unnecessary. I am constantly sidelined. I hate this having to rely on the others, feeling redundant. Never have I felt like this – incapable, like baggage. I am not valued here, and it hollows me out.

After the others returned from their camel ride, Derek went for a walk in the town. He came back triumphantly, balancing our missing table on his head. It was almost unrecognisable as ours. Legs had been added and some of the cross planks strengthening the top removed. But that it was ours was beyond doubt. We all knew intimately its rough and stained surface, the countersunk holes where Derek and James had screwed it together. Derek told us how he had spotted it and demanded it back from the people whose goods were being sold on top of it.

"They said it was theirs, that they had found it on the side of the road out of town. I told them rubbish, that they'd stolen it and it was ours. They started getting aggressive so I just shoved their stuff off onto the ground and walked off with it!"

Over the weeks Derek's forceful attitude, the way he handled strangers with a lightly bridled aggression, had been stressing me out. "Shit, Derek, you can't do that kind of thing!" I expostulated. "It might be true. They might well have found our table. Or someone else could have stolen it and sold it to them. You can't just take the law into your own hands like this."

"You weren't there!" he shouted, moving towards me. "They were all gathered around, screaming at me, pushing at me like this." He shoved me backwards hard, and again as I recovered my balance. This expression of violence, though not severe, was the first we'd had between anyone in the group. I was shattered, and walked out the door to the other room.

I was crying, face down on my bed, when Derek came into the room, ten minutes later, carrying a bowl of pasta as a peace offering. We were both embarrassed by this, he a little more than I. I wiped my cheeks dry and gave him a gruff thanks as he left me to myself. The next day we decided to keep the table but return the legs that had been added by the new owners. We still had our trestles which we would use. Rob and Derek went to the police to report the whole matter and their suspicions.

That evening, after Derek and Rob had had several beers for sundowners, the subject of how trusting we should be of strangers came up again. Derek became upset. "Look, if you guys want me to leave, I'll go. I'll carry on on my own."

"No, Derek. Shit, none of us want that. It's just that I wish we were less hard on the locals, less suspicious. This us and them mentality. We're not in a war here," I said.

"You guys have got no idea what it was like, how it affects you being in the war. When I got back from Angola I found myself diving for cover under bushes whenever an aeroplane flew overhead. My brother had to stop me from beating the shit out of some civilians in a nightclub because they hadn't been up there. You've no idea what it's like."

Derek hadn't spoken much of the Angolan war, but some of it had forced its way out. I was cut by the fragments he told of, the things he had witnessed. On odd occasions he would speak briefly of how it had been, of patrols behind enemy lines and tracer bullets seeking death in the dark; of eighteen year old fingers on startled triggers, bullets ripping through thornbush, and two shepherds falling dead in the sand.

★

Ten days in Agadez, and still there was no news of our visas. We were now hating the town. Its charm had evaporated and we saw only the squalor and poverty, the mounds of rotting garbage being rooted through by goats. The smells of the markets, of dates and meat and camels, began to cloy, reminders that we were held in their grip, impotent to leave. Worst of all was the endless badgering of the crowds whenever we left the hotel. People swarmed over us, holding swords in front of our faces, asking pitifully low prices in their desperation to sell.

On both sides, as we continued not to buy, and they continued to pester, acrimony grew. We stayed in the hotel rooms more than we would have, loath to go out into the waiting crowd. Rob's negotiations with Hassan the silversmith continued. Rob had seen him every day, drawing the haggling out interminably, offering a minutely higher price each time for the silverware he wanted. A wizened, penurious old man had hobbled after us constantly, selling two ancient swords he carried. James eventually bought one of the curved, beautifully fashioned swords for $10, $40 lower than his original asking price.

We began to think we might never get our visas, and started examining the alternatives open to us, other than the obvious one of selling the truck and flying out, which none of us wanted to do.

"There's no way we're going back," James asserted. No one disagreed. "What we could do is have the three with New Zealand or Greek passports – Bronwyn, Sandy and Paul – drive across to Morocco and the others could fly out and meet them there." No one liked the sound of this, especially me who would become solely responsible for the maintenance of the truck across the desert.

"A better plan," suggested Derek, "would be to let them drive across the border while we go around it on the bike. It's all sand out there so there'll be no hassle getting past. We'll only have to go a few miles out of the way."

"But what if we got stopped in Algeria?" asked Sandy. "You'd have no visas or entry stamps in your passports."

"We could just say they'd been stolen, that we'd been held up by bandits. Once we got to the other side the worst they could do is kick us out the country, which is what we'd want anyway."

Derek's daring plan had certain obvious disadvantages, but I realised we'd probably be forced to adopt it if the visas weren't granted.

Beltran, who had been in Agadez for a month now, decided to leave by bus for Arlit, the uranium mining town to the north, where he would continue looking for a lift. His decision to leave without us was prompted both by our seemingly endless delay for visas, and a growing concern on his part for the tough attitudes of our group. He had returned from the camel ride shocked by the cavalier behaviour he had witnessed. I was sad to see him go. The similarity of his thinking to mine had helped restore my self-confidence. I had also enjoyed his literary mind and inquisitive intellect. Before leaving he told me of a short story he had just read. "The central theme," he said in his strongly accented English, "is of a man who has a loving home, work he enjoys, and a peaceful lifestyle. Yet he forsakes all this to go on a journey fraught with danger and discomfort. Everyone is amazed that he should choose to do this and they ask him why he is leaving. He replies to them, 'So that I can come back.'"

★

The next day, a Thursday, Rob and Derek bumped into the consul in town. He said our visas could be collected at ten on Friday morning. Not wanting to spend any more time in Agadez than we had to, we hit upon the imprudent plan of leaving immediately for Arlit, spending the night there and then driving on to the border at Assamakka. Derek would stay behind to collect our visas before driving the 443 kilometres alone across the desert to join us.

We arrived at Arlit, whose uranium mines produce 90% of Niger's income, shortly after sunset. There was a police roadblock at the entrance to the town but the boom was up and we drove through, ignoring the whistle blasts that followed us. We enquired after Beltran and were directed to the main hotel. Walking into the foyer we were mobbed by the usual crowd of beggars, sword salesmen and urchins. A man came up to Sandy. She warned him to step back, but he grabbed her contemptuously by her upper arm where it emerged from her vest. She shouted at him and tore herself free.

Once inside, as we waited for Beltran, we were propositioned by a dozen prostitutes sitting in the hotel's lounge. Undeterred by the men's rebuffs, a few offered their trade to Bronwyn and Sandy.

Beltran was eager to join us, having found Arlit to be even more depressing than Agadez. We told him about leaving Derek behind to fetch our passports.

"So what did you tell the police at the roadblock coming into town?" he asked.

"Oh, we just drove past," James replied.

"It's just as well. What they do is take people's passports overnight, forcing them to spend at least one night here. They then charge $20 or $40 to get them stamped. I had to pay $20 yesterday. But I hear there's another boom on the other side of town. If you haven't got your passports you could run into trouble there."

We discussed the best strategy to combat this. "Let's leave at dawn," suggested Rob. "Hopefully the guard post won't be manned at that time and we can slip through."

"There's no point hanging around this place, that's for sure," agreed Bronwyn.

We laid our mattresses out on the terrace roof of a cheap hotel for a night's sleep under the stars. Rob lay listening to the BBC World Service on his radio. "Hey, listen to this," he called to me.

'In Algeria today, leaders of the Front Islamique du Salut, or FIS, announced that they are to suspend for a month their campaign of terror in which thirty-eight foreigners and several hundred Algerians have been killed in the past four months. They urged all foreigners to evacuate the country in this period. After the month the killings will resume...'

We would be in Algeria in two days' time. Fate continued to smile down on us.

The town's mosque lay next door to the hotel and we were woken early by the wailing cries of the muezzin, his voice blaring from loudspeakers mounted on the minarets. Beltran was waiting for us at his hotel. The last stars were fading as we picked him up and drove north out of the town.

We passed the police roadblock, seeing no one. Relieved, we continued our slow pace forward. Five minutes later a military vehicle drove up beside us on our left, the uniformed man in the passenger seat gesturing vehemently that we should pull over. We slowed to a halt. Two soldiers got out of the vehicle and approached us. They demanded to know why we hadn't stopped at the exit to the town. Rob immediately started offering cigarettes around and steering the conversation away from the subject of passports. Beltran watched amazed as we were left to drive on, waving amiably back at the soldiers, for the price of only two cigarettes.

We were into the desert proper now. The piste stretched ten kilometres wide. Tracks cut along and across it, leading in all directions. A caravan of five camels plodded its way forward in the distance to the east, a withered relic of the days when, three hundred years ago at the height of the salt trade, caravans of twenty to thirty thousand camels, bearing great blocks of rock salt, would have passed over these sands, stretching back for twenty-five kilometres across the desert.

As before, leaving towns behind to enter the wilderness invigorated Bronwyn.

"I looove the desert!" she yelled out of the open door, her arms aloft.

Beltran, by contrast, was quite nervous. Navigation was done by following *balises*, tall poles placed in the sand at one mile intervals. The desert was flat here, stretching out level and unbroken all around us, a brown sea of rough sand. Several of the *balises* were missing. While we drove along, following the most likely tracks, Beltran scanned the horizon anxiously through binoculars, calling out eagerly whenever he sighted the next pole.

He had done a lot of research into travel in the Sahara before coming out, and was filled with horror stories about travellers who had got lost in its unmarked expanses. He told us about a Belgian family who had lost their way. Their dried-out bodies had been found months later, along with the wife's diary. "Her husband died first, of thirst. She decided to drink his blood. The entries become more and more incoherent as she slips into madness, driven there by fear and thirst and guilt. Towards the end, as she drinks the last of the blood, she writes "I feel great. I feel wonderful. I am like Rambo.'" Beltran spoke animatedly, his own concerns lending emotion to his telling. The sands around us, reflecting the heat of the early morning sun, began to look a little more forbidding.

"Oh God, look over there!" Rob called out, pointing to our left. About a kilometre away a Land Cruiser sped across the hard sand, dust billowing out behind it. The angle of its approach made it obvious it was aiming to intercept us. As it neared we could see five turbanned men in the back, sitting around a mounted machine-gun. We felt exposed and vulnerable on the flat expanse of the desert. There was nowhere to hide. They closed in on us as we lumbered forward, a lion moving in on a tortoise. The men looked just like the rebel bandits we'd heard so much about. Rob gripped the staff he'd found in Kenya, seeking security in the weight of its wood. The Land Cruiser cut us off, signalling us to stop.

They were a military patrol, on the lookout for bandits. After asking what the hell we were up to and why weren't we travelling with the convoy, they let us proceed.

Two trucks passed, kilometres distant, heading the other way. We saw no other sign of life. There was no vegetation at all. The gradual desiccation of the Sahara, which had seen horse-drawn chariots cross it in Roman times, had strangled in its dry heat anything that used to live here. Several times we came upon stretches of soft sand, which we chugged through slowly in first gear and four-wheel drive. All along the piste, and in these soft, yielding areas especially, were littered the sand-blasted hulks of cars and trucks, each one legacy to some past personal tragedy. They had all been eviscerated for spares, and mostly lay on their backs, rolled over for easier access to their parts. There was no rust, even on cars that had been lying dead there for twenty years. We drove on through this endless, eerie graveyard.

We stopped for lunch in the lee of high dunes, unrolling the tarpaulin to shade us from the sun. I cooked the meal.

Sandy remarked that it was the first I'd cooked since she'd rejoined us, six weeks before. I realised how long-standing and insidiously enervating my illness had been. At last, though still weak, I was beginning to feel better, buoyed by our regained momentum and the stark beauty of the desert.

We climbed along the back of the nearest dune, our feet sinking into the sand. Looking over the edge, we could see the sharp, curved ridges of other dunes, forbidding in their barrenness and alluring in their beauty, stretching out before us. Looking back towards the west, the truck seemed small below us, fragile against the empty background. As far as we could see the desert lay flat and still, unbroken by even the smallest ripple on its surface. We ran up and down the dunes, taking long, braking strides as we descended, revelling in the wildness of the desert, its alien landscape.

Assamakka, the border town of Niger, started off as a green line on the horizon, growing as we approached into a small collection of huts and palms and a larger one of trucks awaiting authorisation to continue. The furthest town from the sea of any on Africa's bulge, it seemed to be furthest too from any official supervision. We parked near the other trucks, avoiding the aggressive military figures who swaggered around, several of them drunk.

There was no sign of Derek. We had hoped he'd be able to catch us on the piste but now, as the sun began to set, he'd still not arrived. Beltran was very agitated. "He won't be coming now," he said to me as we stood looking south into the encroaching gloom. "There's so much that could have gone wrong. He could have had his passport taken in Arlit. He could even still be in Agadez."

"He'll get here," I replied confidently. "He always does." Though we had decided to drive back towards Arlit the next day if he hadn't arrived, I had absolute faith that he would come through. In these things there was no one more competent than Derek.

With the last blue of the twilight fading, Derek came riding in. He had one litre of petrol left in his tank. And six passports in his backpack. "Hell, I thought I'd never get here!" he said as he climbed off, grinning with relief. "That bloody vice-consul said we all had to be there to sign for the visas so I spent quite a while persuading him that that just wasn't possible. I made it to Arlit early this afternoon and got stopped at the gate and had my passport taken from me. Did you guys stop in Arlit? 'Cause when I asked about you no one had seen you."

"We just drove through. The boom was up," said Rob.

"Anyway, that got me a bit worried. It was like you had just disappeared."

"Did you have to pay to get your passport stamped?" I asked.

"Of course not. I told them you guys had all my money."

Everything had worked out again. We went to bed under a sky brightened by a waning moon and the brilliant trail of northern stars. A single country lay now between us and the sea, the marker of our crossing.

Chapter Twenty

After immigration, James, Rob and Derek went to get us through customs. Beltran went with them. I stayed in the truck with Bronwyn and Sandy, keeping out of the sun, and the confrontation the atmosphere of the border post seemed certain to provoke.

"You have to pay 720 French francs, for temporary import of the vehicles," the uniformed official told them.

"But we've got a carnet," James protested.

"No matter. You must pay this as well."

Rob became angry. "No! This is what the carnet is for. It is enough. See here. Valid for Niger. That's this place."

"You must pay 720 francs."

"Right," asserted Rob, picking up the carnet and turning towards the door, "we'll go back to Niamey and sort this out there. We're not paying this." It was a very hollow threat – Niamey, the capital, lay over 1,300 kilometres away – but somehow it had the desired effect. The carnets were stamped and we were free to proceed.

Beltran was amazed. "I've paid a fortune in bribes in Niger," he said to me as they rejoined us. "How much have you had to pay so far?"

I thought back. "Nothing at all. Not a cent."

"In fact we're actually up," added Rob. "We were meant to pay a $50 road tax, but no one's asked us for it yet."

The Algerian officials at Ain-Guezzam, the Algerian border post ten kilometres further north, were very thorough. After meticulously checking our immigration and currency declaration forms, they searched the truck. We had declared all our traveller's cheques and some of our cash, but had stashed away about a thousand dollars in the hiding place beneath the pole on which the left rear seat swivelled. It was this money that we planned to use for exchanging on the black market. I always felt extremely nervous at times like these, and busied myself in the back of the truck, lest my nerves betray our hiding place. The money remained undetected.

We had been told to purchase temporary vehicle insurance in the town of Ain-Guezzam itself.

"Shouldn't we try to get that insurance?" I asked as we drove down the main street of the small oasis town.

"Forget it," said Rob. "We've got vehicle insurance anyway."

"What? That thing you typed up in Zaire?"

"It's been fine up till now. Anyway, what are the chances of us seeing another vehicle in the desert, let alone hitting one?"

The town was a dry, colourless place, bleached of character by the unremitting sun. Small square houses, their walls daubed a reflective white, flanked the empty streets. Two old men, turbanned and bearded, watched as we passed. A group of small boys and some skinny dogs chased a ball in the heat. There were no women to be seen.

We bought several loaves of a dark and compact bread that was for sale at a price obviously subsidised by the state, and filled up with diesel. Only slightly more expensive than in Nigeria, it cost us $0.06 per litre.

Leaving Ain-Guezzam behind, we continued north. The late morning sun blazed down on the compressed sand, tightening our eyes in its reflected glare. Heat poured into the cab. Mirages danced around us, surrounding us on all sides with vast lakes. The wind made by our progress had a baked, parched quality. The air, distorted by the heat, shimmered above the sand. The firm piste we'd been on turned to *feche-feche*, soft sand covered by a thin crust of harder sand. The wheels broke easily through the upper surface to the dragging reaches below. The engine strained to drive the wheels as they sank deeper into the yielding grasp of the sand. In first gear and four-wheel drive, the truck laboured slowly forward before shuddering and stopping.

"We're going to have to let some air out of the tyres," said James, "to increase the surface area in contact with the sand. That should give us more traction."

The air hissed out of the tyres as four of us depressed the valves in them. Behind the truck twin rifts stretched out, dug into the sand by the chugging wheels. With the tyres deflated we proceeded more easily, like a boat planing across the water instead of churning through it.

For miles the desert had reached out boundless on all sides, a calm sea unbroken by waves or land. Now, to the north, it began to rise up before us, swelling into low, smooth-curved dunes. The shimmering mirages ahead of us resolved, solidifying into huge sandstone formations, their surfaces carved and abraded by sand whipped by the violent desert winds. Backward-sloping and arched, they rose out of the desert like the dorsal fins of sharks, their bodies of rock lying deep beneath the surface. Solid where all around them had long since been reduced to sand, they bore the lines of their age, the slow onslaught of the elements.

"What a wonderful place to camp!" exclaimed Sandy. "Let's stop here for the night."

"It's only three o'clock," rejoined Rob. "There's still almost four hours of daylight left. We need to press on, keep our momentum up. We're making good progress."

"That's all we seem to be doing," said Sandy, "pressing on. Can't we just stop for a while and enjoy where we are?"

"We've just had eleven days in Agadez! And we're going to stay for a couple of days in Tamanrasset. If we stop now we won't get there tomorrow."

"But it's such a stunning place here. We'll never be here again in our lives yet we're going to fly straight past it."

"I'm sure we'll come across somewhere just as beautiful further on," said James, joining in. "I vote we carry on."

The weight of feeling of those not wanting to stop, and the unarrested momentum of the truck, bore us onwards, further north towards London. Towards evening we came upon a thornbush standing solitary in the emptiness and decided to make it our campsite.

As the day cooled, Bronwyn and I had climbed onto the roof, enjoying the unbroken view around us. Gentled by the beauty of the landscape, our talk had turned to discussion of ourselves, of the gap between us where friendship should have formed. Now, as we halted I suggested we go for a walk, to continue the conversation.

The music of the wind had blown the sand into small and regular undulating waves. We walked across this rippled surface, its coarse firmness giving way beneath our feet, the heat of the day leaking up into our bare soles.

"I can't tell you how it frustrates me," I said, "that we just miss each other like this. I don't think you know who I am. It's as though you've pictured me as someone else, made me into an image I can't escape from. Objectively, there's no reason at all why we shouldn't have become friends. I think I treat you better than the other men, yet you seem always to be distrustful of me."

Again the wall was there, the barrier against my words being heard. "I think it's just one of those things. Some personality types just aren't that compatible. Don't take it too personally."

"But I do. I can't help but do. And I can't help but believe that if you saw me for who I am, we would get on really well. But you make me into someone else, as though there's some fiend lurking behind what I do, someone wanting to hurt you. I don't know. Maybe it's got something to do with my being James's friend. I know you've got problems with him at times. Perhaps you're transferring some of that onto me."

We walked back to the truck and the tents sprouting up beside it, as apart as ever, my frustrations uneased. Under the pressure of our long separation from the support of home, and sickness and travel-weariness, we had all, to different degrees, begun to retract into ourselves. This less supportive atmosphere emphasised the loneliness I felt. And in turn made the struggle of my relationship with Bronwyn more damaging.

The night was windless, quiet. No insect sang, no leaf rustled. We doused our lights and sat outside. The stars and gibbous moon dazzled in the deep black of the night air, their glow illuminating faintly the gentle slopes of dunes nearby. The stillness was absolute. It enveloped me, dark and smooth, in its shroud, an intimation of deafness. The magnitude of this so very foreign place diminished us. The stillness contained an impersonal violence. It slept now, the desert, but I knew that as we trod carefully across its back, it could so easily rise from its dormancy and bend to crush us in its grip of storm and heat.

Again a deep weariness enveloped me. The lassitude of my illness and the heat of the day left me drained, dissipated. I sought to escape it in sleep. Lying on my mattress, my last conscious thoughts, as ever, were the hope that the morning would see me well again.

The piste softened as we continued the following day. Metal carcasses were everywhere. In a single hundred-metre stretch of soft, churned-up sand, sixteen wrecks lay abandoned. We moved sluggishly north, like a beetle on a beach. The *balises* were inconsistent and we'd travel for an hour without seeing one, following instead the most densely concentrated lines of tracks. We saw a few other trucks, mostly in the far distance. Presumably their drivers knew the route, and firmer paths off the main piste, and chose to forsake the security offered by the *balises*.

I spent too long on the roof of the truck enjoying the view, and caught sunstroke. I had a splitting headache as we drove into Tamanrasset.

We camped at Camp Zeriba. The Hoggar Mountains stood out to the east. The next day we would travel to Assekrem, a hermitage in the mountains built by a French Christian, Charles de Foucauld, at the beginning of the century. Like Victoria Falls, it was somewhere not to be missed on an Africa crossing.

Tamanrasset is the major town of southern Algeria. After the simplicity of central Africa it was a novelty to be in a place geared for tourism again. We spent the next morning wandering around its shops and telephoning home. Conducting a long-distance relationship by telephone is fraught with difficulty. Added to the need to cram two weeks' emotions into ten minutes' intimacy, and the inadequacy of merely verbal communication, is the background awareness of cost. All these were amplified for Rob. The alien nature of our environment, the extreme difference of our immediate concerns, decreased the overlap between his life and Bridget's. When Rob returned from the hotel it was evident his call had not gone well. He was in a dark mood, withdrawn. Over the coming weeks this frustration would manifest itself as a more resolute propellant in our quest to reach London.

There were a few other tourists at the camp. One of them was a young Chinese woman. We heard that she had been involved in a road accident. The truck on which she was hitching a lift had rolled and she had been flung out, landing on her head. That she was not well was evident from her behaviour. She appeared to be in a permanent daze. Speaking no French and only a smattering of English, so far from home, she wandered lost around the camp.

"God, what's going to happen to her?" I asked.

"Someone needs to get in touch with her family," suggested Sandy. "Let them know what's happened."

"But we can't even speak to her," said Rob. "And even if we could, I doubt she's capable of much sense."

"There is that Spanish guy who seems to be looking after her," James pointed out. "Though who knows what his motives are. He looks pretty shifty to me."

In the end we did nothing, leaving ourselves to wonder ever afterwards what her fate had been.

Having been warned the road to Assekrem was abominable, we decided to leave the truck at the camp and go up in a hired vehicle. On its way down Africa, our truck had taken sixteen hours to complete the eighty kilometre journey. At $80 for six of us, including Beltran, it was worth the protection of our already battered suspension. The hired vehicle could take only six, plus our guide Ahmoud, so Derek had to ride his bike up, to his disgruntlement.

"Thank God we're not in the truck," said James passionately, jolting from side to side as the Nissan Patrol lurched forward over the rocky path. The terrain was the most inhospitable I had ever seen. Vast fields of head-sized, closely-packed boulders, sun-blackened and smooth, stretched out for kilometres until they met the slopes of equally barren hills. The place looked as though it had been seared by an inferno of life-blasting intensity that had rolled across it, leaving behind only these heat-rounded rocks as legacy to its destructive passing. Nothing lived here. No insect scuttled, no lichen covered a rock.

The road, two faint paths, ran across this boulder-strewn waste. The larger rocks had been cleared but we bumped and pitched over the infinite smaller rocks that remained. As we wound upwards into the Hoggar massif itself we passed between giant sandstone formations, towers and turrets stretching up towards the cloudless blue sky, their flanks shaped and carved by the millennial slow pressure of dew and ice, and the attrition of wind-whipped sand. Long and uniform vertical lines and fissures had been sculpted into the rock formations by the artist of these elements, lending them an elegance, a time-etched solemnity. Like patient gatekeepers of this ancient place they stood watch over their domain, the desert around them, slow-drying and expanding, as it moved with them into the unhurried aridity of old age.

We reached the camp, two simple rooms, an hour before dark, and set off immediately up the long, winding path to the hermitage. I walked slowly, my body heavy with the immobility of the past long weeks.

The view, and the tranquillity from within which we could admire it, was supremely beautiful. To the east, the range of mountains stretched out to the horizon, like the layers of a shark's teeth, their jagged peaks forming eerie silhouettes against the silvering background. On all sides the desert stretched empty and bare, lifeless but with its own vitality of heat warming sand and wind carving rock. Shadows crept over its ravaged, unprotected surface. The day's heat bled out of the rocks as the sky in the west sank from red into black. We hurried down to the meal prepared by Ahmoud.

I lay in my sleeping bag, seeking sleep beyond the noise the others were making. An argument, which had been simmering for some time – as I had been vaguely aware – now flared up. It had something to do with menstruation and privacy and Bronwyn and Sandy were in vehement opposition. The force with which they exclaimed their views seemed out of proportion to the content. James, I could hear, was siding loudly with one of them.

*

We rose early to witness the dawn. I went up first with Beltran. The calls and shouts of the others, the clanging of the utensils they were bringing up to have tea in on the top, broke the silence. Other tourists sitting quietly on the rocks looked down towards them in irritation. "Some people always have to be doing to be happy," commented Beltran. "They cannot just be."

Sunrise was even more glorious than the sunset. As the sky burned orange and red behind them, the peaks cast long purple shadows in the valley below. The thinning moon shone brightly, balancing the glow of Mercury and Venus hanging low in the east. As day approached I could see more clearly the mountain slopes below us, flowing endless in a monochrome brown, unmarked by the green of shrub or tree. A camel safari had pitched camp in a valley nearby. Thirty or so camels stood patiently in the sun, seemingly at home amid the barren crags and rock-covered slopes.

While Derek, Sandy and Rob attended Mass in the hermitage's small chapel, I stayed outside, talking to Beltran, enjoying the landscape and his company. "I've come to realise," he was saying, "that people don't have different virtues and defects. These are the same. They are merely different manifestations of a particular characteristic. What determines whether they are deemed virtues or defects is the environment, circumstance. So much of what we love in someone is, in a different context, what we hate too."

I move off by myself, reflecting on what Beltran has said. I think of the other people on board the truck. Is not James's vitality, his passion and spontaneous willingness to do things, which I love, not the same energy, in a different guise, as that which impels him to do things without due consideration for others, which I hate? And Derek, though I hate his toughness, his hardness in dealing with strangers, is this not the same thing which I call his competence, his reliability, which has made me feel so secure having him around in anxious times, and which I respect and admire?

I look down at the harsh paradise below me and see that this dichotomy, this eternal paradox, goes beyond personal relationships. It expresses the contradictory feelings I have towards the country that is my home. I hate that it is such a violent world, so quick to anger, its blood so easily spilled. But what I love in it, its vitality, its exuberance, its readiness to laugh and sing and dance, is that very same energy, differently formed.

Conversely, the security of Europe, its orderliness and control, is what makes it so attractive to those stung by the improprieties and caprice of Africa. But the price paid for this is a uniformity, an absence of spontaneity. Its population too, its number of people, makes it exciting but at the same time claustrophobic. And whereas in the ancientness of its culture it has diversity and sophistication, it has also been calcified by time. It is in some ways arthritic, unbending.

On the way back to Tamanrasset we stopped at a natural spring. The water coming up from the earth was carbonated, just like soda water. We drank from an earthenware bowl dipped into the bubbling water in its basin of rock. That such water swelled upwards from the earth seemed even more miraculous in this barren setting.

In Tamanrasset we said goodbye to Beltran who wanted to stay on for a few days. We had become close in our short time together, he and I, drawn by our common interests and values. His disquiet at the hardness of the behaviour of our group had mirrored my own, building up again my eroded faith in my values. And his own evident fears and anxieties had helped me to feel less alone, less the soft one, the odd one out. It was a wrench to leave the companionable space we had shared in the Hoggar Mountains, to leave behind the security I had felt in their stark and comforting grandeur.

Though still feeling tired, my spirits were up as we did last-minute shopping in Tamanrasset. I sent a postcard to a friend. "Dear Pid," I wrote. "I'm in the Sahara desert. It is 40 degrees in the shade. Even the camels are wearing hats. Two weeks ago I had strange heart palpitations. Last week I had skull-splitting headaches and gastroenteritis. Yesterday I got sunstroke. Wish you were here. Instead of me. Paul."

Rob was more determined than ever to reach London in the first few days of December. To get there, journeying via Morocco before crossing into Spain, would mean almost constant travelling from now on. It was already 12th November. After a night spent camping behind a low sand dune, we continued north. The road was tar now, interspersed with sections of badly corrugated piste. The truck bucked and jolted over these humps, jarring our teeth. The wind picked up, hurling the fine desert sand across the road. Curved mounds of sand crept across the road, clutching at our wheels as we ploughed our way through them.

We reached Ain-Salah, the next major town, in the evening and had supper in a small restaurant frequented by truck drivers. The warmth and friendliness of the Algerians struck me again. The prejudices against Islamic and Arabic people my Western upbringing had instilled in me melted away before their hospitality, their obvious pleasure at having us visit their country. In these things direct experience can undo in a stroke what vicarious learning takes years to wear away.

Derek had found out that South Africans needed visas for Morocco. As we'd therefore have to go to Algiers or

Oran, the two cities with Moroccan consulates, we decided to drive north and avoid the 260 kilometres of rough piste to Reggane that lay to the west, on the direct route to Morocco. With every northward kilometre the temperature dropped. I could sense the European winter ahead of us. There was on board the beginnings of expectancy, like a horse who has scented its stables and fights the reins to head for home.

Suddenly the engine coughed and stalled. The fingers of an old ghost clutched my stomach, but we'd only run out of diesel. The wind blew hard, gusting at the side of the truck as we bled the fuel system, taking only ten minutes in what was now a well-practised ritual.

The stress of our restless travelling was seeping through into our speech. Our conversation was coarser now, more base, in topic and expression. Frustration turned longing for people not here into invective against those who were. There were hidden currents and undercurrents of emotion too, glances and remarks I couldn't understand and just put down to the stress of travelling. Beneath the music and the joking, the atmosphere in the cab, where we five sat close together, was becoming taut and angular.

A police car pulled up beside us and waved us to a halt.

"Oh dear," said Sandy, who was driving. "What could they want?"

"*Douane*," I read. They're customs police. They'll probably search us for drugs."

"Or our currency declaration forms," James added. "Oh shit! We swapped all that money in Tamanrasset. They're not going to tally up!"

With the official exchange rate twenty-three dinars to the dollar and the unofficial one sixty, we'd felt obliged to trade on the black market. So far we'd swapped $160 illegally, and $40 at a bank, using the money we'd declared originally. One of the policemen asked to see all our money and travellers cheques, and our currency declaration forms and bank receipts showing amounts exchanged. The other began to search the truck.

I climbed into the back of the truck anxiously, to get my forms from my locker. The money we could show would fall short of what we'd declared.

Anxiety turned to relief as Sandy produced $60 she'd forgotten to declare, and Rob added to this the $100 we'd received from Beltran. By fluke the numbers on our forms corresponded exactly with the amount we could show them. Rob had managed while they weren't looking to stuff our extra dinars beneath the carpet.

Thwarted for the moment, they turned their efforts to searching the truck. One of them seized excitedly upon the thirty or so million zaire notes Rob still had.

"Ah, what is this? Foreign money. For black market trading, yes?"

Rob laughed. "No, no. Just a souvenir. Worth nothing. Here, here's one for you. A souvenir of us."

The man scowled and refused the offer. They moved to the cab of the truck. I was feeling edgy. Our secure hiding place suddenly seemed to most obvious place anyone would look. Scared that my body language would give it away, I climbed out, and pretended to examine the underneath of the truck.

I noticed diff oil dripping down from the front axle onto the road. Shining a torch and cleaning the area with a rag revealed a huge crack along the outer flange of the left tractor joint. The crack spread fully a third of the way around the circumference of this the joint connecting the wheel to the truck.

"Jesus, James," I called. "Have a look at this!"

James knelt down next to me.

"Good thing we didn't decide to head west across the piste," he said, with a drawn-out whistle. "Another stretch of bad road would have sheared it completely. Just imagine what would have happened if the whole wheel had suddenly broken off while we were moving!"

The customs officials were still deeply suspicious of us. They knew we couldn't have spent only $40 crossing half the country, but could prove nothing. They abandoned their search and let us proceed. After topping up the diff oil we drove on carefully. The next town large enough to provide equipment to conduct proper repairs was Ghardaïa, 260 kilometres away. James and I drove, taking care to avoid any unnecessary bumps – a vision of that crack, and the full brunt of the truck's weight bearing down on it, lodged in our minds. We stopped for the night at the oasis of El-Golea. A bitter wind blew, cutting us as we took hurried showers in the last of the evening light.

I woke up to a drenched sleeping bag and pillow, and the old smell of sickness. Depression at the recurrence of this strange ailment suffocated me. I lay on my back, one hand holding my hair saturated with sweat, desperately wishing it would end, that I could become well again. Wearily I climbed out of the tent and stoked up a fire to warm some water under which I could shower, and scrub off the smell of putrefaction that coated my skin.

We continued our careful pace north. The desert was vibrant now. Mountains of sand towered over us, massive and brooding. Hollowed on one side by dark shadows hiding from the wind, they curved gracefully out to the horizon on all sides. The road wound its way between the dunes, a thin black line in the wilderness of brown, like a fallen hair on a carpet. Clumps of rock lay scattered across the sand, dark shapes like bushes that could never be, blackened by the heat of the sun.

"How are we going to fix that thing, James?" I asked. "Just weld it up?"

"I'm not sure if you can weld it. I think it's cast iron. And there's no way we'll find a spare here, in an ex-French colony. If worst comes to worst we'll have to have one couriered over from London, or drive as far as we can on this one, monitoring that crack."

We reached Ghardaïa late in the afternoon. James, Derek and I immediately set about removing the tractor joint while the others explored the town. By the time they returned, loaded with fresh fruit – deliciously sweet pears and oranges – and vegetables grown locally, we had removed the offending part. The constant pounding of our drive, and the abnormal weight in front, had bent the joint, tearing the metal upwards in a 2mm wide rent. The exposed metal shone silver and jagged where it had torn. I tied a plastic bag over the exposed wheel axle to keep out the sand.

Bronwyn and Sandy were silent, introspective. There had been a confrontation between them. Suspicions had been voiced and the hurtful, numbing truth had been spoken. The last gasps of Bronwyn's hope had been choked by the gloved fist of a now-realised deceit. She sat quietly, writing a letter to a friend. James cleaned his grease-covered hands on a rag which he tossed over to me as we got ready for a walk around the town.

Ghardaïa consists of five towns grouped together, and is the central oasis of the desert. It was a busy place, with huge markets selling food and carpets, and continental-style cafés and patisseries. The European influence was stronger now. We could sense Europe not only in the growing chill of the wind, but in the smells it now bore with it.

*

I woke up feeling wretched – weak and cold. My head throbbed like an anvil being hammered. "I'm going to stay here for a while, James," I told him. "I'll come and find you later."

"Okay. Pity you can't come. I'm not sure how much English they speak here," he replied.

"Oh, we'll be fine, man," said Derek. "We'll just use sign language or whatever. Come. Let's try that engineering works we spotted last night."

One of the employees at the works examined the part. "It cannot be welded," he told them. "You cannot weld cast iron."

"It has to be welded," said James, his arms wide. "We've got no choice!"

"I'll try then. But it won't be strong." Like a dentist filling a tooth, he first neatened the crack using an angle grinder and then welded the split together. When I joined them at the workshop he was turning the part on a lathe, shaving smooth the inner and outer seams of the join he had welded. It looked fixed. As we replaced it I just hoped it would last the remaining 4,000 or so kilometres to London.

★

A pillar of fire rose up from behind hills kilometres distant, bending the air around it. Like a scene from a Biblical Armageddon, it seared the sky, billowing with heat. Curious, we drove as close as we could and scaled the low hill behind which it burned. We looked down on a gas refinery. A long pipe rose out of the sand. From it burst the billowing cloud of flame, excess gas being burnt off in this massive controlled explosion of heat. A low roar filled the air, like the sound of wind in a tunnel.

"No, James! Don't!" I shouted as he started running down the hill to get a close-up photo. "Oh, God, what the fuck does he think he's up to? There'll be all sorts of shit from this."

By the time he got back, and we'd returned to the truck, a security vehicle was waiting next to it. They took James with them and told us to follow.

I continued to curse James as we drove. "Selfish bastard! He's completely irresponsible. They'll probably take all our film and confiscate it. We could be here all night. And Derek'll be stuck somewhere up the road. Bloody Pitman, he doesn't think beyond the second he's in!"

My fears proved unfounded. After a friendly chat we gave the guards some cigarettes, swapped addresses and were allowed to leave, with a mild warning not to do it again.

In the excitement of the day's events we ran out of fuel again but carried on soon enough to where we found Derek waiting patiently at the side of the road. We were out of the desert now, suddenly. Sparse vegetation bordered the road. Dunes had become scrub-covered hills. We had spent so little time in the desert. Relief at nearing the sea was tempered by regret at having passed through the Sahara so quickly. We camped in an old quarry outside Aflou, less than 400 kilometres from the Mediterranean.

In the cab, with Derek driving on up ahead, we had discussed what we thought would be a fair contribution for him to make towards our costs. When we left Kenya together our arrangement had been vague. We'd decided to agree on a figure later on, depending on factors such as for how long Derek actually ended up travelling with us. $200 would be fair, we now thought. James approached Derek.

"$200? What for? That's rubbish, man. I've easily paid my way."

"Come on, Derek, what about all our fixed costs? The camping equipment, all the cooking stuff. Those two car radios we sold. Not to mention the use of the truck for storing all your things in."

"If you're going to come with that kind of argument, I could easily mention all the things I've done like shopping, finding campsites, fetching spares. I don't think I owe you guys anything."

The bad feeling flowed into the next day. "Christ, it makes me angry," James was saying as we left the campsite, heading north towards Oran. Months of frustration found their focus in this issue of money. "It shows a complete lack of generosity of spirit. He could never have travelled like he did without us, leaving all his gear in the truck, using our tools. We saw what it was like for that Scottish guy, weighed down by his kit. And the times he put his whole bike in the back."

"And while our truck is his," I agreed, "it's not like we ever get to ride his bike or anything."

"It leaves me feeling bitter," said James. "Let's just leave it now."

The rancour eased as the day wore on. The road led us into the foothills of the Atlas mountains. Their slopes were chequered with fields, yellow and brown under their autumn harvest. Lined with trees now, the road twisted its way between the geometric shapes of farms and through villages stamped with the mark of the place's ancient and Moorish past. Men dressed in burnouses walked down the streets, or guided horse-drawn carts past solid stone buildings.

As evening drew in, we crested a ridge. There before us was the Mediterranean. We drove down towards it along a winding coastal road reminiscent of that along the Cape peninsula we'd left seven months before. More than anything I felt relieved. My eyes fastened on the sea, on its promise of surcease, the unclenching of tension. There was pride too, at having crossed Africa, at having done so together, but the sounds of triumph were drowned out in me by the long sighs of relief.

We found a campsite on the coast to the west of the city. After pitching the tents, James, Derek, Rob and I walked to the nearby baths, where no women were allowed. None of us had ever been to such a place. The large, tiled rooms were filled with steam and gushing water. The men employed there scrubbed our backs with cloths, horrified at the dirt that rolled off. Though we'd had brief showers each day, and swum where we could, it was now almost three months of hard travel since we'd had a hot bath. Like a balm, the water eased us, carrying away the stress as well as the dirt of our travelling.

For me, much of the measure of this stress had been resolve. Mollified by thoughts of the end, I felt it loosen. My sickness deepened. A sullen torpor began to fall in on me. Whereas before I had looked forward to seeing Morocco, now the thought of more days of hard driving, of the 450 kilometres per day we'd need to cover, filled me with dread. The very thought of climbing into the truck made me flinch, with a revulsion that was almost physical. At rest now, I recoiled at being in it again, feeling it shuddering and bouncing beneath me, smelling its used diesel breath.

"I'm not going to Morocco," I said to the others. "I'll catch a ferry from here and meet you in Barcelona." It was the first time I had contemplated leaving the truck.

"I might go with you then," said Rob.

Seeing where this schism was leading, Sandy protested. "But we've got to go to Morocco! That's the whole reason why we rushed through the desert. I've had my heart set on going there."

"There's the truck to consider as well," added James. That morning I'd noticed that seven of the fourteen leaves of the front left springs appeared to be cracked. "I don't know if we'll be able to get spares here. Also, the roads in

Morocco aren't good and we'd have to drive hard each day to make our deadline."

"Our deadline? It's your deadline! We're killing ourselves to cross Africa to London so that you can fly straight back to where you left from."

Over the day the feeling had grown in me that if I went with the truck into Morocco I would die. A craving for rest consumed me, the opportunity to lie quietly and recover.

"From my side," I emphasised, "I just can't go through Morocco. I don't feel up to it. I don't mind if the truck goes, but I'll be catching the ferry from here."

Now mooted, the idea took hold. In some way my resolve swung the issue beyond debate. Having come so far together none of us wanted to split up now. Sandy gave in. We felt sorry for her, but the extra four months' travelling had hardened us. We needed our journey to end. Like grains of sand in a sandstorm that settle on the roof of a car and buckle it, the weight of the long, unsettled days of driving had bent our concern inwards, away from others and towards ourselves. As a partial compromise, we decided to drive to the ancient town of Tlemcen, 170 kilometres inland.

Derek's bike had broken down and it was in the back as we drove into town to organise visas for Spain. As he was walking in search of spares, a police car drove up beside him. Two men got out and manhandled him into the back. They started questioning him in Arabic, thinking that, with his short hair and heavy beard, he might be an Islamic fundamentalist. They soon realised their mistake and let him go.

After getting Spanish visas, we needed to buy our ferry tickets. These had to be paid for in foreign currency.

"They should let us pay in dinars if we can prove that we've bought more dinars than we need," said Rob, scheming. "What we'll do is forge Sandy's declaration form and receipt from the bank to make it look like she changed $400." Sandy had changed $40 officially, the minimum each person entering Algeria was obliged to exchange. Rob set about doctoring the receipt and declaration form, adding zeroes to the value of the cheques, and the amount realised in dinars. Because a set commission was included, the grand totals could not be changed as easily. Rob simply crossed them out and wrote in the new ones. I looked at the form.

"Christ, Rob, there's no way you can show them this! It's the most obviously forged thing I've ever seen!" Not only was the colour of Rob's pen a darker shade of blue, but his handwriting was noticeably different. "You're bloody mad if you try. We're in the first world now. You might get away with this in Zaire, but not here."

"Pass it here. We'll be fine. See you just now." Rob, Derek, James and Sandy set off for the bank where payment was to be made. Bronwyn and I stayed in the truck.

Three hours later they returned. Sandy looked shell-shocked.

"What happened?" I asked.

"Just be glad you weren't there," said James, shaking his head. "You wouldn't have enjoyed it."

"We might have got away with it, except for two things," explained Derek. "Rob had added up incorrectly, so the grand total was out by a factor of ten. The clerk at the counter noticed and Rob started shouting, telling her the bank in Tamanrasset must have made a mistake and she must phone them to check this up."

"It got worse," James continued. "She called the bank manager across. He looked at the form and said 'There are no $200 travellers cheques. This is a forgery.'"

"My heart sank!" exclaimed Sandy. "I had visions of myself locked up in an Algerian jail. We stood there in silence. I wanted to die."

"So how did you get out of it?" asked Bronwyn, engrossed.

"Rob just became unbelievably indignant," James replied. "He started ranting like mad about all sorts of things, complete bullshit, and somehow managed to steer the conversation away from the issue of forgery. It was getting late as well, so when we offered to pay in francs I think they just decided to forget the whole thing just to get rid of us."

"But it wasn't a total failure," said Derek, pleased. "In all the fuss they just accepted we were students, so we saved $30 each!"

I shook my head, irritated at the risk that had been taken just to save $100 between us. And a similar problem probably lay before us, when we would have to present our declaration forms, including Sandy's forged one, to customs, and explain why we hadn't changed the regulatory $40 each.

It was evening by the time we left Oran. We got lost after darkness fell and stopped to ask directions.

"Are you tourists?" a young man asked, incredulous. "What are you doing out here? You'll get killed. The terrorists are killing all foreigners."

As we drove on towards Tlemcen a black depression bore down on me. Psychologically, going back inland after having reached the sea bent aside my will, letting in despair. The next morning, as Derek overhauled his bike and the others explored the town, I lay in my tent, feeling the threads of my nerves fray as they rubbed against the build-up of stress and anxiety in me. A fine tremor ran through me and I felt myself shaking apart under its resonance, like a wine glass about to disintegrate when a specific pitch is reached. I felt on edge, balanced on a precipice. I wondered if I could hold myself together long enough to reach London.

Chapter Twenty-One

In the afternoon I felt able to accompany the others into the town for supper. We went via the remains of the thirteenth century fort whose walls had guarded the people of what was a thriving town prospering on the trade between Europe and Africa. We climbed onto the massive ramparts that still stood there, guarding the outlines of buildings that had long since crumbled. We left early the next day, to make it back to Oran for the six o'clock ferry. On the way we filled up with 730 litres of diesel, enough to take us to London.

I was dreading our coming encounter with customs. There was a multitude of irregularities we could be caught for. We were illegally exporting diesel from the country. We had Derek's bike in the back, to avoid paying for it separately. Also, our carnet described the truck as a 'Motor Caravan', an obvious lie, and we had used this to buy a ticket for the truck at half the price for heavy vehicles. And we had failed to buy vehicle insurance in Tamanrasset as directed. On top of this there was the whole question of currency. They might find our hidden, undeclared money, and only Sandy had exchanged the required minimum of $40. But her forms were now horribly disfigured with Rob's forgery.

"If I were you, Sandy, I'd tear up that form and say I'd lost it," I advised. "Better to enter customs with no form than that with thing."

"Forget it," responded Rob. "That's the only way we have of convincing them we've changed enough money officially."

"Christ, Rob, remember the bank? Two days ago? It's the most horrendous forgery in existence. It can only get us into shit."

"We'll get through. Leave it to me."

We'd forgotten that the Algerian weekend started on Thursday, and spent a frustrating and fruitless hour searching the town for food to take onto the ferry. As a result, we arrived late at the docks. The last to board, the truck was searched superficially for drugs, and our papers given only a cursory glance. We reversed the truck up the ramp, relieved. Our luck had held again.

*

We stood on the deck, in the chill evening air, looking back at the African continent slipping quietly away from us. Only when it was lost to us in the gloom and the distance did we move out of the cold and into the lounge. There we celebrated Bronwyn's birthday with cake and presents. Dinars were not accepted on board and as we had no pesetas were unable to buy the expensive ferry food for supper. An Algerian man gave us a bottle of water to drink. We lay down on the mattresses we'd brought up from the truck, struggling to sleep beneath the bright lights above us and the wailing singing of Algeria's favourite pop star who smiled down at us from television screens all night long.

The ferry docked in Alicante at sunrise. As the ramp was lowered, three Spanish officials came forward, gesturing and blowing on their whistles as they sought to direct the trucks off the ferry. The Algerian drivers ignored them completely. Revving their engines, they gunned for the exit, the bravest shoulder-charging those more timid out of the way. The officials shouted and gesticulated angrily at this disregard of their authority. Or leapt nimbly out of the way as a freed truck bore down on them. Caught up in the flow, we drove off. The truck rolled onto the ground of Europe.

The clean streets of Alicante made me more aware of the ingrained grime of everything we possessed. I noticed how the clothes I pulled on smelt of cheap soap, old sweat and diesel. The smell of diesel was everywhere, worked into every knot in the carpet or pore of our skins, coating the contents of the back of the truck – the sleeping bags and pots and tents and books – in a greasy film. Six months' hard living had severely worn all our possessions. Against the backdrop of Spanish fashion we stood out, unkempt and dirty.

Barcelona, our next goal, lay two days' hard driving away. We would be staying there with family of Derek's. He rode on ahead, aiming to cover in less than a day what would take us two. The sudden volume of traffic was unsettling. We decided to avoid the major toll roads and drove instead through the towns and villages strung along the secondary roads, relieved at the feeling of smooth tar beneath the wheels.

Vast plantations of citrus trees lined the roads. Stopping for lunch near one, an old woman approached us and gestured that we could pick as much as we liked. Any stops like this were brief. Thoughts of getting to Barcelona hauled us forward like a lure in a fish's palate. We drove late into the night, Rob at the wheel. Darkness made it difficult to find somewhere to camp. Eventually, exhausted, we stopped next to a small thicket bordering the road. The sporadic drone and sudden rush of passing vehicles disturbed the night.

In Barcelona we met up with Derek at the main post office and set off together to see the sights of one of Europe's most beautiful cities. Crowds filled the wide streets of the city centre, jostling down its pavements, flowing into and from the doors of its boutiques and restaurants and galleries. Shopping bags and display windows bulged with goods. Signs urged shoppers to buy any number of things, to take advantage of a sale, to take up an interest-free offer. People walked fast, busily, swerving to avoid others they passed, acknowledgement drowned by the sheer number of strange eyes that seldom met. The noise they made, the drumming of heels on tarmac, the calls and conversations of voices, crashed like a sea against the concrete walls of the buildings. I was filled with a low panic, the need to escape the proximity of the crowds.

James and I found a bench in a quieter street. We sat there, eating baguettes and cheese. A pale sun, filtered by clouds, reflected off the windows of buildings standing over us.

"It's a different world, hey," I said, looking around me.

"You can say that again. God, I'm just struck by how wide the gap is between the first and the third world."

"And it's growing. In two days in Spain I've seen more buildings and roads being put up than in the whole of Africa."

Used now to the open vistas and plains of Africa, I could only see the city by contrast, as the absence of these things. The forces of nature, which had been so intimate, so threatening, over the past months now lay trapped beneath asphalt, or corralled into small parks and pots for trees. Having lived with nature for so long, we were now back to living above it. What security this offered was tainted by a sense of lack.

Derek took us to Sabadell, where his uncle and aunt, Neil and Maria-Rosa, lived with their four children. It was wonderful to be in a family home again, to have baths and sleep in a bed, to have someone cook a home meal for us and do our laundry. We chatted to the children and spoke of the trip, enjoying a greater depth of relaxation than we'd had in a long time.

Neil was running a half-marathon the next morning. James and Derek said they'd join him. Waking early, we drove out to the town of Ripolle at the base of the Pyrénées. Bronwyn, Rob and Sandy had decided to brave the cold and run as well. "Come on, Paul, join us," James encouraged. "I'm sure you'll make it."

I so wanted to join them. I tried to convince myself that I'd be fine. But I felt tired even walking from the car. My weariness had been with me so long now I was used to it. In this acceptance I was no longer wracked by wondering what its source could be. The low-key nature of the illness, which weakened but didn't completely debilitate me, had to be stress-related, I thought. I comforted myself that I'd be able to recover once we reached London, once the stress ended. For now I moved within the lethargy my body imposed on me.

Everyone completed the race, in good times, and we returned to Sabadell. We climbed onto the roof of the apartment where Derek built a fire and cooked a stew in the metal potjie. The next day we went into town to get French visas for the three entering on South African passports. As visas cost $37.50, they opted for the $12 five-day travel permits. "We'll probably take longer than that to get through, if we stop in Paris," said Rob, "but I'm sure they won't even check on the other side."

My disquiet at being back in the city was beginning to ebb. Walking around Barcelona, I began to appreciate the beauty of its art and architecture, especially that of Antoni Gaudi. We prowled the streets in search of his creations, spectacular buildings and churches with eerie leitmotifs of dragons, bats and masks, and organic walls like cliffs rounded by the force of the sea.

Maria-Rosa cooked a paella for us that night, our last in Barcelona. Despite the comfort of their home, and the warmth of their hospitality, I felt eager to press on now, to find more permanent rest. A local journalist came around the next morning to interview us before we set off. He asked a few questions about the changes in South Africa, which sparked off fierce debate as the different politics within the group were expressed. Tensions which had been suppressed or deflected by the rapid change in our environment found focus in the dispute. The journalist had tried to get one of us to represent us all, and had turned to James as spokesman. He watched bemused as James's more liberal sentiments about the country's changes were vociferously opposed.

Afterwards, he asked for a photograph of us next to the truck. While he was preparing his camera, James peered under the wheel arch.

"Hey!" he called. "These springs aren't broken at all. I think only one is. The rest look cracked, but it's just a line in the grease."

James's discovery made me feel slightly guilty. The broken springs had been influential in our decision not to go to Morocco, and I had been the one to point them out. I wondered how much of my mistake had been merely a subconscious wish-fulfilment.

As we wound our way up the Pyrénées to Andorra, the cold intensified. Snow covered the peaks before us, chilling the wind that blew down from them and into the cab. Our progress was slow, and we reached Andorra late in the evening. We had planned to spend a couple of days there shopping and relaxing, and perhaps even getting an opportunity to ski. Unwilling to afford the hotel prices, we camped in an almost deserted campsite. Lights shone from only a few of the hundreds of caravan homes that sat in the field.

A bitter breeze swept across the site, up from the ice-grey river that ran along its bottom boundary, repelling any thoughts of camping. We decided to sleep in the washrooms. We carried our mattresses into the partial shelter they offered. During the day's twisting uphill drive, diesel had leaked from the forty gallon drum in the back, covering the floor and soaking into sleeping bags and pillows that had been thrown off the bunks. The sharp smells of diesel and ice clashed in the cold air above the hard tiles on which we lay down to sleep.

The thrift in spending of the past months was undone the next day as we bought the duty-free clothes and sports goods that filled the endless shops lining Andorra's streets. We drove up to the highest ski slope. It was blanketed in snow brought by one of the coldest Novembers in decades. The ski fields were still closed, but the equipment was being tested. A chair lift moved slowly up the hill. "Let's get on! Come on!" shouted James. We jumped onto the lift, five of us in a four-person chair, with Sandy two rows behind. The workers examining it stopped it, laughing at us from below, and we waited a freezing half hour, suspended fifty metres above the ground, before they started it again. I walked down more slowly as the others ran and slid, exulting in the strangeness of snow underfoot. Less than two weeks ago we had been sweltering in the Sahara.

After another night spent huddled in the washrooms, we drove into France. The countryside was monotonous, suppressed by its coating of ice and snow. We filled our jerrycans with water from a stream running with melted snow and stopped for lunch at the roadside. Bronwyn provoked James and Derek and they chased after her to cover her in snow as she ran away squealing. There was a lightness of spirit on board now, as we neared the end. But there was an undercurrent of venom too, from being too long together, and having to rely on each other.

It became the kind of cold that made it seem like the sun had gone out. A heavy fog clung to the air, sucking from the earth the last dregs of its heat. Wind whistled into the truck from the numerous gaps in the front. James drove with his sleeping bag covering his legs. I had woken feeling very weak, and the cold weakened me still further. I wore all my warm clothes but felt chilled to my marrow. I stared out of the clouded windows, my thoughts bent inwards, the fact of my discomfort underlying and disrupting all else. The cold left my body permanently tensed as we drove along those French roads, the blanket of snow giving the landscape a uniformity and bleakness that heightened my own feeling of desolation. With all my heart I wanted this journey to end. I withdrew into silence, willing the kilometres past, holding on to a vision of London, and the cessation of this endless moving.

We camped at a truck stop. While Derek and Sandy slept in the truck, Bronwyn, Rob and I huddled together in one tent, with James by himself in another. We slept fully clothed to escape the cold. In the morning Derek brought us all cups of tea, as he had done most mornings over the months. We lay in, holding on to the heat of our sleeping, putting off the moment when we had to emerge from our cocoons.

It became too cold for Derek to ride his bike. The wind ripped through his inadequate clothes, numbing all sensation. He wheeled his bike into the back and joined us in the cab. We stopped near Orleans where I phoned the de l'Épreviers, asking Ludovic if he remembered meeting us in Malawi and if his offer of accommodation still held. To our relief it did. I told him we'd arrive the following afternoon. We camped that night in a frozen maize field. Supper was eaten with all six of us huddled in the back of the truck, the gas stove left burning for warmth.

As he had done every night of the trip, Derek showered before bed, rubbing himself vigorously against the vicious cold of the wind.

Waking up, Rob and I had to break our way out of our tent which had iced over completely during the night. The day was the coldest yet. The fog that buffered the ground, holding in the cold, had thickened, adding to the stress of driving. The roads had been salted to melt the ice. A film of dirt kicked up by other vehicles covered the windscreen. James, who was driving, tried to spray it clean. "It's not working. Check if there's still water in the reservoir, won't you Rob. It's next to your seat there."

"I can't believe it!" Rob exclaimed. "It's completely frozen over!"

We stopped and hacked at the ice in the reservoir, which was inside the cab. Rob produced half a bottle of whiskey, which he'd hidden when we started handing out whiskey as bribes at the rain barriers in Cameroon. We poured it into the reservoir to prevent it freezing again.

Following the directions given to me over the phone the day before, we found our way to the suburb of Arcueil and the home of the de l'Épreviers, who gave us a warm welcome. The language difference did make things slightly uncomfortable, as did the fact that there were six of us. Ludovic showed us around the city on our first day there, after which we explored by ourselves.

We decided to stay a third day in Paris. Wanting to be well, to escape by sheer will the clutches of my illness, I set off with the others towards the nearby Metro. But a dizziness shook me. Drained and weak, I returned to the house, to spend the day in bed. I could no longer struggle against the illness, its suction dragging me slowly down like quicksand. All I could do now was hold on, and wait, hope that ease would come in time.

Derek prepared a meal in the potjie as thanks to the de l'Épreviers for having us. Undaunted by the cold, he made a fire in the iced-over garden over which he cooked this by now traditional parting gift. The family joined in in guitar-playing and singing, braving their way past the language barriers.

I retired early. We would set off early the next day on the final stage of the journey. Our destination was the town of Frome in Somerset, 600 kilometres away, the home of Robbie Enthoven, who'd driven the truck down. We planned to spend a few days there before driving to London where the next phase of our lives could begin.

Chapter Twenty-Two

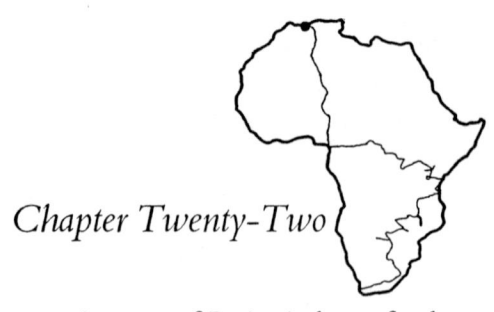

It was slow going getting out of Paris. A dense fog loomed thickly, muffling the light and the sound of the traffic. The roads were iced over. Our headlights illuminated several accidents as we passed. It took two hours to travel twenty-five kilometres. We crept forward in the slow lane. James drove, his foot pumping at the weakening brakes as we moved ahead some metres then stopped. Beyond the ring road the traffic thinned and we made better progress. The cold continued, holding us all the way to the coast. There were no ferries available at Boulogne, so we carried on to Calais.

It was dark already when the ferry left, just before six o'clock. The atmosphere on board was rowdy. Most of the passengers were Englishmen taking advantage of the duty-free alcohol for sale and who hadn't even got off at the other side. They all joined in as we sang Happy Birthday to Rob.

The English officials were friendly and we had no problems clearing customs. Bronwyn was granted a two-year working visa. It was almost eight o'clock, and we still had 300 kilometres to travel to get to Frome. We set off towards the M25.

It felt strange to be on such developed roads again, to be under streetlights. The light seemed to show us up as misfits in this sophisticated world, revealing to us our hardened language and looks. The truck too stood out. Like a beggar it laboured its way down the streets, weaving slightly, black diesel smoke belching from its exhaust. Its tyres were balding now, the brakes worn and the indicators broken. Unlicensed, unroadworthy and uninsured, it lumbered its prodigal way home.

We drove through Surrey and Hampshire and into Wiltshire. We'd been travelling for sixteen hours now. Like a music tape that is stretched, the sound of my nerves was high-pitched in my head, yearning for this movement to end. This movement that my life had become. James was still at the wheel, peering through the mist at the road ahead. "I'll take you past Stonehenge," he said. "It's dead on the way."

We arrived at Salisbury Plain at midnight. A mist hung loosely about us. The moon above was just past full. A hundred metres off, behind the fence around it, stood Stonehenge, mysterious and ancient. Its cold stone slabs reflected dully the light of the moon and the torches shone towards it by the guards patrolling the fence.

"Would you like to have a closer look?" one of them asked in an American accent.

"For sure," enthused Rob.

"Thing is, we charge five pounds per person for the service."

"Thing is," replied Bronwyn, "we don't intend to pay to see Stonehenge. We've just crossed Africa without forking out money like this, and don't plan to start now."

The guard relented and said we could climb over the fence. I sat heavily in the cab, weighed down by the inertia of my sickness. Knowing I could not pass up such an opportunity, I climbed down from the cab and clambered weakly over the fence, joining the others who were standing amid the circle of pillars and beams. I sat beside the altar stone, imagining its anguished and bloody history. The mist thickened at the edges of the light cast by the guard's moving torch, becoming for an instant the robe of a druid once here. It would soon be winter solstice, the anniversary of lives taken to appease more primitive hearts, to affirm the beliefs of a younger world.

We thanked the guard and left. There were still eighty kilometres to cover.

All I want is to sleep, to have quiet, to stop this endless motion, this noise. I sit with my eyes closed, far from sleep. My mind stands on glass, jarred into consciousness continually. The cold is in my bones now and my heart. As we near the end I feel myself starting to collapse. The walls of my will are breaking down. Allowed to at last, my body sags beneath me.

Hapsford House was prepared for our welcome. Food and drink were laid out for us and the house was heated against the cold. I was overtired and could not sleep. I lay in the soft bed, warm under the duvet, with gritty eyes and a desperate weariness. And with relief in me, a thankfulness for the end, for time now to rest.

I woke early. I had been sweating and lay there, clammy and drained. I stayed in bed, listening to the sounds of the house as it came to life. Inside I still felt deflated, the dissolution of the strength that had held me together thus far. I heard in the words of the others too a similar succumbing to strain. The excitement of ending was mixed with vitriol that splashed between them over small things as the need for tolerance fell away.

Excitement surged again as our photographs were brought back from the chemist. As we chose the copies we wanted, reliving the fascination of our journey, the variety of places we had seen and things we had done, the people we'd met and wildlife we'd watched, we felt strongly the accomplishment of what we'd completed. We had made it across the continent without a serious rift between us.

There was much that had been held down, though, suppressed anger and unspoken hurts, and these started to rise up as the need for harmony decreased. The issue of money rose up again over the past week. The argument became fraught with acrimony, fuelled by old grievances that hadn't been voiced. The pattern of relationships that had developed during the past months become sharper now, jagged. Cruel words were directed at Bronwyn, once even a threat of violence, cutting into the heart of her insecurity, her sense of separation. Words that weren't meant, that would be regretted later; but that were spawned in the frustration of his own long separation. Patience had grown thin in the closed walls holding our company. We had been too close together for too long and needed to be apart now.

Sandy phoned home and was greeted with terrible news. Her mother was ill again, with a different cancer. Again Sandy had to make plans for an immediate flight home. She came into the room I was in and lay down next to me. I held her hand, offering what comfort I could. We lay there together, battered in our different ways by the present of our lives.

I felt detached from my body. It was slow to respond, even when prompted by the urgings of its own stomach which was upset. I would get up and walk heavily to the toilet, slowed by the alien feel of my body. My mind was clear as I lay listening, and thinking about the trip, and of this illness that had plagued me since Zaire. I needed to know what it was now, and asked James to take me to the doctor. We went to Frome Medical Centre but they suggested I go to London. We weren't ready to leave yet, so I returned to my bed. Lying on my stomach, I could feel my spleen, hard and pointed, like an extra rib.

It was our fourth day in Frome. Bronwyn and Rob came back from a pub where they had met with Richard and

Lucy whom we'd last seen in Nairobi fourteen long weeks before. James and Derek returned from a pheasant shoot, having shot twenty-three of Lord Oxford's pheasant, and four of his duck. Angela Enthoven, whose house we were staying in, arrived. She came in to see how I was.

"Take this boy to hospital immediately, James! He seems dangerously ill. You should go to London right now."

★

For the last time the bags were packed into the truck. I couldn't bear the thought of getting into the cab again, and sitting upright for the four hour journey to London. I climbed into the back where I lay on a bunk in the pitch black, rolling slightly as we turned and curved down the roads taking us on this the last leg of our journey.

My sickness, still mysterious, is suddenly of urgent consequence. The bouncing of the truck has jolted my unstable bowels. I need the toilet and bang on the wall of the back, shouting at the people in the cab to stop. I can hear the music they are listening to. It drowns out my cries. London is still an hour away. I cannot wait. Frantic, I grope around in the almost total darkness.

The floor is too cold, diesel-smeared, to crouch down on, so I balance myself, bird-like, on the bed and the shelf. Holding with one hand on to the seat belt strap that holds the bed in position, I carefully defecate into an enamel mug before collapsing back onto the mattress.

Five days later it was all over. In that time the wild, brazen behaviour that had become our norm had continued, shocking friends who saw our group, and then slowly begun to calm as we acclimatised, shifting back into decorum. On the fifth day James, Derek and Rob flew back to South Africa, as had Sandy, reversing in eleven hours the past seven months of travelling. Bronwyn had found work in London.

I was in the Hospital for Tropical Diseases near King's Cross. Transferred there from University Hospital, where tests for malaria had come back negative, I had been placed in a room by myself. To rest like that, in clean sheets and kind, competent hands, gave me the comfort I had long since lost.

A doctor came to see me on my second day there. "How long have you been sick for?" he asked.

"About ten weeks, on and off."

"Well, you're a very lucky young man then. It is malaria you've got. Two strains in fact. *Ovali* and *falsiporum*. *Falsiporum*'s the one that becomes cerebral. A lethal attack can develop very swiftly, within hours."

Knowing at last what had been wrong, I felt relief flood through me. In five days I would be out, to begin to recuperate, and to assimilate the dark and the light of the past seven months in Africa.

Epilogue

It is a year later. We are all back on Pamwechete Farm in Raffingora in Zimbabwe. It is Robbie and Bridget's wedding day. The air is humid from the torrential rains that fell all through the night, clearing just in time for the ceremony in the garden. The six of us who arrived in London together stand in a group, laughing as we recount anecdotes of the seven strange, full months we shared together.

Derek has flown in from Singapore, where he has been based. Bronwyn and I have come from England where we stayed to work and travel after the trip ended. Sandy and James have come up from Cape Town.

It has been an eventful year. I am fit and well again, and revelling in being healthy, appreciative of something I lost for so long. Where before I took it for granted, there is a deeper joy in me now in being able to run and climb and dance again.

Healing has taken place emotionally too. There has been much discussion amongst us about everything that happened during the trip. Things that we knew about as well as things we didn't. The truth has been told. Mysteries and ambiguities have been resolved. Letters have passed between continents and in them contrition has been shown and past hurts forgiven. The pain that was felt has also been dimmed by time, and fond memories glow far more brightly in our minds.

Over the past year Bronwyn and I have become close friends. Walking together in the Lake District, and meeting in London and talking about all that happened, we have found the understanding and acceptance of each other that eluded us throughout the trip.

We all dance together in the marquee overlooking the wide valley of rippling wheat. Laughter flows unrestrainedly. It is one of the most joyous days of my life. The love that comes from the union of Robbie and Bridget spills over into and is augmented by the love that flows from our reunion.

There is between us a connection that transcends friendship. Our long days and experiences together have forged between us bonds that make us more like a family, that accept our differences yet are loving all the same. We are close because we have seen each other unmasked. The pressures of the trip made us honest, showing all sides of ourselves, both good and bad.

We are six people of widely differing temperaments. But we have undergone something unique, something that stands out brightly in all our pasts. Together we have shared what has been for all of us the trip of a lifetime.